Meghan

AND THE UNMASKING OF
THE MONARCHY

Also by Andrew Morton

Diana: Her True Story in Her Own Words

*Elizabeth & Margaret: The Intimate
World of the Windsor Sisters*

*Wallis in Love: The Untold True Passion
of the Duchess of Windsor*

17 Carnations: The Windsors, the Nazis and the Cover-Up

William & Catherine: Their Lives, Their Wedding

Angelina: An Unauthorized Biography

Tom Cruise: An Unauthorized Biography

Madonna

Posh and Becks

Monica's Story

Meghan

AND THE UNMASKING OF THE MONARCHY

ANDREW MORTON

GRAND CENTRAL
PUBLISHING

New York   Boston

Grand Central Publishing
Hachette Book Group
1290 Avenue of the Americas, New York, NY 10104
grandcentralpublishing.com
twitter.com/grandcentralpub

Originally published in hardcover and ebook by Grand Central Publishing
in April 2018 under the title *Meghan: A Hollywood Princess*
First Trade Paperback Edition: October 2021

Grand Central Publishing is a division of Hachette Book Group, Inc. The Grand
Central Publishing name and logo is a trademark of Hachette Book Group, Inc.

The publisher is not responsible for websites (or their content)
that are not owned by the publisher.

The Hachette Speakers Bureau provides a wide range of authors for speaking events.
To find out more, go to www.hachettespeakersbureau.com or call (866) 376-6591.

Library of Congress Cataloging-in-Publication Data has been applied for.

ISBNs: 978-1-5387-4733-9 (trade paperback), 978-1-5387-4734-6 (ebook)

Printed in the United States of America

LSC-C

Printing 1, 2021

To my wife Carolyn and all our friends in Pasadena.

Contents

Acknowledgements

Sometimes it helps to be in the right place at the right time. My wife Carolyn is from Southern California, and for some of the year I live in Pasadena, a few miles north-east of downtown Los Angeles. When Meghan Markle's engagement to Prince Harry was announced, it was remarkable how many local people had stories about the *Suits* actress. Pasadena was truly Meghan Markle Central: Edmund Fry, owner of Rose Tree Cottage, a little slice of England in the town, served her tea; her old boyfriend, now a realtor, sold a house just across the street; parents sent their children to the school where Meghan has either studied or performed; local photographers had boxes of slides with unseen shots of the royal-in-waiting; and the Hippie Kitchen where she volunteered as a teenager was just a short drive away.

So, starting in Pasadena, I would like to thank my friend Dr Wendy Kohlhase for introducing me to the enthusiastic and helpful staff and administrators at Immaculate Heart High School. School President Maureen Diekmann and Callie Webb delved deep into the archives stored in the basement to discover all matters Markle while senior teachers Christine Knudsen and Maria Pollia added their insights with regard to their former pupil. My thanks, too, to photographer John Dlugolecki for uncovering a charming series of shots of Meghan as she blossomed into a beautiful young woman.

Gigi Perreau, a Hollywood child star herself and Immaculate Heart alumni, and Emmanuel Eulalia, director of drama at St Francis High School in La Cañada, described Meghan's emerging talent. Elizabeth and Dennys McCoy spoke warmly of the young

Meghan, while the thoughts of Catherine Morris, Jeff Dietrich and the staff at the Hippie Kitchen, who work tirelessly to help those without a roof over their head, were much appreciated.

With regard to Meghan's complicated and extensive family tree, I would like to thank genealogists Elizabeth Banas, Gary Boyd Roberts and historian Christopher Wilson, as well as Professor Carmen Harris, University of South Carolina Upstate, who put the lives of her ancestors in context. Family members Tom Markle Junior, Roslyn Loveless and Noel Rasmussen all helped tease out her equally complicated upbringing, while several friends, including Leslie McDaniel and others who remain anonymous, added their perspective. Tameka Jacobs and Leyla Milani talked perceptively about the girl they knew from the *Deal or No Deal* days, while several members of the crew of *Suits*, who for professional reasons did not want to be named, also pitched in. My thanks, too, to Samantha Brett, author of *Game Changers*.

I would also like to thank Professor Prochaska and Trevor Phillips OBE, former chairman of the Equality and Human Rights Commission, for their views on her impact on the monarchy and the country. I have discussed this issue with other former members of the royal Household, who have understandably asked not to be named. Thanks, too, to those in the popular press and social media who have carefully followed Meghan's evolving life and career.

A huge thank you, too, to my researchers, Phil Dampier and Emily Stedman in London and the indefatigable Lisa Derrick in Los Angeles. Additionally, without the consummate professionalism of my editors Fiona Slater and Helen Cumberbatch in London and Gretchen Young in New York, as well as the dedication of editorial assistant Katherine Stopa and copyeditor Nick Fawcett, we would never have got over the finish line.

Finally, a big shout-out to all my Pasadena friends, acquaintances and neighbours, whose thoughts, suggestions and advice energized this whole project.

Pasadena
September 2021

The Meghan Paradox

When I was researching *Wallis in Love*, my biography of the Duchess of Windsor, I came across a photograph that seemed to encapsulate her relationship with her royal husband and his world.

It was taken in a ploughed field or some bleak, flat ground. While the Duke of Windsor, dressed in loud check trousers, merrily blasted away at pheasants and other flying creatures, Wallis Simpson, seated uncomfortably on a wooden shooting stick, looked a picture of abject misery, wincing at the noise of the guns. Dressed in an off-white fur coat, a stylish hat and fashionable ankle boots, the duchess seemed attired for shopping on a winter's day in Knightsbridge or some other ritzy neighbourhood. Boredom seeped out of every pore. Wallis, a city girl down to her elegantly manicured fingertips, clearly wished she was somewhere, anywhere else rather than watching her husband kill things.

I was reminded of that photograph and what it represented when it became clear that another American had won the heart of a dashing prince, himself acknowledged as one of the finest shots in England. Not for nothing did his mother, the late Diana, Princess of Wales call her sons 'the killer Wales', as Harry and William were exceptionally accomplished and enthusiastic when it came to hunting.

How would Rachel Meghan Markle – whose favourite word was 'classy', who supported animal rights and whose politics tended to the left – fit in with a family to whom hunting, shooting and fishing was a way of life. Diana passed the so-called Balmoral test, the unspoken assessment of royal girlfriends – and boyfriends – by the family, when she fell in a bog and came up laughing. The royals and their party thought her misfortune hilarious. As her grandmother Lady Ruth Fermoy later cautioned her, the Royal Family has a very different sense of humour to the rest of us. Diana didn't listen and went ahead with her ill-fated royal match.

Would Meghan, a girl raised on the West Coast of America, catch the arcane family codes and obscure references that had them chortling and chuckling? At least her love of dogs was a conversational starting point with the Queen.

As Kate Middleton discovered, Meghan was poised to join a family in which who enters a room first, who sits where, who bows or curtsies to whom, forms part of a labyrinthine pecking order. Meghan was on the cusp of swapping her world of taste-makers, influencers and brand ambassadors for a confusing flurry of equerries, valets, beaters and ghillies.

I wasn't the only one pondering these issues when news broke of Prince Harry's romance with the star of *Suits*, a legal drama on cable TV. As Diana's biographer, I was frequently asked by journalists: 'Would it last?' This question about the dating couple was clearly predicated on the unhappy marriage and eventual divorce of the Prince and Princess of Wales.

At the time I felt it was the wrong question, as anyone with even a passing knowledge of Prince Harry would have realized that he was the eager supplicant in this romantic drama – not the other way round.

The single unifying observation made by one and all concerned what she was about to give up – a successful TV career, a thriving social media presence, and charitable positions as global ambassador for World Vision Canada and a UN advocate role – in order to marry into the Royal Family.

It was also clear that she was not some shy girl from the shires fresh out of finishing school, but rather a divorced woman of the world who was an active promoter of gender equality, women's rights and, to use a Markle phrase, 'being the change'. It is a slogan that does not spring readily to mind when considering the monarchy, an institution defined by the past and precedent. As Diana joked, the only thing they change is their clothes.

The Meghan Paradox cuts two ways. Feminists saw her as being swallowed whole by the royal system, seriously compromising her agenda as an equal rights activist. She was about to swap her values and principles for the appellation 'Her Royal Highness' – and the chance to curtsy to the Duchess of Cambridge for the rest of her life.

On the other hand, traditionalists feared that she was a well-groomed stalking horse, her values and lifestyle inimical to a thousand-year-old institution that is studiously hierarchical, and which encourages deference and acceptance of the existing order. This was no European-style designer cycling monarchy. How then would this progressive in 4-inch heels cope in a world where a misplaced decoration can earn a royal rebuke?

Of course the ultimate irony was that, even though Meghan was successful in her own right, we only began to take collective notice of her because she was marrying a man whose place in society was secured by virtue of his birth rather than his abilities.

Perhaps the reason why the Meghan Paradox holds good is that she was marrying into a family – and an institution – defined as much by its contradictions and incongruities as its position at the apex of society. It shouldn't make sense, but it does. As Thomas Paine, author of the eighteenth-century tome *Rights of Man*, observed: 'A hereditary monarchy is as absurd a proposition as a hereditary doctor or mathematician.'

The real issue was who would accommodate whom: Meghan or the monarchy? Or to put it another way, who would blink first?

Meghan was very different from other royal brides – at least in the House of Windsor. She came from a country, culture and profession where the self and the service of self comes first, second and third. The institution she hoped to join was about self-effacement, about being, to quote one pundit, 'brilliantly bland'. The causes she espoused – gender equality and female empowerment – sat ill inside an institution that was about rank, place and hierarchy.

She may have been something of a unicorn but she was not the only one. Americans have married foreign princes, forged successful careers and lived to tell the tale. Think of the actor Grace Kelly, who went on to marry Prince Rainier of Monaco, and Princeton-educated Lisa Najeeb Halaby, an airline executive who became Queen Noor of Jordan following her marriage to King Hussein of Jordan. Both women are renowned for their philanthropic work, as is Texan Sarah Butler, who earned a degree in international relations and has an impressive résumé that includes stints working at the United Nations, Human Rights Watch and charities dealing with women's issues. She found her happily ever after in Prince Zeid bin Ra'ad Zeid al-Hussein of Jordan, the couple marrying in 2000 after which Ms Butler became Her Royal Highness Princess Sarah Zeid.

They were living proof that different cultures and nationalities were not barriers to individual happiness and wider public respect. The difference was that, unlike the other American royals, Meghan was a mixed-heritage woman who could trace her lineage back to the cotton fields of Georgia and the world of slavery and suppression. Her racial background, indeed her very existence, provoked a debate in Britain about ethnic tolerance.

The new dual-heritage kid on the block arrived at a time of genuine and profound change in both the nation and the monarchy itself. Harry and Meghan started dating just as the UK began licking its wounds after the rancorous departure from the European Union following a referendum in 2016. Rightly or wrongly, Britain was seen as a more insular and nationalist country just as the Royal Family was viewed as more relevant and inclusive thanks to the girl from California. First signs looked promising, with anecdotal evidence suggesting that predominantly ethnic minority communities were more interested in the work of the monarchy thanks to the presence of Meghan.

Inside the institution itself, the retirement of Prince Philip and the Queen's reduced workload, particularly her decision not to undertake long-distance travel, placed a heavier burden on the younger generation. There was an expectation that Meghan would help to share the load.

While Meghan was beginning her royal adventure at a critical moment in regal and British history, she was following in Diana's footsteps by giving the House of Windsor an international, glamorous gloss. Unlike Diana, she was camera-ready, not camera-shy. It is doubtful that the global media would have been so excited had Harry chosen a nice upper-class girl from the county set.

Long before Prince Harry was mentioned in conjunction with Meghan, her high school, Immaculate Heart in Los Angeles, regularly screened the speech that she made at the UN Women 2015 conference on gender equality as inspiration for the current generation of female students.

She arrived at the gates of Buckingham Palace fully formed: a successful actor, a popular blogger and an acknowledged humanitarian. The puzzle remained as to whether this ambitious, intelligent, modern and successful woman would stay the course.

She boasted a bloodline of slaves and kings, servants and swordsmen. Hers has been a remarkable journey, and one that began where else but in the city of dreams: Los Angeles.

1

In Search of Wisdom

For years she was troubled by nagging questions at the back of her mind: where does my family come from, what is my history? For Rachel Meghan Markle – known as 'Bud' and 'Flower' by her family – it was an endlessly perplexing issue. The fact that her mother, Doria Ragland, was an African American from Los Angeles, California, and her father, Thomas Wayne Markle, was a white Pennsylvanian only added to the confusion. She felt she had to find her place, where she belonged, in both the black and the white world. In the hierarchy of colour that still defines so much about place and position in American society, she was light-skinned and therefore seen as 'whiter' than her black cousins. So, along with her perplexity came a fluidity, a readiness to view the world from different perspectives, from both sides.

She had listened wide-eyed as her Uncle Joseph had told and retold the story of the Raglands' cross-country drive from Cleveland, Ohio, to Los Angeles in a borrowed car when her mother was a babe in arms. Their adventure turned nasty when they pulled into a one-horse town in Texas in the teeth of a blizzard. They were looking for a room for the night, but soon realized they were not wanted in the redneck town. One guy pointed off into the snow and yelled, 'The highway is that way. Get going. You are not welcome here.'

While it may be family lore – the road from Cleveland to Los Angeles goes nowhere near the Lone Star State – for Meghan's uncle, then around seven or eight years old, it represented his first real experience of racism. He further recounted that during this journey the family were told to use the back door for 'coloureds' when they stopped at a diner. As Meghan was to learn, the history of her mother's family was one of exploitation, discrimination and injustice. Some of it she would experience first-hand, such as when she felt the rush of blood to her cheeks when someone in a parking lot used the 'N' word to her mother because she did not leave briskly enough. It was a word that her ancestors – slaves who worked on the cotton plantations of Georgia – would have heard on a daily basis.

It is no wonder that Meghan was left bewildered by her family tree. Tracing her family back through her mother's line is a difficult business. Prior to emancipation, evidence about the lives of black people in the South was inevitably scarce. There were few written records, and most information was passed on by word of mouth. What we do know is that for years the family were the property of a Methodist, William Ragland, whose family originated from Cornwall in the south-west of England, before emigrating to Virginia and then North Carolina.

Ragland lived in Chatham County, North Carolina, with his slaves before moving to the rural town of Jonesboro in Georgia, where land was regularly given away by the authorities in lotteries to encourage settlement. Traditionally, slaves were only known by a first name, given to them by their owner, and on occasion they also took their owner's surname. The scanty records that are available show that the first 'black Ragland', that is to say Meghan's first documented Ragland ancestor, was born in Jonesboro in 1830. This was Richard Ragland, who married a woman named Mary. Though much of his life was spent in enforced servitude, at least his son, Stephen, who was born in 1848, lived to see the emancipation that came when the Union, the anti-slave northern states led by President Abraham Lincoln, triumphed over the pro-slave Confederacy in 1865. According to records unearthed by Massachusetts-based genealogist Elizabeth Banas, at the end of the war Stephen Ragland became a sharecropper. But this was merely slavery by another name, as the overwhelming majority of what he produced was taken by the white landowner in rent and other dues, leaving an average sharecropper like Stephen constantly in debt.

Though freed at the end of the war in June 1865, it was not until the 1870 census that most former slaves were able to register a name for themselves officially. Stephen Ragland stuck with his former master's surname and his given name. Not quite as romantic as 'Wisdom', the name that Meghan believes great-great-great-grandfather Ragland chose when he was given the chance to make a fresh start. As she wrote for *Elle* magazine in July 2015: 'Perhaps the closest thing connecting me to my ever-complex family tree, my longing to know where I come from, and the commonality that links me to my bloodline, is the choice that my great-great-great-grandfather made to start anew. He chose the last name Wisdom.'

Sadly, the professional genealogists and researchers who have carefully investigated her history point out that the records, albeit sketchy and contradictory, show that he kept his original name. They also indicate that his first wife was named Ellen Lemens and that the couple married on 18 August 1869 and went on to have four children: Ann (who was also known as Texas), Dora, Henry, and Jeremiah, born in either 1881 or 1882, who is Meghan's great-great-grandfather. Based on census and tax records, it seems that for some years Stephen and Ellen continued to live around Jonesboro on the Ragland plantation where they had been slaves. In fact, when Lemuel Ragland died on 19 May 1870, Stephen was recorded in the census as working for Lemuel's widow Mary, who was then aged sixty. Other family members living in the vicinity, probably in the same plantation bunk-house or rough-hewn wooden shacks, included Vinny and Willy Ragland, as well as Charles, Jack, Jerry, Mariah and Catherine Lemens.

After a time in Jonesboro, the town now famous as the setting for the epic novel about the American Civil War, *Gone with the Wind*, the family moved the short distance to Henry County, an agricultural district noted for its rich soil and premium cotton. Stephen and his sons, Henry and Jeremiah, worked the land as either sharecroppers or hired hands. However, beyond the cotton profits, Henry County also had a darker reputation as a home of the Ku Klux Klan, which had risen in the area in the spring of 1866. The Klan's first action in the county was to lynch former slave Dave Fargason during a local conflict centring on educating black children. Stephen's son Henry was also later confronted by a gang of armed white men, but managed to escape with his life. Local historian R. H. Hankinson observes that, soon afterwards, the Klan was wound up in the area – although the threat of violence remained.

Indeed, the threat of violence combined with grinding poverty prompted many to migrate north or west in search of better prospects. Sometime after the turn of the century, Stephen Ragland's daughter Ann, her husband Cosby Smith (whom she married in 1892) and their six children decided to make the 3,000-mile journey to start a new life in Los Angeles, in the days when oil and oranges were more important to the town's economy than making movies.

Their decision to move inspired Stephen's youngest child Jeremiah, his wife Claudie Ritchie, daughter of the wonderfully named Mattie Turnipseed, and their growing brood to leave Georgia as well. Around 1910, when Claudie was twenty-five, they made their way to Chattanooga in Tennessee in the hope of building a better life for themselves.

It is likely that neither Ann nor Jeremiah saw their father Stephen ever again, even though he lived to the relatively ripe old age of seventy-eight, breathing his last in Paulding County, Georgia, on 31 October 1926.

By then, Jeremiah and Claudie had raised five children, though one died in childbirth. Claudie, who was officially designated in the census as a 'mulatto' or of dual heritage, worked as a maid at Miller Bros department store, then the company's flagship. Jeremiah found casual jobs working in a barber shop and as a saloon porter before setting up his own tailoring business. At that time, black people were barred from well-paid jobs or obtaining loans. Self-employment was the only route for self-improvement.

Just as the women in the family raised the children, they also made more of their opportunities, as they became available.

Jeremiah's daughter and Meghan's great aunt, Dora, was the first Ragland to go to college and the first to set herself up as a professional, becoming a schoolteacher. Her younger sister Lillie did even better. She studied at the University of California as a mature student before training as a realtor and establishing her own business in Los Angeles. She was so successful that she was listed in the African-American *Who's Who*.

Their brothers did not climb so high: one worked as a waiter, while Meghan's great-grandfather Steve found employment as a presser in a cleaner's shop in downtown Chattanooga. As Meghan's Uncle Joseph admits: 'Culturally, our family did not have male figures.' Steve married Lois Russell, the daughter of a hotel porter, when she was fourteen or fifteen. In the census of 1930, the couple were recorded as living with their baby son, Alvin Azell, later Meghan's grandfather, as well as Lois's father James Russell and assorted nieces and roomers.

When Alvin was old enough he made his way to Cleveland, Ohio, in search of work. There he met Jeanette Johnson, the daughter of a bellboy and elevator operator at the five-star St Regis Hotel. Soon after the end of the Second World War, Johnson had married professional roller-skater Joseph Johnson, by whom she had two children, Joseph Junior and a daughter, Saundra. It was not long before Johnson, who travelled from town to town to show off his skills, skated out of her life, leaving Jeanette to raise their children on her own. Enter the smooth-talking, snappily dressed Alvin Ragland, who soon had Jeanette's heart beating a little faster.

They married and moved into a basement apartment in a three-storey building in Cleveland. Their first child, Doria, Meghan's mother, was born in September 1956 and it was soon afterwards that Alvin uprooted the family and embarked on that famous cross-country ride to begin a new life in Los Angeles, where their Ragland relations had settled. For a time he worked for his Aunt Lillie in real estate and then he opened his own bric-a-brac and antique store called 'Twas New in downtown Los Angeles. A larger-than-life character who was well known to other dealers, Alvin specialized in selling second-hand designer shoes and other fashion items at local flea markets. As a big, imposing fellow, he instantly attracted attention – not all of it positive. Eddie Ingram Junior, the son of his business partner, recalled: 'He spent so much of his life on the receiving end of really ridiculous, abominable treatment to black people. He resisted that all his life. He was never ashamed of who he was and what he believed, and he didn't care what you thought about it. He would fight prejudice, but it wasn't just that he would fight it: he would live his life the way he wanted to live it.'

That way of life, though, no longer included his wife Jeanette, who was once again left holding the baby. He married for a second time on 6 May 1983, and his wife Ava Burrows, a teacher, gave birth to their only son Joffrey a few months later.

By this time, Doria Ragland was all grown up and with a child of her own. Two years earlier she had given birth to her daughter, Rachel Meghan Markle, at 4.46 a.m. on 4 August 1981 in the West Park Hospital in Canoga Park, Los Angeles. Meghan's arrival would change the narrative of her family forever.

✳

The blooming of Meghan's family, from picking cotton under the blazing sun to seeing one of their own taking her wedding vows to a royal prince under the camera lights, is an extraordinary story of upward mobility. And what a sublime contrast it makes with the not-so-distant past. The last American to marry a member of the British Royal Family was Wallis Warfield Simpson, who hailed from Baltimore, Maryland. Though she was twice divorced with both ex-husbands still living, King Edward VIII insisted on marrying her despite overwhelming opposition from the Church, the government and the Empire, all of whom objected to a divorcee becoming royal consort. As a result, Edward VIII abdicated the throne, marrying Wallis at a modest ceremony in a French chateau in June 1937. Billed as the royal romance of the century, the King gave up everything for the woman he loved.

Fast-forward eighty years. While the Duke and Duchess of Windsor, as Edward and Wallis became, would doubtless have been delighted that the House of Windsor had embraced the reality of divorce, they would surely have been astonished that Prince Harry's bride was to be of dual heritage. For Wallis's family, the Warfields, had built their various fortunes on the back of slave labour.

For their part they did consider themselves benign and enlightened masters, as Wallis's third cousin, Edwin Warfield, who was elected forty-fifth governor of Maryland in 1903, gave several speeches on the topic of 'Slavery as I knew it'. However, Edwin's tolerance only went so far; in the election for governor, he stood on a platform of white supremacy, believing that 'ill-educated blacks' should be denied the franchise.

While Wallis was brought up in relative poverty – she and her mother were the poor relations of the wealthy Warfield family – she enjoyed the services of a black nanny, butler and maids. They were part of her life, albeit as downstairs folk who never crossed the line of familiarity. Indeed, she once observed that the first time she shook the hand of a non-white person was when she and her husband, the Duke of Windsor, glad-handed the crowds in Nassau during his time as governor of the Bahamas in the Second World War. People of colour simply did not feature in the lives of Wallis or her husband, except to hold out a tray of drinks. Wallis was from a class, an age and a region where, quite unselfconsciously, she and her friends were nonchalantly racist. In letters and table talk, she casually used the 'N' word and other derogatory terms. When Wallis was born in 1896, Meghan's great-great-great-grandfather Stephen Ragland was scratching out a meagre living as a sharecropper. The very idea that a woman of dual heritage would marry a prince of the realm in the august setting of St George's Chapel at Windsor Castle, the scene of numerous royal weddings including those of King Edward VII and, more recently, the Queen's third son, Prince Edward, would have been unthinkable.

But Meghan wasn't the first to challenge that particular notion. In 2004, the daughter of a prince, Lady Davina Windsor, married sheep-shearer, surfer and father Garry 'Gazza' Lewis, a Maori, or New Zealand native, in a private ceremony at Kensington Palace. Now thirty-fourth in line to the throne, Lady Davina and her husband were invited to the wedding of Prince William and Kate Middleton in 2011. The Royal Family barely batted an eyelid at the union between the daughter of Prince Richard, the Duke of Gloucester, and a member of New Zealand's second-largest ethnic grouping. However, the marriage didn't last – the couple divorced in 2018.

Unsurprisingly, not all members of Britain's aristocracy are quite as welcoming. When the glamorous food writer Emma McQuiston, the bi-racial daughter of a Nigerian oil tycoon, married Viscount Weymouth, the heir to the famous Longleat estate, in 2013, his mother's reaction was: 'Are you sure about what you are doing to four hundred years of bloodline?'

Ironically, Meghan herself is not such an outsider as some may think, and her European bloodline is far older than 400 years.

Popular interest in Meghan has perhaps inevitably largely rested on her family's history of slavery and how, through hard work and endeavour, her ancestors made a life for themselves in an unforgiving world; what is less familiar is that Meghan has, through her father's family, links to the royal families of Scotland, England and beyond. When she wrote, 'Being bi-racial paints a blurred line that is equal parts staggering and illuminating,' she never realized for a moment that the blood of kings as well as slaves ran through her veins.

For starters, it is possible to trace a direct line through twenty-five generations to Robert I of Scotland, perhaps the most colourful of all Scottish kings. Better known as Robert the Bruce, he is the legendary warrior who, as he hid in a cave to avoid capture by the English enemy, watched a spider trying to spin a web. The spider repeatedly tried and failed to swing itself up from a long thread, an echo of Robert's own failure on the battlefield. He gave the spider one last chance. If it succeeded in swinging itself up, he would wage a final battle to liberate his country.

The spider triumphed, and so did Robert the Bruce, defeating the English at the bloody Battle of Bannockburn in 1314. He remained king until his death in 1329, acknowledged as one of the most successful and best-loved of all Scottish monarchs.

Such a fascinating connection to this distant world of kings comes through her father's family, the Markles, whose bloodline tells a story shared by so many – ancestors whose roots were in the Old World but who sailed west to seek a better life.

The Markles, who have their origins in Germany and Holland, lived in Pennsylvania for generations, working as farmers, lime burners, carpenters, miners, soldiers and, in the case of Meghan's great-grandfather, the giant Isaac 'Ike' Markle, as a fireman for the Pennsylvania Railroad Company. Ike's son Gordon Arnold Markle, Meghan's grandfather, started his own filling-station business, worked in the shoe industry and wound up in an administrative position for the post office in the small town of Newport, Pennsylvania. In March 1941, just months before the USA entered the Second World War, he married Doris Mary Rita Sanders, who hailed from New Hampshire. Following the attack on Pearl Harbor in December, Gordon was called up for duty, travelling to Hickam Air Force Base in Honolulu, Hawaii, that same month. The state of war that had arisen between Japan and the United States also put on permanent pause Doris's ambitions to be an actress. Instead, she became a homemaker.

It is the lineage of Meghan's grandmother that can be traced directly to the Scottish royals and more. Through her ancestor Roger Shaw, Meghan's trickle of blue blood was ultimately transported to America. The son of a wine merchant and shipper in the City of London, Roger sailed from Plymouth in south-west England to Massachusetts around 1637. Like many other young men, Roger saw America as the land of promise and opportunity. Thanks to his father's influence, the authorities gave him licence 'to sell wine, and any sorts of hard liquor, to Christians and Indians, as his judgement deemed, on just and urgent occasions, and not otherwise'. In time he became a substantial landowner, farmer and an acknowledged pillar of the community.

Through Roger Shaw's family, who originated from Yorkshire in the north of England, we find the critical link to royalty. Locally they were well-respected landowners and in 1490 it was the marriage of one of the clan, James Shaw, to Christina Bruce, the heiress daughter of Sir David Bruce, 6th Baron of Clackmannan, a direct descendant of Robert the Bruce, that sealed the royal connection.

Going back down the generations, Doris can also boast another interesting royal association, this time through her ancestor Mary Bird, who appeared in the household records for Windsor Castle in 1856 and probably worked as a maid. There is some satisfaction here in that, like some latter-day Cinderella, Mary's descendant would go on to marry her own prince.

This, though, is not the only royal and English bond. Meghan is also descended from the English immigrant Christopher Hussey, who lived on the whaling island of Nantucket off the coast of Massachusetts, as well as the Reverend William Skipper, who landed in New England in 1639. The Reverend Skipper's bloodline is of particular note. His royal connections and subsequent links to the Markle family ensure that, according to Boston-based genealogist Gary Boyd Roberts, Meghan is a twenty-fourth-generation descendant of the medieval King Edward III. Born in 1312 at Windsor Castle, he successfully ruled England for fifty years until his death in 1377.

Furthermore, research by Roberts has revealed that Meghan is distantly related to most European royal families thanks to her English kinswoman Margaret Kerdeston, who lived during the fifteenth century and was the paternal grandmother of Anne of Foix-Candale, Queen of Hungary and Bohemia. There are other, more tangential, royal links. Skipper's ancestors, Sir Philip Wentworth and Mary Clifford, have distant blood connections to the late Diana, Princess of Wales, and the Queen Mother. As a result of royal intermarriage, Prince Harry, according to Roberts, is descended from Margaret Kerdeston in more than 240 lines, making the prince and his bride very, very distant cousins.

As Gary Boyd Roberts observed of Meghan: 'Much of American and English history is reflected in her diverse ancestry.'

Of course, many people with European ancestry can claim distant links to royalty, but for Meghan, such connections naturally gain new significance. Her mixed European and African-American heritage has constantly reminded her, especially when she was growing up, about her difference and distinction. It is something she has learned to acknowledge and embrace.

2

Growing Up Markle

Growing up Markle in the 1950s was like a chapter from *The Adventures of Tom Sawyer*. Young Tom Markle, Meghan's father, and his two older brothers, Mick and Fred, enjoyed an idyllic childhood in the small Pennsylvanian town of Newport where they lived in a modest clapboard house. The boys played on monkey vines in the woods at the end of their dirt road, went fishing for catfish in the Juniata River, and in summer picked blackberries, their mother, Doris, turning their trove into delicious pies and jellies. As a teenager Tom earned his pin money literally, setting the pins in the local bowling alley. Or he would join his father Gordon, who worked in administration for the post office, watching his beloved Philadelphia Phillies score home runs on their black-and-white television.

By the time Tom graduated from Newport High School, his brother Mick had joined the United States Air Force where he worked in telecommunications, though some say he was eventually recruited into the Central Intelligence Agency. Brother Fred headed south, found religion, and eventually ended up becoming the Presiding Bishop of the Eastern Orthodox Catholic Church in America, located in Sanford, Florida, where he is known as 'Bishop Dismas'.

Tom took a different attitude towards his future. After graduating, he left small-town Newport and drove to the Poconos, a mountainous resort area in north-eastern Pennsylvania. There he worked at a local theatre, learning the technical backstage side of the business and gaining valuable experience that gave him a step up the professional ladder. He then travelled to Chicago, Illinois, after getting a job as a lighting technician at WTTW, the local affiliate for the Public Broadcasting Service. He also worked at the Harper Playhouse operating alongside the new owners, Bruce and Judith Sagan, who wanted to give the Hyde Park district, also the home of a certain Barack Obama, a vibrant new cultural centre. He soon became the theatre's lighting director, working on the controversial musical *Hair*, dance shows and classic Russian dramas, as well as jazz and chamber-music concerts.

Tom worked hard and played hard, spending downtime with his student friends from the prestigious private college, the University of Chicago. During one rowdy party at the on-campus International House in 1963, Tom, then nineteen, met eighteen-year-old Roslyn Loveless, a student who worked as a secretary in the nearby Amtrak offices. Both tall – she is 5 feet 9 inches, he 6 feet 4 inches – and with similar red hair, the attraction was immediate, Roslyn being amused by his quirky sense of humour and 'light air'. They married the following year, their only daughter, Yvonne, born in November 1964 and their son, Tom Junior, in 1966. In those early years, life was a grind, with Tom often working eighteen-hour days and Roslyn holding down a secretarial job herself while bringing up two children. It was a constant juggling act, though Roslyn's mother Dorothy helped out when she could.

Despite the daily pressures, they still enjoyed a busy social life and had a fun circle of friends, Tom keeping everyone amused with his offbeat brand of humour. Roslyn remembers one time at a Greek restaurant where he pretended to have a parrot called Stanley, passing the imaginary parrot from one person to the next and imploring the waitresses not to stand on him. 'It was hilarious,' she recalls. When Yvonne and Tom Junior each started to lose their milk teeth, he sent them long letters from two tooth fairies, Hector and Ethel, who described their lives and explained what would happen to the teeth. From time to time he'd take the children to work with him. It was a thrill, especially as at that time he was lighting the hugely popular puppet show, *Sesame Street*. A trip to Wrigley Field to watch the Chicago Cubs baseball team, driving his dad's car in the parking lot at WTTW, being lifted into the air on the studio lighting gantry, hunting for quarters on a stage filled with foggy dry ice: these were some of the good times that Tom Junior treasures.

In his eyes, Tom Senior was the fun dad, the dad who played the best games and made you laugh the hardest – when he was around. Which, sadly, was not often. Childhood expectation was invariably tinged with disappointment. Tom Senior was consumed by his work, the fruits of his labour coming in local Emmy nominations – and a fat pay cheque. The price he paid for such success was his marriage, the constant late nights, the boozy cast parties, and the endless distraction and fatigue taking their toll. One of Tom Junior's earliest memories is the sound of raised voices, slamming doors and angry words. At some point in the early 1970s, when the children were still in elementary school, the couple decided to go their separate ways.

For a time, Tom lived in Chicago and had the children at weekends. But it didn't last long. He had a dream and that dream was Hollywood. Sometime before their divorce in 1975, Tom left his estranged wife and children behind as he started his new life on the West Coast. The children would not see their father again for several years.

At the urging of her brother Richard, who lived in New Mexico, Roslyn and the children travelled to Albuquerque to make a new life. For a while it was a happy time. Uncle Richard was not his father, as far as Tom Junior was concerned, but at least he was around, teaching him to drive his VW Bug in a parking lot and showing him how to shoot. Plus, Richard and Roslyn got on well together. For the first time in their lives the children did not have to live with a rancorous atmosphere at home.

The downside was that, as the only redhead at his new school, Tom Junior found himself bullied and picked on by his new classmates. Fellow pupils would steal his lunch money, while others started fights. He used to dread going to school, often coming home with yet another black eye. Worse was to come. One night he went to see the movie *Smokey and the Bandit* with his mother and her new boyfriend, a martial-arts expert called Patrick. They arrived back home to find a full-scale robbery in progress. When Patrick tackled the thieves he was shot in the stomach and the mouth, the bullets whistling past Tom Junior. Although Patrick survived, Tom Junior was traumatized.

Between bullying and burglary, Tom Junior decided to leave Albuquerque and go and live with his father, who was now enjoying life in the beachfront town of Santa Monica in Southern California. He arrived in time to enrol in high school.

Though he still idolized his father, there was one big fat fly in the ointment of his new life: his sister, Yvonne. She had moved there a few years earlier when she was fourteen, converting her father's office into her bedroom. Tom and Yvonne had always fought like cat and dog; the sibling rivals from hell.

When the trio moved from Santa Monica to a large home on Providencia Street in Woodland Hills, adjacent to the local country club, Tom Junior snagged the downstairs den as his bedroom, which he decorated with posters of the *Charlie's Angels* pin-up, Farrah Fawcett. He was especially thrilled when a friend sold him a king-sized waterbed but his excitement turned to dismay when, not long after its arrival, he sat on it only to be soaked in water. Inspecting the evidence, he discovered several holes in the brand-new bed. There was only one suspect. His sister Yvonne immediately admitted responsibility but argued that it was retribution, as she had wanted that room for herself. Another episode in a bitter, resentful dance between the siblings. As Tom Junior told me: 'If she didn't get what she wanted out of you, she was your worst nightmare.'

Enter into this bickering dynamic the figure of Doria Ragland. Small, watchful, with liquid-brown eyes and a jaunty Afro, this was the woman who had turned their father Tom into gooey mush. Before he ever brought her home, the children noticed a change in their father. He was more relaxed, cheery and light-hearted, frequently taking time off work. In short, he was happy. The couple had met on the set of ABC's drama *General Hospital* where she was training as a make-up artist and he was well established as the show's lighting director. In spite of the twelve-year age difference

– Doria was closer in age to Yvonne than to her boyfriend – the couple very quickly fell for one another.

A graduate of Fairfax High School, Doria had seen her education badly affected by the 1971 San Fernando earthquake. The quake had destroyed nearby Los Angeles High School so the two schools doubled up, Doria studying from seven in the morning until noon and then pupils from LAHS taking over their classroom for the afternoon. In spite of the difficulties, she was a member of the Apex club, a class for academically advanced youngsters. After graduating from Fairfax, Doria sold jewellery, helped in her father's antique store, 'Twas New, and tended a bric-a-brac stall at a Sunday flea market. She also worked as a travel agent. It was a way of obtaining cut-price air tickets so she could see the world on the cheap.

Not that Tom Junior took much notice of the new addition to the Providencia Street household. What with his skateboarding, go-karting and working for a florist, he barely missed a beat when Doria moved in. He was too busy enjoying himself with his new circle of friends.

As for Yvonne, it was indifference, not to say dislike, at first sight. She resented the fact that the new arrival was taking her father's focus away from her, as she had been eager for Tom Senior to use his showbiz connections to get her work as a model or an actress. During her time in Albuquerque with her mother, Yvonne had modelled jewellery and wedding gowns. Now the truculent teenager was seeing dollar bills in the Hollywood sign. When her friends came over to the house she dismissed the presence of her father's African-American girlfriend, referring to her, according to her brother, as 'the maid'. By contrast, her best friend, now a successful realtor, doesn't recall Yvonne using that kind of language and, even if she did, she ascribes it to her sour Chicago sense of humour. Nonetheless, Yvonne was not, as her mother recalls, a particularly tolerant young woman.

Doria's arrival also coincided with Yvonne embracing the dark tenets of black magic. Even as a little girl Yvonne had had a fascination with the macabre, once bringing into her bedroom a mouldering gravestone that she had found in the basement of their apartment block in Chicago. This time around, as her brother Tom recalls, she bought a copy of Anton LaVey's *Satanic Bible*, installed an altar in her bedroom, played with a Ouija board, burned black candles and dressed in the all-black uniform of the goth. It may have been no more than a rebellious teenage obsession, and her brother never witnessed her performing any satanic rituals, but he described to me how he was still disturbed by her 'weird' behaviour. She left the house when it was dark and rarely returned before dawn. One of Yvonne's friends remembers those years, describing how she and Yvonne would dress up and go out dancing, especially if a British band was in town. 'We put on our make-up and got all decked out,' she recalls. 'We were out having fun.' The ritual of boy meets girl, rather than anything satanic, was their aim.

Much of the back and forth between brother and sister was more taunting and teasing than witchcraft. On one occasion Yvonne came to the flower shop, where Tom Junior worked part time, to borrow money from her brother. While he and his colleague Richard, a devout Christian Scientist, were dealing with customers, she picked up Richard's Holy Bible and drew a pentagram, the sign of the Devil, on its pages with her red lipstick. Before leaving she wrote '666', the mark of the Beast, on another page. Young Tom had his revenge when he called home telling his sister that Richard was so traumatized by her desecration of his Bible that he had run into the road and been hit by a bus. His ruse had her racing back to the store to check on Richard's condition.

Certainly Doria could be forgiven for wondering what she had got herself into when faced with this bickering, back-biting brood. It was one thing falling in love with a man twelve years her senior, but quite another being thrown headlong into his fractious household with brother and sister continually squabbling. A strong personality with a level head on her shoulders, Doria brought a sense of family to the gloomy house.

When she arrived, everyone was used to going their own way. Tom Senior worked every hour of the day and night, Yvonne was out clubbing with her friends, while Tom Junior was smoking weed with his own crowd. Doria brought them together as a family and was seen as the cool hippie peacemaker. She soon became friendly with their near-neighbour Olga McDaniel, a former nightclub singer, the two spending hours together shooting the breeze. 'The best way I can describe Doria is that she was like a warm hug,' Olga's daughter told me. Her masterstroke was to take Tom Junior to the animal shelter and help him pick out a dog, which he named Bo. The noisy new arrival, a golden retriever-beagle mix, soon ruled their five-bedroomed home in the leafy Valley suburb of Woodland Hills.

At Thanksgiving, Doria invited the Markles to join the Ragland clan, including her mother Jeanette, her father Alvin, her half-brother Joseph and half-sister Saundra, for a true Southern feast of sweet potato pie, gumbo, ham hocks and beans. 'Good times,' recalls Tom Junior. 'When I first met them I was uneasy and nervous, but they were really warm and inclusive, the kind of family I had always wanted. They were happy-assed people with a real sense of family.' Even his sister was impressed, admiring Doria's imaginative use of home-prepared seasonings in her cooking. She noted that everyone had seconds.

That sense of family was formalized when, on 23 December 1979, Doria and Tom Senior were married at the Self-Realization Fellowship Temple on Sunset Boulevard, just east of Hollywood. The venue was Doria's choice, the new bride adhering to the teachings of Yogananda, a Hindu yoga guru who had arrived in Boston in 1920 and preached a philosophy of breathing and meditation as part of the yoga routine to help followers on their path to enlightenment. Hollywood stars such as Linda Evans and Mariel Hemingway, Apple founder Steve Jobs and ex-Beatle George Harrison all followed his teachings. But even in such an enlightened setting, mixed marriages were still uncommon.

Less than half a century before Tom and Doria's wedding, California had repealed anti-miscegenation laws that banned marriages between black and white people. However, it was not until 1967 that anti-miscegenation laws were declared unconstitutional throughout the nation by the United States Supreme Court, with their landmark decision in *Loving v. Virginia*, their story since being dramatized in a Hollywood film starring Ruth Negga and Joel Edgerton.

In 1958, Richard and Mildred Loving, a white man and black woman, were married in Washington DC. When they returned to their home in Virginia, they were arrested in their bedroom under the state's Racial Integrity Act. Judge Leon Bazile suspended their sentence on the condition that the Lovings leave Virginia and not return for twenty-five years. The couple appealed the judgment, but Judge Bazile refused to reconsider his decision, writing, 'Almighty God created the races white, black, yellow, Malay, and red, and he placed them on separate continents, and but for the interference with his arrangement there would be no cause for such marriages. The fact that he separated the races shows that he did not intend for the races to mix.'

The Lovings, supported by the NAACP (*National Association for the Advancement of Colored People*) Legal Defense Fund, the Japanese American Citizens League and a coalition of Catholic bishops, then successfully appealed to the US Supreme Court, which wrote in its decision, 'Marriage is one of the "basic civil rights of man", fundamental to our very existence and survival ... Under our Constitution, the freedom to marry, or not marry, a person of another race resides with the individual and cannot be infringed by the State', condemning Virginia's anti-miscegenation law as 'designed to maintain White supremacy'. While this judgment decriminalized miscegenation, mixed-race couples were still looked upon with suspicion by many, confronted by casual racism and sometimes outright hostility.

On their big day, a nervous Tom Senior, wearing a herringbone sports coat and button-down shirt, and Doria, in a flowing white dress with baby's breath flowers in her hair, took their wedding vows in the presence of Brother Bhaktananda and various family members. He stressed that the merging of the couple was for the 'highest common good' and to achieve union with God. The children of followers of Self-Realization have a reputation as being open, inquisitive souls. So when Dodi – the family's nickname for

Doria – found herself pregnant just a year after tying the knot, she and Tom – or Bunky, as he was known – couldn't wait for the new arrival. Further good news came when Doria's pregnancy coincided with Tom's first nomination for a Daytime Emmy Award for his design and lighting work on *General Hospital*; he would later be nominated a further eight times. Not bad for a man who was officially colour-blind. If 1980 was a good year, 1981 was going to be even better.

As the months ticked by and the summer thermometer inched upwards, Doria became impatient for the waiting to be over. With the daytime temperatures often in the mid-thirties, she was grateful that they had a 'swamp' evaporative cooler and that the rambling home was dark and shady. In his spare time, Tom Senior decorated the nursery, painting the walls and hanging Disney characters and angel pictures around the white painted cot. Even their two cats, Brandy and Xander, realized that change was a'coming. Finally, at 4.46 on the morning of 4 August 1981 at West Park Hospital in Canoga Park, obstetrician Malverse Martin announced that Doria and Tom were now the parents of a healthy baby girl. This latest addition to the sorority of 'Valley girls' was, as her mother noted, a Leo. Typical Leos are supposed to be 'Warm, action-oriented and driven by the desire to be loved and admired. They have an air of royalty about them. They love to be in the limelight, which is why many of them make a career in the performing arts.' Never has an astrological star sign been more accurate.

The arrival of Rachel Meghan Markle transformed her father's life. 'He was just so, so happy,' recalls Tom Junior. 'He spent every single minute he could with her. My dad was more in love with her than with anyone else in the world and that included Doria. She became his whole life, his little princess. He was just blown away by Meghan.'

Meghan's seventeen-year-old sister Yvonne ignored her, more interested in clubbing and make-up than playing with a newborn. '"Babies, yuck, no thanks," that was our feeling,' recalls one of Yvonne's friends. She was a teenager having fun, and fun certainly did not involve babysitting the new arrival. Not only was Yvonne indifferent to her sibling, now nicknamed 'Flower' or 'Bud', but she felt left out on the sidelines, her father utterly devoted to his infant daughter. Doubtless she recalled his frequent absences when she was growing up and felt somewhat jealous of the attention now focused on her half-sister.

It became an understandable source of friction that her father did not spend, in her eyes, as much time as she would have liked in using his contacts to fix her up with acting or modelling jobs. That said, sometime down the road he did get her a walk-on part on *General Hospital* and an episode in the drama *Matlock*, in which she was killed off before the first commercial break. It seems, though, that she never fully exploited these opportunities.

Not only did Tom spend every waking minute with his second daughter, but in his own quirky fashion he tried to impose a little discipline on the somewhat laissez-faire household in order to protect his little 'Flower'. Previously, he had always said to his son that if he and his friends wanted to smoke weed they should do so only in the house, but this instruction changed with the arrival of the baby. Tom Junior told me that on one occasion he and his friends were smoking a spliff in the sitting room while Meghan was in the nursery crying. His father announced loudly that he was going upstairs to change her nappy. Shortly afterwards he appeared in the sitting room carrying a full nappy. He joined the boys on the sofa, took a spoon out of his pocket and started eating the 'contents'. Grossed out, the boys fled the house. Only later did he reveal that he had earlier substituted the soiled nappy with a brand-new one that he had filled with chocolate pudding. It was his way of stopping the boys from smoking weed when Meghan was around.

But that was about as far as discipline went. Their house was still generally party central, with Doria's friends coming over, playing music, practising yoga – which Doria now taught – and barbecuing. From the outside it seemed to be one big, happy family, Doria's relations, especially her mother Jeanette, babysitting for the couple. Even Tom Junior pitched in, to give his dad and Doria a break. For the most part, Tom and Doria seemed content, but then their bickering started. As much as Tom loved Meghan, he loved his job, too; he was still a workaholic and thought nothing of spending eighty or ninety hours a week on set. And in his eyes, it was paying off, with Meghan proving to be his lucky charm. After two nominations, in 1982 he and his colleagues on *General Hospital* finally won a Daytime Emmy for 'outstanding achievement in design excellence'.

But it all came at a price. Doria had not signed up for this, dealing with his children, raising her own, keeping frisky Bo away from the baby, kick-starting a career and trying to run the family's cavernous house. And, though it was not Tom's fault, they were also living in a predominantly white neighbourhood where, because of her dark skin and Meghan's light skin, people often thought that Doria was the nanny. They regularly stopped her and asked, quite innocently, where the baby's mother lived. It was a petty humiliation that she could do without.

It seemed too that Tom was wedded to work more than he was wedded to her. It was a feeling that had been shared by his first wife, Roslyn. Gradually, the harsh words and the fighting became the norm rather than the exception, Tom Junior and Yvonne recognizing the all-too-familiar sounds of a relationship breaking down. According to family friends, Tom's constant criticism of Doria over matters small and large wore her down. There came a point where Doria decided that enough was enough and she went back home to her mother. As a family friend observed: 'Doria is not a doormat, that much I know. She spoke up for herself, protected herself and her daughter fiercely. Her head was on straight. I trusted her judgement.'

The couple split up when their little 'Flower' was just two years old, but did not divorce for another five years. Tom would have custody of his daughter at weekends and drop her off on Sunday evenings. Then, as Meghan told writer Sam Kashner, the trio would sit together and eat dinner off their knees as they watched *Jeopardy!* 'We were so close-knit,' she recalls, a memory perhaps seen through the forgiving prism of a child desperate for her parents to be united, rather than accepting the bleak reality of a mother and father at odds. Others were not so sanguine, pointing to Tom's bewilderment, not to say bitterness, that Doria had given their union so little time to prove itself. By the time Meghan was old enough to appreciate *Jeopardy!* the couple were divorced and living separate lives.

✳

Founded in 1945 by Ruth Pease, the Hollywood Little Red Schoolhouse is a favoured institution for the sons and daughters of LA's showbiz elite. While parents rarely saw Johnny Depp, whose daughter was a pupil, waiting outside the school gates, Flea, bassist for the Red Hot Chili Peppers, used to pick up his daughter after school in a spray-painted Mercedes-Benz. Now known as the Hollywood Schoolhouse, its teaching – based around the four-stage programme of Swiss psychologist Jean Piaget – is eclectic, imaginative and expensive: $25,750 for kindergarten rising to $28,300 for grade six at today's prices. As the school only chooses the brightest and the best, older children have to take an exam before they are considered for entry. In 1983 Doria, who was now training as a social worker, and Tom enrolled two-year-old Meghan for the crèche-cum-kindergarten at the exclusive establishment.

The set-up was convenient for all involved. The school was close to the ABC studios in Los Feliz where Tom worked, and just a few minutes away from Doria's work and her new home just south of Hollywood. Meghan would stay there until she was eleven years old. While reading, writing and arithmetic were at the core of the school day, children could dip into a whole range of subjects, from Spanish to quantum physics. In summer, its pupils worked in the community garden, and went on nature trails at Leo Carillo beach or nearby Griffith Park. After school Meghan would go on bike rides or jogging with her mother, who also encouraged Meghan's early interest in yoga. Doria would insist that she help prepare the evening meal, a daily routine that Meghan credits with fostering her love of food and cooking. Her parents also instilled into her an awareness of the needs of others. Meghan later described how her mother and father gave a lot even though they had little. They performed, she wrote, 'quiet acts of grace – be it a hug, a smile or a pat on the back to show ones in need that they would be all right'.

At the same time, the school's stage shows, watched by proud parents, encouraged Meghan's budding interest in the theatre. When she was five, Meghan entertained the parents with a rendition of the song 'The Wheels on the Bus', and later featured in *Bye Bye Birdie* and *West Side Story*. On Halloween, Meghan and her friend Ninaki 'Nikki' Priddy played two corpses discussing the size and comfort of their respective coffins. Another time, she shared the lead in an adaptation of *How the Grinch Stole Christmas*. Unfortunately, her co-star Elizabeth McCoy came down with stomach flu just hours before the show began, leaving Meghan desperately trying to memorize both parts. 'That was the worst experience of my life, trying to learn your lines,' Meghan told an apologetic McCoy afterwards. Ironically, no one gave a thought to asking a little girl with an unkempt mane of blonde hair, thick glasses and an awkward, clumsy manner, who was lurking in the chorus, to take the part. Her name was Scarlett Johansson, now one of the world's highest-paid actresses and who was briefly a pupil at the school.

McCoy, who these days is a renowned chef and scriptwriter, had another reason to thank Meghan. Two years Meghan's junior, Elizabeth was the self-confessed 'weird kid'. Intense, fiercely intelligent and overweight, she was interested in quirky subjects like UFOs, the occult and ghosts. Other children thought her odd. Nor did it help that she suffered from petit mal seizures, a form of epilepsy that saw her going into a trance-like state from time to time that made her unreachable. As the seizures last for only a short time, children are often thought to be daydreaming or not listening.

Meghan, Elizabeth was to discover, was not like many of the other kids, who either walked on by or mocked her. The first time Meghan saw Elizabeth suffering from a seizure she came to her aid, sitting next to her while holding her hand and comforting her. Elizabeth also remembers how Meghan provided friendship when she was being taunted by 'the mean girls', as she describes them. She recalls: 'I was bullied and miserable and my only salvation were the kids who liked me. I really liked Meghan a lot. She didn't turn me away if I started talking about offbeat subjects. She listened. She was cool and had cool things to say. I liked being around her.'

It was clear that Meghan had inherited her mother's strong sense of right and wrong, and was prepared to stand up for herself and for others. On one occasion the so-called 'mean girls' announced that they were starting a 'White Girls Only' club and wanted Meghan to join. 'Are you kidding me?' said Meghan to the gaggle of fellow pupils, dismissing them in a sentence. They went very quiet after that.

But that playground confrontation highlighted something that Meghan was battling with herself. Around this time, Christmas 1988, she tells the story of how her father bought two sets of Heart dolls containing the traditional nuclear family unit of mother, father and two children. He bought one with black dolls, one with white, and mixed them together to represent Meghan's own family. Then he wrapped them in sparkly Christmas paper and placed the box under the tree.

Meghan's struggle to understand herself instinctively made her more aware of those who had difficulties fitting in. As Elizabeth McCoy recalls: 'You never forget the people who were mean to you and who was nice. That's why I have never forgotten Meghan. She was one of the most righteous people I have ever met. If someone was being treated unfairly she stuck up for them. On one occasion I made the girl who bullied me cry. I tried to apologize and Meghan sided with the other girl because she was the one in tears.

'Meghan called it like it was. She was going to defend those who needed it. Her attitude was: "I can see you are hurt and I'm going to protect you." She was a genuinely decent human being who looked out for people who needed help. She gave a damn about people other than herself.'

Even Elizabeth's father, Dennys McCoy, an internationally known animation scriptwriter, singles out Meghan. He recalls: 'She stood out because she was a level-headed kid who was smart and mature for her age. We were surprised that she became an actress. We thought she would be a lawyer.'

By the time she was ten, Meghan was fiercely switched on and loved to debate an issue, taking part in discussions about racism in America, most notably after the notorious beating of Rodney King by Los Angeles cops in 1991, the Gulf War that same year and the build-up to the 1992 presidential contest between Bill Clinton and George H. W. Bush. During one classroom discussion about the looming war in the Gulf, a fellow pupil was in tears because he didn't think his older brother, who was serving in the US military, would make it home. The issue became such a hot topic that the children, led by Meghan, staged a protest on the school grounds. They made banners and signs daubed with anti-war slogans. Such was the interest that the local TV station, KTLA, sent along a camera crew to film the protest. It was Meghan's first TV appearance.

Even nearer to home were the LA riots in late April and early May of 1992, which were ignited after four Los Angeles Police Department officers, who had been filmed savagely beating Rodney King, an unarmed black man, were acquitted of assault and using excessive force. As the burning and looting spread like fingers along LA's thoroughfares, Meghan and her classmates were sent home. Meghan watched with wonder as ash from burning buildings floated onto her lawn. She thought it was snowing, but her mother knew better and told her to get into the house. Even when they returned to school there was a brooding sense of anxiety and menace. On one occasion the children, including Meghan, crowded around a second-floor school window as they watched police arresting a man. In total, the six days of rioting left sixty-three people dead and more than 2,300 injured, and led to over 12,000 arrests.

The experience awakened the nascent activist in her, Meghan becoming determined to use her influence when she could. She gained something of a reputation for writing to companies, especially food giants, about damaged or faulty packages and foods. Invariably, she was sent bags of crisps, biscuits or whatever by the food companies as compensation, and she regularly brought the fruits of her letter-writing to share among her schoolfriends.

Her most memorable coup was when she wrote to the household products company Procter & Gamble for making a sexist commercial that used the tag line 'Women all over America are fighting greasy pots and pans' to sell its Ivory dishwashing liquid. She and the rest of her classmates had been watching commercials as part of a social studies assignment. It was, however, the reaction of two boys in her class to the dishwashing liquid ad that particularly incensed her. She recalls them saying, 'Yeah, that's where women belong – in the kitchen.' Meghan felt confused. She was angry and annoyed, knowing that they were wrong, but she also felt, as she later recalled, 'small, too small to say anything in that moment'.

She went home and told her father, who suggested that she channel her feelings into handwritten letters of complaint. She wrote not only to the soap company chairman, saying that the phrase should be changed to 'People all over America', but also to Hillary Clinton, who was then the First Lady, Nickelodeon's *Nick News* anchor Linda Ellerbee, and prominent women's rights lawyer Gloria Allred, who was based in Los Angeles.

While Clinton and Ellerbee wrote letters of encouragement, and Allred also offered her support, according to Meghan she never heard from Procter & Gamble. However, when the ad aired again just a month later, she saw the fruits of her handiwork. The slogan had been changed to 'People all over America are fighting greasy pots and pans.' Her success once again had the TV cameras arriving at the school, this time with Ellerbee interviewing Meghan and her fellow pupils about her one-schoolgirl campaign.

'I don't think it's right for kids to grow up thinking these things, that just Mom does everything,' Meghan told Ellerbee. 'It's always, "Mom does this" and "Mom does that".' Sometime afterwards, this and other incidents inspired her to join the Washington DC-based pressure group, the National Organization for Women. Meghan, as she proudly recalled, became one of the youngest, if not *the* youngest, member of the group founded in 1966, which campaigns for women's rights.

More than twenty years later, in 2015, Meghan reflected on this chapter of her life while giving a speech as the newly minted UN Women's Advocate for Political Participation and Leadership. 'It was at that moment that I realized the magnitude of my actions. At the age of eleven, I had created my small level of impact by standing up for equality,' she said.

While her childhood experiences were the crucible that set her on the path to activism, her mother believes that she was hardwired from birth to try to make the world a better and more equal place. In short, she had a moral compass. Doria played her own part, strict at home but also ready to show her daughter that there was more to the world than Woodland Hills. She raised her to be what she called 'a global citizen', taking her to places like Oaxaca, Mexico, where Meghan recalls seeing children playing in the dirt roads and peddling chewing gum so that they could bring home a few extra pesos. When Meghan, then aged ten, and her mother visited the slums of Jamaica, the schoolgirl was horrified to see such grinding poverty. 'Don't look scared, Flower,' her mother told her. 'Be aware, but don't be afraid.'

Her experience is reminiscent of the times the late Diana, Princess of Wales, privately took her boys, William and Harry, to visit the homeless and the sick in central London so that they would hopefully appreciate that life did not begin and end at the palace gates.

Meghan's letter-writing campaigns, her interest in current affairs, her purposeful travelling and gender awareness were all of a piece with a young girl embarking on a journey where feminism could coexist with femininity, as well as an ethos of hard work that was matched by a willingness to try the new and the interesting.

Curiously, just as her letter-writing campaign got underway, another protest was kicking off, this one regarding the raunchy comedy show *Married ... with Children*, for which her father was now the lighting director. Meghan often sat on the floor of the studio after school, waiting for her father to finish work so that he could take her home. Indeed, she thrilled her fellow classmates when she was given permission to bring several friends on set to meet the cast.

As she sat quietly reading or studying, all kinds of ribald scenes were being played out on set, some involving various stages of undress and semi-nudity, as well as off-colour jokes about sex. Hardly the normal after-school fare for a young schoolgirl. In January 1989, a Mormon from Michigan, Terry Rakolta, led a boycott of the show after the screening of an episode entitled 'Her Cups Runneth Over', which involved the purchase of a bra. That episode showed the character of Al Bundy ogling a naked model in a department store.

The resulting media storm led to some sponsors withdrawing advertising and the conservative Parents Television Council describing the show as 'the crudest comedy on prime-time television … peppered with lewd punchlines about sex, masturbation, the gay lifestyle and the lead character's fondness for pornographic magazines and strip clubs'.

Meghan later described her own misgivings about spending time around the long-running comedy when she appeared on Craig Ferguson's late-night show. She told her host, 'It's a very perverse place for a girl to grow up. I went to Catholic school. I'm there in my school uniform and the guests would be [former porn star] Traci Lords.' While she wasn't allowed to watch the show when it aired, her mother would let her kiss the screen as her dad's name went by in the credits at the end of the programme.

Perverse it may have been, but it paid the bills – and Meghan's private-school fees. At this time, unbeknownst to her, her father enjoyed a slice of luck that meant he no longer had to work such a brutal schedule. In 1990 he won the California State Lottery, scooping $750,000 with five numbers, which included Meghan's birthdate. The win was ample payback for the thousands of dollars he had spent over the years buying lottery tickets.

As he still had outstanding financial matters concerning his divorce from Doria, he kept the win secret. But he was too greedy, and his duplicity proved to be his undoing. In order to avoid registering his name with the lottery authorities, he sent an old Chicago friend, who is now dead, to pick up his winnings. The plan, according to Tom Junior, backfired when his pal ended up swindling him out of the lion's share of his fortune in a failed jewellery business.

Before he lost his loot, Tom gave his son a substantial handout to start a flower shop and bought daughter Yvonne a second car after she wrecked the first one he had given her.

Within three years of his windfall, Tom had declared bankruptcy, the lottery win proving more of a curse than a blessing. At least he had kept some money aside to pay for the next stage of Meghan's education, at Immaculate Heart, a private all-girls Catholic school just yards from his home in Los Feliz. From now on it made sense for her to live with her father during the week, as his home was within walking distance of the school. It was a decision that would have far-reaching implications for the way she was seen by her new teachers and classmates.

3

A Street Called Gladys

Sixth Street in downtown Los Angeles is not a place for the unwary. And after dark, even the wary give it a wide berth. Danger lurks in the shadows, desperation loiters on the sidewalk. This is the heart of Skid Row, the mushrooming and endlessly shifting encampment of the homeless and the helpless that is a makeshift home to more than 2,000 people. Los Angeles is the homeless capital of America. At the last count there were over 66,000 men, women and children sleeping rough in Los Angeles County, tent towns frequently springing up around the city underpasses, in empty buildings and other open spaces.

This particular stretch is more organized than most of the impromptu enclaves of Skid Row, with volunteers handing out water, food and clean socks. And there is one place in particular, at the corner of Sixth and Gladys, which offers a welcome oasis of calm and tranquillity amid the shouts, moans and shrieks of those who live in the tents and cardboard sheds that line both sides of the road.

This is the Hospitality Kitchen, more popularly known as the 'Hippie Kitchen', which is part of the Catholic Worker community founded more than eighty years ago by Dorothy Day and Peter Maurin. Their stated goal is to 'feed the hungry, shelter the homeless, care for the sick, clothe the naked, visit the prisoner'. In an average day, volunteers will hand out a nourishing but simple meal to around a thousand folk who line up around the block; for many it is their only food for the day. There is no prayer or proselytizing, just beans, salad, a hunk of bread and a thick slice of goodwill.

The charity's uncompromising ideals have, at times, placed them in head-on conflict with the Catholic hierarchy, local police and even other homeless charities. Catholic Worker activists are known to protest against unfair treatment of the homeless, American militarism and nuclear policy as well as the death penalty. Acts of civil disobedience, including lie-ins and noisy marches, have led some to suffer arrest and even jail. Former nun Catherine Morris, now eighty-six, and a stalwart of the Hippie Kitchen for more than forty years, has lost count of the number of times she and her husband Jeff Dietrich have been arrested for peaceful acts of civil disobedience. They like to think of themselves as the 'Merry Pranksters', the name derived from the early hippie followers of counter-culture author and poet Ken Kesey.

Though protest is an integral part of the Catholic Worker credo, feeding the homeless and the destitute takes priority. And it was in the garden of the Hippie Kitchen – a small outdoor haven that's filled with colourful murals, the chirping of Brazilian finches in an aviary and water bubbling over a fountain – that Meghan Markle had what could only be described as an epiphany.

With her mother's encouragement, she first visited the Hippie Kitchen when she was just thirteen and found the experience 'very scary'. By the time Meghan had enlisted as a volunteer in the early 1990s, the composition of the homeless neighbourhood had drastically changed, from mainly old, white, male drunks to a new younger and more volatile community of those high on crack cocaine and other deadly drugs. 'I was young, and it was rough and raw down there, and though I was with a great volunteer group, I just felt overwhelmed,' she later recalled.

She might well have chalked the visit up to experience and never ventured there again but for a classroom conversation with her Immaculate Heart High School theology teacher, Maria Pollia, some three years later. During class, Maria, who had already been a volunteer at the Hippie Kitchen for years, described her own early experience and how she faced up to her fears and doubts.

'It's one of the worst corners of Skid Row,' she says. 'One of the most distressed and distressing. It is heartbreaking. Driving through at night it looked like something Charles Dickens would be writing about. People huddled around blazing oil drums. It was very, very frightening. An awakening for me.' Her message to the class, though, was to put their fears aside and make contact with the homeless on a human level. They are people too, people with names, people with a past and hopefully a future.

'Life is about putting the needs of others above your own fears,' she counselled. It was a message that resonated with sixteen-year-old Meghan. 'That has always stayed with me,' she later recalled.

After class, Meghan spoke with her teacher, who advised on the practicalities of volunteering at the Hippie Kitchen. Heartened, Meghan began to go regularly, working as a server and clearing tables, which put her directly in contact with the Hippie Kitchen's guests. Maria Pollia recalls: 'What she learned was what I learned – that it is the human contact people crave. It's someone saying hello and knowing your name.' Meghan earnestly absorbed all the advice and began to come back with her own stories.

'It was remarkable that, once in the situation, she got right in it,' Maria added. 'She wasn't just handing out stew and letting everyone go by, but she was connecting with people, she was learning their names and listening to their stories. And that is what gave her joy – really connecting with people.' The teenager came to realize, as Catherine Morris observed, that everyone on Skid Row has a story. It might be a hard-luck story, a never-catching-a-break story or a wrong-turn story; they would all be eye-opening for Meghan, offering a new perspective on what kind of life you could be dealt.

Meghan's experience was echoed by others, such as schoolgirl volunteer Sophie Goldstein, who described how she too confronted her fears and concerns. 'When I first came here, I have to admit, I was kind of nervous,' she wrote on the Catholic Worker blog. 'I saw the area and I was scared. Then I met the people. What the Workers told me was that a lot of the time these were people who couldn't meet up with their bills, and now they're stuck, or that they have drug problems. I got to put a face on my own prejudice.

'I realized that these are real people. They are not just the crazy homeless that you hear about all the time, or that my friends talk about, or the flippant remarks that people make about the homeless.' For Meghan it was a life-affirming and life-changing experience.

Up to that point, Meghan's only other experience of work was at Humphrey Yogart, a frozen yogurt shop where she worked when she was thirteen, serving customers and taking out the rubbish for $4 an hour, employed under the California law that permitted youngsters enrolled in school to work ten to twelve hours a week. Owner Paula Sheftel told the *Daily Mirror* that Meghan was a hard worker and popular with the customers: 'She had to prove she had an outgoing personality and would work well with staff. A lot of the kids can't handle the pressure. It takes a special personality for somebody that young to deal with it. Meghan had that early on.'

Meghan had ample opportunity to practise her people skills at the often fast-paced fro-yo shop, but she also gained another valuable lesson that would later serve her well. One afternoon, Meghan saw Yasmine Bleeth, one of the stars of *Baywatch* who was a particular idol of hers. Finishing up with the trash bin, Meghan approached the star and blurted out, 'I loved you in that Soft & Dri commercial.' Bleeth smiled, asked Meghan her name and shook her hand. Later Meghan would say, 'That moment with Yasmine is exactly what I base every interaction with fans on.'

A yogurt shop in Beverly Hills was a far cry from the Hippie Kitchen at Sixth Street and Gladys, which, like her travels with her mother to Mexico and Jamaica, honed her awareness. As she later observed for a book called *The Game Changers*: 'Yes, make sure you are safe and never ever put yourself in a compromising situation, but once that is checked off the list, I think it's really important for us to remember that someone needs us, and that your act of giving/ helping/doing can truly become an act of grace once you get out of your head.'

If this was a practical application of her spiritual journey, her encounter with the work of Catholic theologian Thomas Merton emphasized her intellectual curiosity and emotional maturity. In a world of black and white, Merton's mercurial thinking, with its endless shape-shifting vista of grey, of muted maybes and possibilities, is hard to pin down. 'As well as grappling with her personal issues, Meghan was taking on Merton, whose thinking was at the core of her theology class,' says her former teacher Maria Pollia.

Merton is arguably the most influential American Catholic author of the twentieth century, his autobiography, *The Seven Storey Mountain*, selling more than a million copies. He lived a raucous and challenging life, fathering a child while studying at Clare College, Cambridge, in the UK, and briefly joining the Young Communist League before finally being confirmed in the Catholic Church in 1939 when he was in his mid-twenties. In 1941, he joined the Abbey of Gethsemani in Kentucky, where he gained a reputation as a monk who was a spiritual seeker, not a settler; a man who did not recognize absolute truth but saw the grand ambivalence, the contradictions and duality of existence.

For the average American sixteen-year-old, weaned on an academic diet of short sentences and multiple-choice questions, Merton is a complex and demanding character. Yet perhaps because of the racial duality of her own background, Meghan was attracted to and inspired by the work of the American theologian. 'She was someone questing for knowledge; she had a profound desire to connect with people,' recalls Ms Pollia. There was a practical side to her perplexity. When she was in seventh grade at Immaculate Heart, she was asked to fill in a form during an English class on which one of the questions related to her racial background. There was no box for dual heritage. It was a quandary that would have welcomed the Merton touch.

Instead, she put her pen down and left the box empty, not wanting to offend one of her parents. 'So, I didn't tick a box,' she later recalled. 'I left my identity blank – a question mark, an absolute incomplete – much like how I felt.' When she discussed her experience with her father that night, she could feel his impotent fury wanting to protect his daughter. He told her, 'If that happens again, you draw your own box.'

In her 1997 theology class entitled Experiencing God, Meghan was encouraged to think outside the box, proving herself undaunted by the intellectual challenges posed by Father Thomas Merton and other mystics. She embraced concepts that demand considerable maturity and considered reflection. For the first time in their school career, students were thrown into a subject without obvious answers, the course requiring more than an ability to memorize pages of a set text. Maria Pollia observed to me, 'As we become more mature in the adult life we understand that there are many inconsistencies, many dichotomies, and that life is a continuing encounter with mystery.

'For a young person to feel comfortable with that conversation is very unusual. They get there in the end but rather than fearing these concepts and backing away, Meghan was already interested in pushing deeper and deeper into these questions. She was remarkable. Someone said [to me], "Would you have remembered her, Prince Harry notwithstanding?" Absolutely. She is one of the top-five outstanding students in my career and I promise you I am not just saying that.'

During this philosophy course, Meghan and her classmates were faced with a real-life paradox; namely, how could a young mother, a glamorous humanitarian in the prime of life, die in the cruel banality of a car accident. She and her friends watched the funeral of Diana, Princess of Wales, in early September 1997, tears coursing down their cheeks at the poignant moment when the cameras zoomed in on the royal coffin. Perched among the white flowers was an envelope with the one word, 'Mummy', containing Prince Harry's last note to his beloved mother. Meghan was not the only one to ask how this tragedy could befall a living icon; dozens of conspiracy theories sprang up on the internet and elsewhere as millions tried to make sense of the senseless.

Nor was she the only one to feel Diana's loss in a keenly personal way. After Meghan heard about the tragedy, she and her friend Suzy Ardakani had sat and watched old videos of the 1981 wedding between Prince Charles and Lady Diana Spencer. According to family friends, she was intrigued by Diana not just for her style but for her independent humanitarian mission, seeing her as a role model. Inspired by the princess, she and Suzy collected clothes and toys for less privileged children. In fact, such was her interest in the princess that Suzy's mother Sonia even gave her a copy of my biography, *Diana: Her True Story*, which remained on her bookshelves for the next few years. As her childhood friend Ninaki Priddy observed: 'She was always fascinated by the Royal Family. She wants to be Princess Diana 2.0.'

Diana's death was a painful reminder for the Ardakani family, who just two years previously had also experienced the life-changing force of a random act of fate. One afternoon in 1995, Matt Ardakani, Suzy's father, was working at his downtown car-body shop when a deranged Vietnam veteran who had murdered his own family came into the garage and started shooting indiscriminately. Mr Ardakani was hit in the spine and lung and was rushed to hospital. When Suzy was told about the shooting, it was Meghan who was the first to console the sobbing teenager and the one who accompanied her to the hospital, where they kept vigil for hours.

Sonia Ardakani recalls: 'She and Suzy sat beside Matt's bedside for many hours, praying he would pull through. We feel sure those prayers helped him survive.' Though permanently paralysed, Matt did survive and is still working.

Meghan's instinctive empathy with others and her interest in giving back – a central tenet of Immaculate Heart's mission – as well as her evident maturity, thoughtfulness and positive attitude made her the clear first choice to be a group leader at a Kairos retreat in the autumn of 1998. Like hundreds of Catholic schools across America, Immaculate Heart regularly organized Kairos (Greek for 'critical moment') retreats for students, which were designed to help teenagers contemplate the place of God in their lives.

During the four-day event, which was held at the Holy Spirit Retreat Center at Encino, six girls were chosen to lead groups of eight in various discussions, their role being to encourage participation and debate. As a leader, the most daunting assignment was to make a thirty-minute presentation dealing with a challenging list of issues ranging from self-image and trust to core values and finding yourself.

Christine Knudsen, who has been organizing the Kairos retreat at Immaculate Heart for twenty-three years, described the qualities she seeks in the girls chosen as leaders. 'You are looking for a girl who has been through something and who has a certain amount of depth to her. The kinds of insights and comments Meghan made gave her a depth because she had had to struggle with her own issues.'

It was clear that her dysfunctional family background, the separation and subsequent divorce of her parents when she was still a youngster, were the concerns she grappled with. 'I know that was difficult for her, one parent over here and one over there and neither particularly fond of each other,' recalls Mrs Knudsen. While Meghan was not the only girl on campus with divorced parents, what marked her out was the way she had managed them. Like many children of divorced parents, she had learned to become a skilled diplomat, mediating between the warring parties. This nihilistic parental interaction taught Meghan a valuable lesson: how to control her emotions. 'She is very poised,' observes a schoolfriend. 'It could be hard for her. Sometimes she felt she had to pick sides.'

The older she became the more she felt she was the one who was mothering her father. It was a source of friction, especially when she started dating. As a friend notes: 'Typical teenage stuff.'

There were other issues, too, which clearly troubled her, though she did not discuss them publicly at the time. Fitting in was a constant concern. As she later recalled: 'My high school had cliques: the black girls and white girls, the Filipino [*sic*] and the Latina girls. Being bi-racial, I fell somewhere in between. So every day during lunch, I busied myself with meetings – French club, student body, whatever one could possibly do between noon and 1 p.m. – I was there. Not so that I was more involved, but so that I wouldn't have to eat alone.'

Photographer John Dlugolecki, who photographed Meghan and other students throughout high school, noticed that Meghan never appeared to be part of the African-American, Asian or any other ethnic group of girls. Dlugolecki also remarked that Meghan 'was not considered mixed race by her peers', adding, 'We only ever saw her with Tom, never with the mom.' And so it came as a mild shock to members of faculty when they finally got to meet Doria.

'Everyone thought [Meghan] was Italian because she was so light-skinned,' recalls one former teacher. 'Then we met her mother and realized she was bi-racial.'

As poised and confident as she seemed at Kairos when she discussed her own demons, at least those related to her family discord, having had those experiences clearly enabled her to encourage her classmates to confront their own. As Meghan revealed in a 2016 issue of *Sharp* magazine: 'In middle school and high school, there was this huge span of my life where I was just the girl with the crazy curly hair, a big gap between my teeth, with skinny legs. I was always the smart one. My self-identification was wrapped up in being the smart one.'

Mrs Knudsen recalls: 'You have to be very honest about who you are and be willing to share all the things that you struggle with, your successes and failures. She was articulate, confident, feisty and spunky.

'I remember her saying, "Why can't we do it this way, has anybody thought about that?" She was always thinking about a better way to do something, not just complaining.'

For many students, the retreat is a turning point in their young lives, a time when they face up to their own emotional issues honestly. Realizing that their classmates have their own problems is seen as a critical catalyst. 'It's a time of truth-telling and the leaders are the ones who set the tone,' observes Mrs Knudsen. 'The atmosphere is: "I am willing to share my truth with you, and that makes you willing to share your truth." So there is a lot of crying, but it is healing crying. Everything out in the open, you realize everybody has to struggle and that nobody is perfect no matter how they look.' Given her emerging leadership qualities, it came as no surprise to her teachers that she decided to run for class president under the slogan 'Meghan Markle – make it sparkle'. She also gave a speech on social change at her middle-school graduation, where she described her fellow pupils as 'women of great heart' who were dedicated to making the world a better place. It was a phrase and speech that marked her future direction.

※

While her fractured family background and her sense of isolation caused Meghan a great deal of heartache as she grew up, it also helped to provide some of the psychological drive that would propel her towards her overarching ambition. From a young age, Meghan dreamed of becoming a famous Hollywood actress. She fantasized about winning an Oscar one day, practising her acceptance speech in front of her bedroom mirror. As James Lipton, the venerable inquisitor for the long-running *Inside the Actors Studio*, never tired of reminding his audience, most actors come from broken homes. This often bitter experience gives them the emotional rocket fuel to power a star-making screen performance.

From day one at Immaculate Heart, Meghan threw herself wholeheartedly into the drama department. Besides being a stepping stone towards following her dream, at school the drama department has a rather different function. It acts as a welcoming club, an unofficial sorority and a close-knit family. As a six-time Daytime Emmy Award-winner told me: 'You might be a misfit everywhere else, but here you have a sense of belonging.'

As well as taking to the boards, Meghan held numerous offices, including president of the school's Genesian Society, a group devoted to the preservation of the performing arts that actively hosted or attended plays, dramatic festivals and apprentice stage productions. However, as she didn't hold a formal office, she was always at the edge of the student council, never quite a part of it.

Immaculate Heart was able to call on a rich roster of Hollywood luminaries to direct and produce plays and musicals. There was leading voice coach Rachael Lawrence, choreographer and *Jersey Boys* star Joseph Leo Bwarie, and, most prominently, Gigi Perreau, a former child actor whose work is honoured with a star on the Hollywood Walk of Fame. Ms Perreau started her career in movies at the tender age of two, when she played Greer Garson's daughter in the 1943 film *Madame Curie*. By the age of ten she had appeared in twenty-five films, including working on set with Nancy Reagan in the 1950 thriller *Shadow on the Wall*. When she retired from acting work, Ms Perreau, now eighty, brought her experience to staging plays and musicals at her alma mater, as well as to teaching drama classes.

Gigi remembers Meghan as a skinny kid who developed and blossomed into a beautiful and confident young woman during her time at Immaculate Heart. She told me, 'We never had a moment's problem with her, she was spot on, learned her lines when she had to, very dedicated, very focused. She was a wonderful student, a lovely girl even then, and very hard-working. She was very dedicated. I knew she would be something special.'

In drama class they often discussed topics of the day and Gigi remembers Meghan as an inquisitive youngster who loved hearing tales of Gigi's time in France and other European countries. She was keen to explore the world beyond the nearby Hollywood sign.

When she was rehearsing for a play, her father was always around. As a Daytime Emmy winner who had been nominated almost every year while working on *General Hospital*, he was soon roped in to becoming the technical director for every school production Meghan was involved in. The majority of students were not aware that he was Meghan's dad. He was known simply as 'that guy in the overalls'. Those in the drama group were rather more respectful, calling him 'Mr Markle'. 'He liked to be thought of as gruff,' recalls Ms Perreau, 'but he was always very generous with the girls. If we had a late rehearsal he would go out and buy a boxful of McDonald's to feed them. Modest, too. He never asked to be credited for any work he did.' He was single and shy and Gigi admits to having a 'bit of a crush' on the burly guy in overalls who was clearly trying to bring up his teenage daughter on his own. She asked him out, and they went to see a play together at the Doolittle Theatre, just south of Hollywood and Vine. Though they had a good time, nothing ever developed.

Tom's focus was on Meghan. A keen photographer, he took endless pictures of Meghan on stage, teaching her how to pose and coaching her on angles. He was proudly watching from the wings when, on 28 March 1996, she made her first solo singing performance, playing the secretary in the school's production of the musical *Annie*. Director Perreau remembers that the fourteen-year-old budding actress was 'very excited and nervous about her song', and describes her performance as 'delightful'. Meghan went on to play an aspiring actress in the 1937 comedy *Stage Door*, was featured in *Back Country Crimes*, a black comedy by American playwright Dr Lanie Robertson, and also sang along with Katharine McPhee, who became an actor and singer in her own right, in the musical *Yankee Doodle Dandy*. In the March 1997 programme notes for Immaculate Heart's production of Stephen Sondheim's musical *Into the Woods*, in which she played Little Red Riding Hood, Meghan announced her ambition to the world. In between thanking her friends and her 'adorable' boyfriend, she revealed that she wished to attend Northwestern, a prestigious university near Chicago. This, she predicted, would be her next stop on her way to Broadway. Meghan was clearly not a girl lacking in confidence.

For her junior year she appeared yet again in a school production, *Steppin' Out*, but for her senior year she decided to test her ability beyond the confines of Immaculate Heart. It was a new challenge and offered the chance of branching out on her own without her father looking down on her from the lighting gantry. There was also the small matter of spending time alone with her then boyfriend. Thus she found herself in a room with forty other girls waiting to be auditioned for Sophocles' Greek tragedy *Oedipus Rex*, staged in the autumn of 1998 by the all-boys St Francis High School in La Cañada Flintridge.

As it was drama director Emmanuel (Manny) Eulalia's first big production at St Francis, he wanted to make an impact, so he carefully chose the girl who would play the lead role of Jocasta. It was no contest. 'Meghan was a standout,' he recalls. 'She had that something of the "it" about her. As a director it is what you are always looking for. She had charisma, no doubt.'

After signing a formal document pledging to arrive on time, dress appropriately and refrain from sexual and racial innuendoes – a code of behaviour somewhat ahead of its time – Meghan and the rest of the cast got down to a gruelling two-month schedule of rehearsals. Early on she impressed the show's director with her timekeeping, preparation and command of the stage. In the show's musical numbers her voice packed a punch, even if she quavered somewhat on the higher notes.

While she was the only girl from Immaculate Heart to audition, she had star status at the all-boys school. She had already dated several pupils from St Francis, including her first long-term boyfriend, Luis Segura. In time-honoured fashion it was his sister Maria who had set them up on their first date, the couple seeing one another regularly for nearly two years. She got to know the Segura family well, including Luis's younger brother Danny, who played Creon in *Oedipus Rex*, and always credits Meghan, who was then sixteen, with encouraging him to take to the stage. In turn she accompanied Danny to the Junior-Senior St Francis school prom in April 1998, which was held at the InterContinental Hotel in downtown Los Angeles. Through them she also became friendly with other boys from St Francis, everyone hanging out at each other's homes.

Describing her as 'sweet and fun', Luis – now a successful realtor in downtown Pasadena – was no doubt one of a number of voices encouraging her to enter for the contest for St Francis Homecoming Queen that autumn.

This pinnacle of high-school social standing came with serious competition from dozens of other girls. Hopefuls had to write an essay listing their accomplishments – Meghan's regular work in the Hippie Kitchen made her an instant standout – before facing a grilling from members of the student body and faculty. The names of the finalists were read out at the fifty-yard line on a hastily erected stage during the half-time interval at a St Francis football game. Amid whistling and cheering, Meghan was proclaimed that year's queen and was duly crowned by the previous incumbent. The entire 'court' then left the field in a procession of classic convertibles so that the game could continue. It was an indication of her popularity and appeal that a girl who was neither a cheerleader nor hailed from one of the local all-girls Catholic schools was chosen.

Even though she was now 'Queen Meghan', her drama director Manny Eulalia recalls that she didn't let the adulation go to her head. She remained grounded, joking around as she accepted the congratulations of her fellow cast members. Once word got out that 'Queen Meghan' was the female lead in the show, tickets sold briskly for the sombre tragedy. For three nights in early January 1999, the teenage cast played to a full house in the 250-seater theatre at nearby Flintridge Preparatory School. In previous years, interest in school productions had been disappointing. Not this time. When Meghan first appeared, there was a rustle of applause, despite the audience having been warned to curb their enthusiasm.

'A lot of pupils went to the show just to see Meghan,' recalls Manny with a smile. 'She certainly had a fan club. Quite a few of the boys had crushes on her.' At the end of the eighty-minute production, the audience gave Meghan and the rest of the cast a standing ovation.

In the programme notes she wrote, 'I would like to give thanks to Mommy, Daddy, Sushi, Aubergine, Danny boy, Brad, Gabe, all the beautiful, amazing, gorgeous sweeties at Immaculate Heart, the great guys at St Francis, and the phenomenal cast and crew.'

Though she was deemed a standout in *Oedipus Rex*, Meghan Markle's high-school acting career is best remembered for her performance as the sexy South American vamp Lola Banana in the 1955 musical comedy *Damn Yankees*. As the production was being staged by another all-boys Catholic school, this time Loyola High School in downtown Los Angeles, once again she had to compete against girls from other Catholic schools. Fresh from her triumph in *Oedipus Rex*, she snagged the star role. The story, based on a modern retelling of the Faustian pact, involved the vampish Lola, her deal with the devil, and her attempts to seduce a baseball fan turned star player, Joe Hardy. When Meghan, dressed in long satin gloves and a sequined leotard, shimmied across the stage in the sassy burlesque number 'Whatever Lola Wants', she brought the house down.

'It was like WOO,' a member of the audience told me. 'She was extraordinary. I remember sitting there thinking: "Oh my goodness, this is an Immaculate Heart girl." She was wearing the little spangly number, doing the shimmies, the whole bit. It wasn't lewd, she was playing a character. It was sweet in a way, but it was also like WOW. This was a girl with star quality.'

At another time, in another country, something very similar happened when the normally demure student Kate Middleton sashayed down the catwalk in a sheer shift dress over a bikini at a college fashion show. Prince William, watching the parade from the front row, whispered to his companion, 'She's hot.' The rest is royal history. On this occasion, it was an eye-opener for those teachers and classmates who were witnessing a very different side to Meghan. Normally seen as fun but thoughtful, mature and controlled, Meghan performed an amorous song-and-dance routine that was nothing less than revelatory. After the show, her theology teacher, Maria Pollia, and her teacher's boyfriend, went backstage and presented her with a bouquet of red roses. It was a touching moment. Meghan, who had been beyond excited to win the role, burst into tears. 'Oh, you didn't have to do this,' she sobbed, suddenly overwhelmed by the moment. As Ms Pollia recalls: 'She had appeared in many productions and she was always good. This time, though, she was a star. And that night a star was born.'

It was perhaps appropriate then that it was a Loyola High School boy who accompanied Meghan to the Junior-Senior Immaculate Heart school prom in April 1999, again at the InterContinental, now Omni, Hotel. Meghan and her beau, Giancarlo Boccato, now a New York property manager, looked very glamorous as they danced cheek to cheek. They were, as photographer John Dlugolecki observed, 'a star couple'.

An academic star, too. Her graduation ceremony in June 1999, which was held at the Hollywood Bowl, was another chance to shine. She walked away with a clutch of glittering prizes that touched on her intellectual, artistic and charitable work. She was presented with the Bank of America Fine Arts Award and the Notre Dame Club of Los Angeles Achievement Award, earned a commendation in the National Achievement Scholarship Program for outstanding black students, and won a service award for mentoring younger students.

The future was looking very bright. As she had predicted three years earlier, she had been accepted at Northwestern University, where she intended to study English as she wanted to explore her writing ability. She resisted the idea of studying drama, considering it a cliché of the California girl going to college and then returning to her roots in Hollywood without attempting another discipline. She was accomplished in so many fields that some expected her eventually to enter politics or the law. All felt that she would do something worthwhile with her life and at the same time give back to the community. The word 'classy', which she used to describe herself in her final yearbook, and her choice of a quote attributed to former First Lady Eleanor Roosevelt to illustrate her senior-year photograph, reflected her rounded personality. It read: 'Women are like teabags; they don't realize how strong they are until they're in hot water.'

As her drama teacher Gigi Perreau recalled: 'I wasn't sure which direction Meghan would ultimately be going in because she also had interests in humanitarian activities. She had a good heart, had absorbed the school's philosophy that there is nothing we cannot do, and she seemed to be focused on her future.'

❋

A couple of years after she graduated from college, Meghan returned to her alma mater. She chatted to a few of her old teachers and caught up on the news. 'Keep in touch, sweetheart,' Gigi said, as Meghan was preparing to leave. The budding actor was still struggling to get a foothold on the greasy pole that is Hollywood and was working as a hostess in a Beverly Hills hotel restaurant to pay for acting lessons. Somewhat ruefully she told her former acting mentor, 'I don't want to come back until I have really made it.'

The staff and pupils of Immaculate Heart figure it might be time.

4

'Can You Say, "Hi"?'

Summertime, and the living was easy for Meghan. Freshly graduated from Immaculate Heart and with her Northwestern University future beckoning, Meghan filled her last Los Angeles summer with memories and then packed her suitcases for her first semester away from home. She would effectively be starting a new life. Not one of her classmates from Immaculate Heart or anyone she knew from LA was going to Northwestern and she was determined to make a good impression. The orthodontics she'd had during her high-school years had gradually adjusted her bucked, gap-toothed grin, and now she was smiling widely without feeling self-conscious.

Once her dental work was complete she had some head shots taken to send out for auditions. As she was leaving for Chicago in the autumn, the best she could hope for was a day or two's work on one of the many music or short videos that were being filmed around town. She had already earned around $600 for a couple of days' work in a Tori Amos video, '1000 Oceans', which was shot in a car park in the downtown LA streets. Meghan, dressed in a low-cut, blue spaghetti-strap top, appeared as one of a crowd curiously examining a glass box containing Amos, writhing around as she sang. It comes across as a kind of performance art – but to a melody. The four-and-a-half-minute video, directed by Erick Ifergan, climaxes with scenes of rioting kids facing police horses and hoses, a musical reprise of the LA riots. Amos's video is, for dedicated Markle watchers, the first public appearance of one of Meghan's most distinctive mannerisms: continuously brushing back her long hair from her face with her hand.

That weekend, she had another audition lined up, this time for a Shakira video. It was to be a high-energy dance fest, a world away from Amos's vision of urban alienation. Meghan's best friend Ninaki 'Nikki' Priddy was going to drive with her to the audition, then they would go shopping to find something new for Meghan to wear at the Northwestern students' reception at the Beverly Hilton Hotel. The meet-and-greet was her first chance to scope out her fellow undergraduates and to make some first impressions herself. During the day, Nikki and Meghan also planned to goof around, filming LA street scenes – and themselves – with Nikki's new video camera.

The audition for the Shakira video didn't go quite as well as Meghan had hoped. It was fun to dance crazily, but afterwards she told Nikki: 'I am burning up; I was really nervous I was going to fall out of my top I was just shaking around so much.'

She knew her performance hadn't won her a gig as a $600-a-day featured dancer, but she was hoping for a spot as an extra. It was less money and no real camera time, but still, it would be fun. As she waited in the audition room, she ran into a girl she had met at the Tori Amos video shoot. It was the last time they saw one another – Meghan did not get a call back.

After hitting the mall, Meghan and Nikki drove through Los Angeles in Doria's Volvo station wagon with the personalized number plate MEGNMEE. Meghan kept up a running commentary while Nikki was in charge of the camera. The duo dismissed the gay majority of West Hollywood with the jejune, 'We could walk down the street naked and no one would care.' They zoomed in on a woman who seemed to have just had collagen injections in her lips, and they marvelled at the houses along Beverly Glen and other wealthy enclaves in Beverly Hills and the surrounding area.

Back home at her mother's house, Meghan tried on her new outfits for the student gathering at the Beverly Hilton. She had a vision of how she wanted to project herself at Northwestern and had decided that she would focus on a monochromatic look, black and grey, a colour scheme that would make her look stylish, sophisticated and pulled-together. With that in mind, she'd chosen a pencil skirt, tube top and white, structured, open-front blouse that doubled as a jacket. It was a prescient foreshadowing of the office-wear she would don to play Rachel Zane in *Suits* over a decade later.

Meghan made that last summer at home count, but she was also troubled. She and her father weren't getting along, and she was deliberately avoiding him. The emotional shutters had come down – Meghan went to stay with her mother and did not even visit her father's house to pick up her mail. It was a situation that perplexed her friends, as they knew that Meghan was the apple of her father's eye and could get away with blue murder. Not that any of his children, Tom Junior and Yvonne included, had taken advantage of his laissez-faire attitude; they always did their homework on time whatever the distractions. It was Meghan's mother who was more of a stickler for boundaries. Though she would join Meghan and her friends dancing to music on the radio or talking about make-up, she was stricter than her ex-husband. Meghan could twist him around her little finger. Yvonne often told the story of the time before Christmas when Meghan was looking at a jewellery catalogue and picking out a ring, which Tom Senior had promised as a gift. She teased her much older sister by saying that whatever her father bought Yvonne, Meghan would receive the most expensive gift as she was the most favoured child. So while the split between father and daughter was unusual, her friends dismissed it as simply a summer storm. It was not the best send-off for her college career, though.

As well as leaving behind her childhood home, she was also leaving the girl she considered her 'sister', Ninaki 'Nikki' Priddy, who had been her closest friend since they could barely walk. Meghan and Nikki became best friends at the Hollywood Little Red Schoolhouse, spending countless sleepovers together, playing in the pool at Nikki's parents' modest three-bedroom home in North Hollywood. They remained close when they transitioned to Immaculate Heart, the duo travelling around Europe together with Nikki's parents, Dalton and Maria, and her little sister Michelle. Nikki loved Paris so much that she studied at the Sorbonne the following summer. When they landed in London and posed in front of Buckingham Palace, they never for a moment thought that one day Meghan would be welcomed inside the black wrought-iron gates. Now college and separation loomed, and they were trying to crowd every moment with laughter and fond memories.

❋

Meghan looked around her dorm room and began unpacking. She was bunked in the freshman dorm known as North Mid-Quads, next door to the Kappa Kappa Gamma sorority house. She hadn't decided yet if she would 'rush' – the peculiarly American college system where students visit all the sorority or fraternity houses and find one that suits them, then hope they will be selected to join it – or just stick to friendship groups in her dorm and classes. The first few weeks at a new college are difficult enough; there is a lot of judging and sizing up as hundreds of anxious teenagers, bubbling over with hormones and excitement, try to orientate themselves both physically and psychologically. Rush merely exacerbates that feeling of vulnerability, of wanting to belong. Without a friend, or even an acquaintance, from back home, Meghan, a naturally gregarious character, worked hard at making new friends.

But her self-esteem was about to take a most unexpected blow. She had grown up in the melting pot that is Los Angeles. Her school, Immaculate Heart, was a kaleidoscope of girls of different colours and nationalities. Now, she discovered that even though the town of Evanston, where Northwestern University is based, is just a few miles from Chicago, the college itself was overwhelmingly white. African Americans made up a third of the town, but only 5 per cent of the student body. There were even fewer dual-heritage students. Here at Northwestern she stood out.

Just one week into her first semester, as Meghan sat reviewing her class schedules for her chosen major, English, a dorm mate came up and asked, 'You said your mom is black and your dad is white, right?'

Meghan smiled weakly and nodded, suddenly uncomfortable. 'And they're divorced?' her dorm mate continued. Meghan nodded again. The girl gave her a knowing look. 'Oh. Well, that makes sense.'

Meghan felt a stab. The snide remark cut her deeply. 'Makes sense how?' she wondered. Of course, she understood the implication: that the failure of an inter-racial marriage was inevitable. The interaction stayed with her and was one of the memories she referred to years later in an article she wrote for *Elle* magazine in 2015.

Los Angeles had been a huge multicultural bubble, and now Meghan was being exposed to narrow minds and outdated, provincial thinking. This wasn't the first, nor would it be the last, time she would hear or be subject to a crass racial slur. As she was light-skinned, many fellow students didn't realize she was of dual heritage, which left her as a fly on the wall as they made racist jokes or expressed bigoted opinions. The above incident, in particular, remained with her, shaping her reflections about how others viewed her, her family and her heritage. 'My lasting memory of Meghan is her profound sense of self,' remembers Professor Harvey Young. 'She was thoughtful and understood what it means to face prejudice and discrimination.'

But Meghan was tough enough not to let it bring her down – she was too busy cutting loose. Now that she wasn't under the watchful gaze of her mother, she started wearing heavier make-up and experimented with highlighting her hair. Having made up her mind, she rushed Kappa Kappa Gamma and was initiated into the sorority, which was full of girls who were considered 'intelligent hot messes'. As KKG member Melania Hidalgo observed: 'The thing we all have in common is that we're all very driven, ambitious and passionate.' The sorority embraced her warmly, Meghan eventually being elected as the sorority's recruitment chair, responsible for bringing in new girls into the KKG clan. As an outgoing, confident and articulate young woman, she was well suited to the role of selling the sorority. Sometimes she was a tad too persuasive, some students, according to classmate Ann Meade, thinking her overly assertive. For the most part, fellow students remember her thirst for life and her 'explosive personality' – a dynamic, self-possessed young woman.

As a sorority member, she also participated in the Northwestern University Dance Marathon, one of the biggest student-run charities in America. The year Meghan danced was the first time since the event's inception in 1975 that a woman, Ginger Harreld, was the emcee, though she shared the duties with a male student. While the dance marathon was no longer the gruelling win-or-die dance fest of the Depression era, the thirty hours that Meghan spent on her feet, day and night, certainly helped her work off her 'freshman fifteen' – the weight she had packed on from drinking, munching starchy dorm food and making late-night trips to the twenty-four-hour Burger King.

Of course, all this socializing did have a focus for many students: the search for a boyfriend. More sophisticated and put-together than most of her contemporaries, Meghan was seen as a cool catch. Normally, she went for well-dressed Latino boyfriends like Luis Segura, but she changed gears during her time at Northwestern. Her first boyfriend was Steve Lepore, a chiselled, white, six-foot-five-inch sophomore basketball player from Ohio. He made Meghan, at five foot six inches, feel petite. Her association with Lepore raised her stock with her KKG sorority sisters, who were 'impressed that she had snared such a hottie'. 'They made quite the pair,' recalled a former classmate. But their relationship was short-lived. For his junior and senior year, the high-scoring basketball star accepted a transfer offer to Wake Forest University in Winston-Salem, North Carolina. Goodbye Meghan, hello pro-basketball prospects. He now coaches at Eastern Kentucky University.

While they made a perfect-looking college couple, they had their differences. Steve's sporting ambitions meant that he had to forgo partying, turn in early, and the night before any game Meghan was not welcome to stay over. Meghan, on the other hand, was a party animal – at least at weekends. She enjoyed the freedom that college offered away from her parents, but during the working week she diligently completed her academic assignments or babysat to earn extra cash.

While she may have lost her freshman-year boyfriend, she had no shortage of admirers, her later boyfriends including Shaun Zaken, who became a scriptwriter, along with another wordsmith,

Brett Ryland who would go on to write scripts for the popular comedy, *2 Broke Girls*.

During her time at Northwestern, she may have dallied with romance but it was a place where she found true friendship, forging lifelong bonds with two sorority sisters, Genevieve Hillis and Lindsay Jill Roth. It was while attending a literature class, discussing the work of African-American writer Toni Morrison, that she first met Lindsay, a petite blonde from Lattingtown, New York, a wealthy Long Island suburb with million-dollar homes overlooking Oyster Bay. Her parents were attorneys, though her mother had retired. Unlike Meghan's friends from Immaculate Heart, Lindsay was Jewish.

Besides her gal pals, her other best friend could not have been more different. The son of two pastors, Larnelle Quentin Foster was a flamboyant, larger-than-life African American who hid the fact that he was gay from his family and friends – although he eventually confided in Meghan. Meghan and Larnelle took classes together in the School of Communications after she changed her major from English to a dual major of theatre arts and international relations. The twin major reflected her indecision – she was unsure whether to pursue a career in politics and the diplomatic world or strive for screen stardom. Though the latter was, as she recognized, something of an LA cliché, she was in good company – Warren Beatty, Stephen Colbert, Zach Braff and David Schwimmer had all learned their trade at the university. Larnelle, however, couldn't help but notice that her enthusiasm was more for Hollywood than the State Department. The couple, who attended everything from student productions to avant-garde offerings, enjoyed discussing the theatrical structure and language of a play as much as performing. During her time at college, Meghan took part in short films made by fellow students or, if her schedule allowed, would leave campus to attend auditions for TV commercials.

On weekends Meghan would often go to Larnelle's family home for meals, the two friends trying out different recipes, including Meghan's then speciality, Indian food.

The Foster family adored Meghan, attracted by her quirky sense of humour and her effervescent smile. She even accepted their invitation to join them at church. 'If my mother had had her way, of course I'd be with Meghan,' he explains. 'She would say: "Oh, I love Meghan so much." I was like, "Yes, Mom, I do, too."' He also knew that he would break his mother's heart if she discovered that he was gay. For the time being, Meghan was his cover, and he in turn provided her with companionship and an escort, a role which made him the envy of many of the straight guys on campus. 'How do you go out with her?' they asked him. 'Because I'm not trying anything!' Larnelle told the *Daily Mail*.

Meghan's closest friends represented the duality of her heritage: the iconoclastic, eccentric and independent African American and the white professional. Their presence helped her to explore and integrate these sides of her personality, absorbing and synthesizing as she grew into her own identity.

Between semesters, it was a relief to return to Los Angeles, not only for the weather but also to be back in such a diverse city, where the blonde and blue-eyed are in a minority. As she learned, though, the image of tolerance and acceptance was a veneer that was easily scratched.

She tells a story about the night she and her mum went to a concert. As Doria was slowly backing her Volvo out of the parking space, another driver impatiently yelled at her, using the 'N' word. Meghan flushed, her skin prickling with frustration, sharing Doria's pain and rage. She looked at her mother, and saw her eyes welling with tears. Meghan whispered the only words she could manage: 'It's OK, Mommy.' But it wasn't OK. They drove home in silence, blood pounding in Meghan's ears, Doria's fingers gripping the steering wheel tightly.

※

The experience of growing up with dual heritage was used as a jumping-off point for discussions that Meghan and seven other classmates had with their history and theatre professor Harvey Young, whose seminars focused on African-American plays, their meaning, their impact and their history. Meghan, who had moved between two communities throughout her life, was very aware of how people responded to race, racial differences and the idea of otherness. Young said, 'She had a very sophisticated understanding of what it means to live in a racial body that gets perceived and is treated differently based upon communities in which you find yourself.'

Young's class brought into focus Meghan's ambiguous place in society. She later recalled: 'It was the first time I could put a name to feeling too light in the black community, too mixed in the white community.'

Her experiences at Northwestern, both in and out of the classroom, and the self-knowledge she gained would serve her well, arming her with insight and inner strength when she tried to penetrate the smooth, evasive structure that is Hollywood

※

By the start of her junior year, it was clear that if Meghan continued at her current pace she would earn most of her credits for her degree way ahead of schedule. Just for fun she took a course in industrial engineering, her professor choosing the French classic *The Little Prince* by Antoine de Saint-Exupéry as a set text. As she later wrote in her blog, The Tig: 'It was a seemingly odd choice, but at the end of the day, the takeaway was a self-empowerment and motivational bent that I apply to decision-making in my life to this very day.'

With time on her side, and still unsure about her path after university, she decided to go into the field to gain some practical experience in international relations. She knew that her uncle, Mick Markle, was employed as a specialist in communication systems for the US government – the talk in the family was that he worked for the CIA, the government's overseas spying arm. So she approached him to ask for his help in getting her an internship abroad with the State Department. 'Meghan, I will help you if I can,' he replied. Help her he did. Uncle Mick pulled a few strings, and even though Meghan was quite late in submitting the application paperwork, that was overlooked because of her excellent academic record and her uncle's influence. Soon afterwards, she was informed that she had secured a six-week internship as a junior press officer at the American Embassy in Buenos Aires, Argentina. It was quite the adventure for the twenty-year-old, flying from Los Angeles to Buenos Aires on her own. She joined a team of around twenty-eight State Department officials and guards in the mid-sized American enclave. Before starting work she was given an orientation of the building complex and the city, safety being the primary focus. The young student was warned about where to avoid, what to do in an emergency and which telephone numbers to call. Basic but vital information. With the anniversary of 9/11 approaching, all American embassies around the world, including that in Buenos Aires, had been placed on Code Orange security, the second-highest level.

For the most part, her day-to-day life was the routine and mundane world of the office grunt, filing, answering phones and drafting letters. As a consummate team player, she impressed her superiors with her enthusiasm and demeanour.

She was a willing worker, undertaking the tedious, run-of-the-mill jobs quickly and efficiently. Her superior, Mark Krischik, now retired, remembered her as a young woman who was good to work with and who carried out her assignments with 'efficiency and ingenuity'. Though memories are hazy, there was talk of a dalliance with a US Marine tasked with guarding the embassy compound, and an Argentinian businessman who sent his chauffeur-driven limousine to take her out for dinner. There were even reports of a Buenos Aires clairvoyant who, it later emerged, had conveniently described her marrying a man with 'curly red hair'.

As it was her twenty-first birthday on 4 August 2002, she was given permission to travel in the convoy that was picking up the US Finance Secretary Paul O'Neill, who was paying a whistle-stop visit to South America. It was a treat. However, her opportunity to be treated like a VIP for an hour or two rapidly turned into a terrifying ordeal.

She was waiting in the motorcade when Secretary O'Neill landed at Ezeiza International Airport, 15 miles outside the centre of Buenos Aires. Argentina had recently defaulted on a $141 billion debt and neither the International Monetary Fund nor the American government were in any mood to bail them out. Before he left Washington DC, O'Neill had announced that South American nations should have policies in place to 'ensure that aid is not diverted to Swiss bank accounts'. Though his target was the corrupt political elites, siphoning off billions of dollars into their own personal bank accounts, the suffering man and woman in the street blamed the United States for the economic calamity that had befallen them. After he landed at precisely five o'clock, O'Neill's motorcade drove to a meeting with President Eduardo Duhalde, head of the interim government. Though O'Neill was expecting a bumpy ride, even he was perturbed when banner-waving demonstrators surrounded the convoy. 'I remember the arrival because protesters banged on my limo with their placards. It was a memorable event,' he later dead-panned.

The junior press officer was terrified, recalling that it was the scariest moment of her life. It was all the more concerning, not only because of the impending anniversary of 9/11, but because of intelligence reports suggesting that Islamic militants could be setting up a network in South America. Meghan would have already been wary, and it's easy to imagine how frightening she would have found an angry mob of protesters attacking her car.

However, the experience didn't seem to put her off pondering her future inside the government agency. 'If she had stayed with the State Department she would have been an excellent addition to the US Diplomatic Corps. She had all that it takes to be a successful diplomat,' Mark Krischik later recalled.

Certainly she was sufficiently committed to a career with the State Department to take the Foreign Service Officer Test while she was still in Argentina. The three-hour exam is a mix of politics, history, general knowledge and maths, requiring an awareness of everything from the origin of be-bop to East Asian labour laws. It proved a stretch too far; Meghan, much to her disappointment, failed the exam. She did, though, fly to Madrid to take a six-week course in Spanish on the International Education for Students programme. It was an added string to her bow just in case she wanted to give the world of diplomacy another try.

When she returned to Northwestern, she was able to regale her friends with tales of tapas and tango, and tried to brush off her regret over missing the mark on her Foreign Service Officer Test. In any case, fate, it would seem, was pushing her into the world of entertainment. Her lighting-director father pulled favours to put her forward for a casual role in *General Hospital*, just as he had done with his eldest daughter almost a decade earlier. In November 2002, Meghan auditioned for a 'day player' role in which she said around five lines. Thanks to her father's influence, she got the part of a nurse named Jill. The episode aired just before Thanksgiving.

A few weeks later, she was at a holiday party with friends when she was approached by a man who introduced himself as Drew. Instead of wanting to date her, he wanted to manage her. A friend had slipped him a copy of a student film in which Meghan had appeared, and he was impressed, calling Meghan to tell her: 'You know what? You're going to make money and I'll take ten per cent. I think you should stick around.'

But at that time in her life, Meghan couldn't stick around. She had courses to finish back at Northwestern and a graduation to attend. She promised, though, that she'd be back. As she saw it, as one door had closed, another one had opened. If the State Department didn't want her, maybe Hollywood did.

※

Once home from Northwestern, diploma in hand, Meghan went out and auditioned for commercials, none of which were successful but they were good experience. By now this was a well-trodden route, Meghan having attended numerous auditions when she was still at Northwestern. Then she got a call. Her best friend from college, Lindsay Jill Roth, was working in casting for a film called *A Lot Like Love*, starring comic heart-throb Ashton Kutcher. She had snagged Meghan an audition for a one-word role.

'Can you say "hi"?' asked the director.

'Yes, I can,' replied Meghan. 'But I read the script and I really respond to this other character, and I would love to read for that.' Naturally, the other character had a bigger role.

The director and the casting staff exchanged glances. 'This girl certainly has some balls,' their looks said. Meghan didn't get the role she pitched herself for, but she did land the part for which Roth had recommended her. Once on set, the director allowed her to improvise, expanding her lines from one to five. In movie terms, that was a triumph.

Next up she secured another small part in the futuristic law-office drama *Century City*, starring Viola Davis and Néstor Carbonell, among other old hands. She played a staff member and delivered one line: 'Here's to Tom Montero, who had the vision to install this amazing virtual assistant.' Her scene was over in one day, and she was back to casting calls, at the mercy of the Abominable No Men. It was a scratchy hand-to-mouth existence, one experienced by thousands of Hollywood hopefuls who hand out their résumés by the box-load. Meghan's was little different from those of other aspiring actors, except that she boasted special skills in kick-boxing, tap-dancing, ballet and Spanish.

On the way to an audition one day, the electric button that unlocked the doors to her Ford Explorer failed to open. She tried the key but to no avail. Trying not to panic, she went around to the hatchback trunk, which used a different key. By some miracle, it opened. Running short on time, she had no choice but to crawl in through the back and clamber over the seat. Thank goodness she was in shape from yoga and running, and thank goodness the car started and had a full tank of petrol. When she got to the casting studio, she pulled into a deserted part of the parking lot and exited the same way.

Too broke to get her SUV repaired, Meghan repeated this routine for months, parking far from other cars and waiting for the coast to become clear before emerging from the hatch, feigning that she was searching in the back of the car for a script or photos before climbing back inside.

Of course she knew there would be setbacks; Meghan had been around the entertainment industry for too long to believe in rags-to-riches stories. So she stayed optimistic. Her motto was 'I choose happiness', and she made it a point to stay happy, getting together with friends over pizza and wine, taking yoga classes, and going out as often as her budget permitted. One night her budget took her to a dive bar in West Hollywood that had been popularized by the 'Young Turks' in the entertainment industry (young hotshots keen on challenging the older Hollywood establishment) who liked to feel that they were slumming it in an authentic beatnik environment. A loud drawl, tinged with a New York accent, caught her attention. The owner of the voice was chatting with a couple of friends.

Over six feet tall with reddish-blond hair and blue eyes, Trevor Engelson looked like a surfer or volleyball player, an archetypal California golden boy. He had the tone and the air of a Matthew McConaughey Lite, although he was born and raised in Great Neck, New York, the son of a successful orthodontist and great-grandson of Jewish immigrants.

Like Francis Ford Coppola, Trevor had attended Great Neck North High School and, also like Coppola, he originally wanted to direct movies. 'I realized you needed talent to do that, so that was out the window,' he says self-deprecatingly. While still in high school, he managed to get himself hired as a production assistant on shoots in New York City, working tirelessly on weekends and during school breaks. The experience paid off and he was admitted to the Annenberg School of Cinematic Arts at the University of Southern California. He was on his way.

After he graduated in 1998, Trevor worked on the low-budget movie *Safe Men*, notable only for the appearance of Paul Giamatti as the strangely monickered Veal Chop. Then Engelson, who liked to think of himself as a hustler, was hired on *Deep Blue Sea* – a film which needlessly demonstrated the inevitably bloody consequences of genetically engineering super-intelligent Great White Sharks – as a staff assistant. During his time in the office he studied how his bosses, the movie's producers, worked. He liked what he saw. It didn't seem that they were working very hard and yet they made a lot of money and got the prettiest girls. He approached one of the producers, Alan Riche, and told him earnestly: 'Alan, I want to do what you do. I want to produce.' Riche advised him that, first, he had to work as an agent. Once *Deep Blue Sea* wrapped, Riche got the ambitious assistant a referral to the Endeavor Talent Agency. He started at the bottom of the ladder in the mailroom working as a driver, delivering scripts and other agency-related packages around town.

Trevor was personable and eager, and in due time he worked his way up to become assistant to the motion-picture literary agent Chris Donnelly. He was on the fast track to higher things. Then his ruthless ambition got in the way. While Donnelly was on vacation, Trevor sent out uncommissioned scripts, known as spec scripts, to actors and directors under the Endeavor letterhead. 'I thought I was being a self-starter,' Trevor admitted later. While there were no lasting hard feelings, he was fired for overstepping his remit. Never down for long, he quickly found work as an assistant to fellow USC alumni Nick Osborne and his partner Jeffrey Zarnow at O/Z Films. As Trevor put it: 'They needed a hustler who could bring food to the table.' After he sold his first script, *The Road to Freaknik,* to Fox Searchlight for $25,000, he celebrated by partying hard.

When Osborne began his own movie company, Underground Films, Trevor became his assistant, several years later taking over the company. Beneath the banter and the wisecracks, Trevor was a driven soul, a young man out to make his mark in an uncompromising industry. When Meghan first met him on that night out in West Hollywood, she liked what she saw, attracted to his passion, drive and ambition. Trevor was a typical New Yorker: brash, blunt, no bull and ballsy. At times, though, he was maybe a little too gauche for a sophisticated girl who liked classy rather than crass. He was a guy, too, who had an aphorism for every occasion. 'Hope is the greatest currency we have in this business,' he told the wide-eyed wannabe. True or not, it's a great pick-up line.

His favourite saying belonged to the legendary Hollywood producer Neal Moritz, the man behind *The Fast and the Furious* franchise: 'Don't give it five minutes if you're not gonna give it five years.' Trevor said it so often that, in time, Meghan began to use it herself, presenting the phrase as though it had sprung fully formed from her head. Her version is more refined: 'Don't give it five minutes unless you can give it five years.' But Trevor had aphorisms

– and chutzpah – to spare. As he once told a former USC buddy in a podcast interview for *Scripts and Scribes*: 'I'm a gigantic believer that all this shit can come to an end any minute now, and you've gotta take advantage of [it]. I'm Jewish and all that, but I think you got one shot at this life, so if you have a chance to have some fun and you're not hurting anybody else and you can still take care of everything else to be taken care of and – I always find a way to have a lot of fun. That's never an issue.'

He was the quintessential example of the young man who burned the candle at both ends, playing and working hard. Cuba, Palm Springs, New York: the world was his oyster – at least until he reached his credit-card limit. As he said: 'If I'm on a plane going somewhere, when I land I'm working, on the plane I'm working, when I'm drinking I'm working. But I'm always having a lot more fun than most other people I know.' A passionate producer and an ambitious actor. It was a classic Hollywood combination.

When Trevor's movie *Zoom* began production in early 2005, Meghan had recently bagged a brief appearance on the sitcom *Cuts*. It was one line, one measly line, but for Meghan she felt that she was on her way to the stars. Later, in an anonymous blog entitled Working Actress that she had been credited as writing, she described that feeling: 'At the start of my career, I remember freaking out, and celebrating over getting one line on a shitty UPN show. At the time, that was a big success. It was phone calls of congrats, and flowers, and celebratory dinners with wine glasses clinking. It was a landmark of more work to come, and a glimmer of hope that said, "Holy shit, you're really doing this."'

While she waited for her close-up, to pay the bills she was making ends meet as a hostess in a Beverly Hills restaurant, working at a local store where she taught classes on the art of gift-wrapping and used her other skill, her impeccable handwriting, to earn decent money as a calligraphist. She had learned the skill back at Immaculate Heart, and as she later commented: 'I've always had a propensity for getting the cursive down pretty well.' At that time, her claim to fame was writing the envelopes for the June 2005 wedding of singer Robin Thicke and actor Paula Patton.

The roles were coming, but not as quickly as she would have liked. In the summer of 2005 she was booked for a role on the show *Love, Inc.*, and later in the year, around Thanksgiving, for a TV movie called *Deceit*, followed by an appearance as an insurance salesperson on a short-lived sitcom *The War at Home*.

While Meghan was steadily but slowly chugging along, Trevor went from boom to bust as *Zoom*, which was released in the summer of 2006, was proving an unmitigated disaster. The family action film, described as a 'dull and laugh-free affair', received a 3 per cent rating on Rotten Tomatoes. The movie's star, Tim Allen, even received a Razzie nomination for Worst Actor.

It was not much better for Meghan. So far, 2006 had been a bust both for film and TV roles. The couple's social life, though, got a bit of a boost when, in August, they were invited to the Hamptons for the Coach Legacy Photo Exhibit. The event celebrating the American handbag manufacturer saw the couple sipping champagne and rubbing shoulders with wealthy socialites and the celebrity fringe – but it didn't help them up the Hollywood ladder.

The daily rejections would have broken someone with less grit, but Meghan knew it was a numbers game. As girls dropped out and headed home, defeated, the greater her chance of booking something became. As Trevor said, don't give it five minutes unless you can give it five years. And her five years were not even close to being up.

Like other girls doing the rounds, she had a gym bag containing the essential wardrobe for every possible part she might be called for: red for feisty Latina, pastels for the girl next door, mustard yellow for African American. Short skirts, long skirts, blazer, bikini and tops; everything she needed was in her trusty tote. As she acknowledged, being ethnically 'ambiguous' allowed her to go for virtually any role. 'Sadly, it didn't matter,' she later wrote for *Elle* magazine. 'I wasn't black enough for the black roles and I wasn't white enough for the white ones, leaving me somewhere in the middle as the ethnic chameleon who couldn't book a job.'

She was sitting in her sweats, fabric tubes covering her forearms to keep skin oil off the envelopes she was hand-addressing for a calligraphy client, when her agent Nick Collins called. Collins, Boston-bred and a graduate of Brown University, knew all about the struggle to get on the Hollywood ladder – he had made ends meet waiting tables at a Brentwood restaurant before Bob Gersh made him his assistant at his eponymous talent agency. So he sympathized with her struggle to stay afloat.

He had secured an audition for her. There was one hitch. She had to appear in what the producers coyly described as a 'body-conscious outfit', that is to say, a bikini, swimsuit, short skirt or shorts, so that they could get an idea of what her body looked like. Yes, it was a cattle call for the position of briefcase girl in the popular TV game show *Deal or No Deal*, but with nothing else lined up she agreed to go. After all, it was only a short drive from the West Hollywood home she now shared with Trevor to Culver City where the auditions were taking place. As she picked out her shortest skirt, she could have been excused for wondering: 'Is this why I earned a Bachelor's degree?'

5

Short Skirts, High Heels

Like so many teenagers, Tameka Jacobs arrived in Hollywood wide-eyed and eager to make her mark as a model or an actor. At five foot ten inches she was a head above the competition. Striking, too, having Creole, Norwegian, African American, French and Spanish in her genes. And that's just what she knows about.

First, she did some modelling before auditioning for a new entertainment show, *Deal or No Deal*, hosted by Howie Mandel. The show, based on the Dutch original and replicated across the world, was predicated on the tension between greed and prudence, a sure-fire ratings winner. Contestants choose from twenty-six briefcases that contain a cash value ranging from a cent to $1 million. During the game, the contestant eliminates various briefcases in the hope of being left with the million-dollar case. Periodically, the contestant is offered a deal by an unseen banker. The offer to quit the game and take modest winnings is matched by the possibility of going on to win the big prize. The audience is always eager to see them risk it all.

The briefcases themselves are held by twenty-six beautiful, smiling girls, arranged temptingly in front of the contestant. This is where Tameka came in. She was asked to be briefcase girl 21, a position she held from the day the show opened in December 2005 to the end of its run in 2010.

When she was first asked to join, Tameka was over the moon. It was almost everything she could have asked for. She was paid $800 per episode and they regularly recorded seven episodes a day. That was $5,600 – more than $23,000 a week when the going was good. Then there were endorsements and personal appearances thrown in. Fame and riches for standing for hours on end holding a briefcase full of pretend cash. The irony was not lost on her.

Plus it was fun being a briefcase girl. The other girls were rowdy, catty and goofy; it was just like being in a sorority house. They only had two enemies – the cold in the studio and the achingly high heels they were all asked to wear.

Meghan joined the gang in 2006 for season two after successfully passing the audition. Along with model Chrissy Teigen, she began as a back-up in case regular girls were ill or failed to show up. Eventually, she got a full-time slot as briefcase girl number 24 – close to Tameka. When she first arrived, Tameka clocked her as another multiracial girl. 'It was never discussed between us,' she recalls. 'We just looked at one another and knew.' It was an unspoken code, a shared understanding of a lifetime of misunderstandings, quizzical glances and snide comments condensed into one knowing look. They had connections in common, too – early on, Tameka had been taken under the wing of model, talk-show host and all-round superstar Tyra Banks, who was, as Meghan well knew, a legend back at her old high school. Now it was Tameka's time to return the favour, giving Meghan the low-down on the personalities, on who and what to look out for. She briefed her on the daily routine and what to bring to set – a pair of cosy Ugg boots after a day in high heels in near-freezing temperatures was a must. As they chatted it was clear to Tameka that Meghan saw this as a stepping stone to earning some money before trying for more serious acting jobs.

The average *Deal or No Deal* day began at 5.30 a.m. as Meghan and the other briefcase girls gathered for hours of hair, make-up and the final fitting for their skimpy attire. With outfit changes every episode, and multiple episodes filmed per day, they often had to endure three separate fittings. A rack of beautiful matching ballgowns would arrive, to be unceremoniously hacked to pieces so that the girls' legs and décolletage were on full display.

After rough checks and measurements for length and shape, there would be a final wardrobe session in which the girls sucked everything in and the dresses were pinned down. Some outfits were so tight that the girls couldn't even bend down to put on their agonizingly high heels, so an assistant would be on hand to help.

The briefcase girls all wore Spanx shapewear, not only to make their stomachs flatter but also to keep themselves warm in the Arctic studio temperatures. As a final touch, they inserted what briefcase girl number 13, Leyla Milani, liked to called 'chicken cutlets' – or sometimes wodges of tissues – into their bras to enhance their cleavage.

As Meghan stood there for hour after hour, trying not to shiver, her feet sore from the cheap high heels, a painted smile on her face, she thought of the pay cheque at the end of the week. This was not what she had in mind when she went into acting but, at only twenty-five, she was earning more money than she had ever made in her life, and the shooting schedule was perfect: long blocks of filming followed by weeks of downtime, which gave her the opportunity to attend more auditions and go travelling with the man she playfully called Trevity-Trev-Trev, a nickname he had originally been given by the rapper LL Cool J.

While the Hamptons had been sampled, there were other spots she wanted to visit, schedules permitting: Greece, Mexico, Thailand, anywhere in the Caribbean, were all on her list. The foodie in her fantasized about going to Bangkok and sampling the menu at Chote Chitr, the restaurant which had been featured on National Public Radio and in *The New York Times*. Their mutual ambition as well as their love of adventure, of hopping on a plane to somewhere unusual and faraway, was a central plank of their relationship. Over time, Meghan gained something of a reputation for knowing about the newest restaurants or the quirkiest hotels in odd parts of the world.

He would join her – if he had the time. They were both driven individuals, Trevor as busy, if not more so, than his girlfriend. It was noticeable that, unlike the boyfriends and husbands of her *Deal or No Deal* 'sisters', Trevor never visited Meghan on set. It was so unusual that his absence was commented upon by the other girls. However, there were plenty of other celebrities, mainly sports stars, who dropped by, some clearly trying to get up close and personal with the girls. One regular guest caused quite the frisson: Donald Trump, then organizing the Miss Universe pageant, once made a guest appearance as the banker on *Deal or No Deal* to cross-promote *The Apprentice*. The frequently bankrupt real-estate mogul toured the set, giving girls his card and inviting them to play golf at one of his courses. Tameka Jacobs told me: 'He was a creep, super-creepy, but some girls were attracted to money and power, and took his number.'

Meghan was one of the girls who gave the future president a wide berth. Not that she was known for joining in much with any of the 'after-work' events – occasions when a bevy of beautiful women, several minders in tow, trawled the bars of West Hollywood. As Meghan is now known as a thirsty socialite, it is surprising that she rarely, if ever, joined in these raucous nights of karaoke and chasers.

For a girl who would end up living her life on Instagram, it is remarkable, too, that she never posed for a silly picture, mugging for the cameras like the rest of her colleagues. Meghan knew her angles – after all, she had been taught by the best, her father – and always posed sweetly. If caught with a drink in her hand, it was only ever champagne, and she was never heard to swear.

Aside from promotional photos in costume on the *Deal or No Deal* set, Meghan's only promo work for the show was self-serving; at the 2006 Emmys she appeared at a gifting suite, where celebrities are given products in exchange for posing for a photograph by the company logo, and was duly photographed looking at yoga mats and resort wear. Meghan's lack of involvement in 'office' gossip – she was always studying lines for an audition, recalls Leyla Milani – and after-work play was just one of the reasons she stood out. Another was her eating habits. While the other girls 'sucked hard candy and ate raw vegetables' between scenes, Meghan would eat pizza or bags of potato chips, seemingly unconcerned about bloat or weight gain. And while many of the other girls thanked their lucky stars for this opportunity, Meghan saw the gig as a temporary berth. As Tameka recalls: 'She was super-sweet, adorable, a little sheltered, wholesome, with a good head on her shoulders. Looking back, it was clear that she had a brand and wanted to protect that brand for a future career as a serious actor.' She knew where she wanted to go, and it certainly wasn't spending her days on *Deal or No Deal*.

During the shooting break in November, Meghan auditioned for and got the role of a Latina murder suspect on *CSI: NY* – the part once again had Meghan flashing the flesh when her character was introduced wearing a corset and suspenders. Then it was back to the cold NBC sound stage in Culver City.

During Meghan's time on *Deal or No Deal*, Trevor had a film in production, a marital comedy called *License to Wed*, starring funny man Robin Williams and Mandy Moore. Meghan secretly hoped there would be a role for her, but the bit parts that might have suited her went to more experienced actresses who had previously worked with the director, Ken Kwapis, on the TV series *The Office*. It was to become a source of conflict between the couple, Meghan becoming disappointed that Trevor didn't try harder to include her in some of his productions. After all, as she complained to her friends, he had plenty of connections.

No matter. She had the feeling that this could be her year. During the February round of auditions for the 2007 pilot season, she came away from a meeting with top casting agent Donna Rosenstein with a positive spring in her step. Rosenstein had been senior vice president at ABC for many years, overseeing the casting of such series as *NYPD Blue*, *Roseanne* and *Twin Peaks*, and had since set up her own company. She was Meghan's best chance yet at the big time.

Meghan loved the part she had been asked to read for, a former stripper and street walker called Kelly Calhoun, who had been rescued from her seedy life by a born-again Christian cop who had fallen in love with and married her.

The show, named *The Apostles*, was part police drama, part *Desperate Housewives* complete with similar voiceover narration, and was set in a suburban Southern California cul-de-sac north of Los Angeles where all the residents were police officers and their spouses. Shortly after her reading, Meghan received the news she had been longing to hear: 'Meghan, you got the part,' her agent excitedly advised her. When she told her father, he wrote her a loving note of congratulations, the actor keeping his tender letter in a hand-carved box by the side of her bed.

Meghan's character wasn't the most feminist of women, but compared to her role as a briefcase babe, Kelly Calhoun was at least a step in the right direction. Her African-American husband, played by Keith Robinson, finds himself conflicted, berating her for her immoral past but drawn to her sassy, yet vulnerable, personality. In the tight-knit enclave, Kelly finds empowerment and friendship with the other wives. She startles them first by sharing sex tips on how to keep things hot in the bedroom and then by teaching them the tricks of the stripping trade, demonstrating how to disrobe seductively. Meghan had a good feeling about the show. It ticked all the boxes: a strong cast – Shawn Hatosy from *Alpha Dog*, who specialized in playing tightly wound, edgy characters, was one of the leads; a solid back story; feminist themes; and plenty of room for conflict and tension in the insular cop community.

The pilot, shot as a full-length feature, was delivered in June 2007. After several viewings and much back and forth, Fox Studios decided to pass on making a full-blown series, airing it the following year as a stand-alone movie. It was a real blow for Meghan, who had harboured high hopes for the show. At least she could now add 'stripper' to her acting résumé. Which she promptly did.

While Meghan worked on *The Apostles*, Trevor was in production on a Sandra Bullock/Bradley Cooper comedy, *All About Steve*, written by two of his clients. Bullock had taken control of the film as producer, leaving Trevor to manage his growing stable of writers and directors.

He was always hustling to get them work and to find new clients. When he went to coffee shops he handed out business cards to whoever was tapping away at their laptop. 'What's the worst thing that happens? I read a shitty script?' he laughed. He read scripts non-stop, going so far as to keep a stack of them in their bathroom at home, as well as a supply of waterproof pens so he could make notes.

As for Meghan landing a role through her boyfriend – that had proved to be a bit of a washout. At least, so far. Not so with casting agent Donna Rosenstein, who called her in to read for the role of Sadie Valencia, the spoilt daughter of a Las Vegas casino owner in the story of a crime boss's family who were struggling to go straight. There were solid expectations that the comedy, *Good Behavior*, which also starred *Chicago Fire*'s Treat Williams as her father and *Schitt's Creek*'s Catherine O'Hara as the family matriarch, would be well mannered – and funny enough – to make a series for the ABC network.

When the show, which was filmed in Las Vegas and Los Angeles, and also starred the Canadian actor Patrick J. Adams, was tested to a wider audience, it got the thumbs down. In the end it was just another pilot that wound up being broadcast as a stand-alone TV movie.

Work did keep coming, though. Now twenty-seven, Meghan, once she was finished with *Good Behavior*, was cast as Wendy in *90210*, a reboot of the long-running series *Beverly Hills, 90210*, which she had watched as a teenager. The new version was trying to be equally iconic, but updated and raunchier.

In the series premiere, Meghan's character once again had a bawdy introduction, first being shown outside West Beverly Hills High performing oral sex in another student's car while pupils went back and forth. Her character lasted for just two episodes before vanishing without any plot explanation. The series, however, would run for five seasons. With various guest spots in established series like *Knight Rider*, *Without a Trace* and the sitcom *The League*, Meghan was almost becoming a familiar face to TV audiences. Real fame, however, or even just a steady pay cheque – she was barely earning enough to pay for actors' health insurance – continued to elude her. She was always on the cusp of making a breakthrough.

When director J. J. Abrams – who even before his mega successes with *Star Wars* and *Star Trek* was lauded as the mastermind behind *Mission: Impossible III* and *Lost* – had Meghan playing a junior FBI agent, Amy Jessup, in his sci-fi procedural *Fringe*, she once again had high hopes that something would come of it. She appeared in the first and second episodes of the second season, and though director Akiva Goldsman, best known for his hit *A Beautiful*

Mind, hinted that audiences might be seeing more of Agent Jessup, she never returned to the creepy tale of spooky shapeshifters and parallel universes. In fact, she was next seen altering her personal universe in a more conventional way, snorting a couple of lines of cocaine in the knowing TV-movie comedy, *The Boys & Girls Guide to Getting Down*. Based on the award-winning 2006 independent film that featured her *Deal or No Deal* co-model Leyla Milani, the show charts the vagaries of the LA dating scene.

In the sex, drugs and anything goes movie, Meghan is shown as a single girl pouring herself into a super-tight black dress – shades of *Deal or No Deal* – before heading out for the night prowling the singles scene of downtown LA, where she knocks back some blow to keep the mobile debauchery moving.

With roles to her name in which she had snorted coke, performed oral sex and taught striptease, what better credentials could she have had to share an on-screen smooch with former junkie, funny man and now British movie star Russell Brand. Her 'exotic' looks won her the role of Tatiana in *Get Him to the Greek*, which filmed in the spring of 2009. With no lines, she remained uncredited in the official cast list. Still, she fared better than Brand's ex-wife Katy Perry and singer Alanis Morissette, whose scenes were deleted.

During this time, it was her partner who was getting the plaudits. Trevor was named by *The Hollywood Reporter* as one of the 'Top 35 Under 35' in the Next Gen Class of 2009 for his work as a manager and producer. All those years of meetings and schmoozing were paying off – and he already had the pretty girl he had always dreamed of. Along with that glowing write-up in *The Hollywood Reporter*, the honour came with a party at My House, a Hollywood club famous for its velvet ropes and bottle service, where Meghan did her best to shine as the beautiful and talented, as well as supportive, girlfriend of a bona fide mover and shaker.

Trevor could now afford to give Meghan a few crumbs from his groaning pile of scripts. At least it would stop her continuously nagging him to get her a part in one of his productions. Two clients, Marcus Dunstan and Patrick Melton, the writers behind the *Saw*

IV, V and *VI* movies, had put together a nineteen-minute film, *The Candidate*, based on the short story by Henry Slesar. Meghan was cast as the secretary, in one scene showing off a beautifully written, hand-addressed envelope – an in-joke about her calligraphy skills.

Trevor then found a small role for her in *Remember Me*, a 9/11-themed melodrama starring the British heart-throb Robert Pattinson. The movie, which was shot in June, was written by his client Will Fetters and, following its release in March 2010, turned out to be the producer's biggest hit to date, a ratings and box-office success. Meghan might be proving to be his lucky charm.

Not that she thought so. Earlier that year, in January, the young actor had started a blog that she called Working Actress, where she described in often heartbreaking detail the life of a jobbing actor. In one post she wrote: 'I'm not gonna lie. I've spent many days curled up in bed with a loaf of bread and some wine. A one-woman pity party. It's awful and ridiculous.' She described what it was like to have her minor scenes cut from a movie, the endless rejection, bitchy fellow actresses at auditions, and test shoots gone wrong. 'All you are doing is setting yourself up for heartbreak,' she said of this most demanding of professions. Though her blog, which abruptly ended in 2012, was anonymous, the *Daily Mail* reported in February 2018 that fellow bloggers and actors had confirmed she was the author. 'Yes, it was definitely Meghan Markle who wrote it,' said actor Lance Carter, who communicated with her before reproducing one of her posts on his own site.

A few months after beginning the blog, in July 2010 Meghan was ready for her own close-up. She was cast opposite comedian Jason Sudeikis in the comedy *Horrible Bosses*. In her thirty-five-second scene she played a FedEx girl whom Sudeikis creepily hits on, saying that she is too 'cute' for the job. Meghan was cool and polite, a professional just doing her job. That was it. Blink and you would miss her. She did, though, get to meet her screen idol, Donald Sutherland, who played Jack Pellit in the movie. 'I was so excited to work with him,' she enthused in her Working Actress blog. 'The woman in the hair department said he was a gem and that I would love him, so when I met him (and his oh-so-debonair self), I said: "Mr Sutherland, I hear I'm going to fall in love with you before lunch-break." He laughed, it broke the ice. And I resisted the very major urge to squeal.'

Despite enjoying her fan-girl moment, she had to recognize that this was yet another acting job that traded exclusively on her looks and sex appeal. Time to recalibrate. She was approaching thirty, an age in a notoriously cruel place like Hollywood when she would soon be considered over the hill. If she was not careful, her agent would be dropping hints about changing the date of birth on her résumé.

Another casting season had passed her by and she had nothing apart from a series of auditions in her diary. It was hard not to feel discouraged, especially when she heard of the successes of her contemporaries. Those five years were up and she just hadn't quite made that extra leap.

Time to dip into Trevor's pick 'n' mix bag of aphorisms. Along with 'give it five years' he had another favourite: 'This is not a business for the weary. You're either gonna buy an island or be sent to one.'

Meghan straightened her skirts, focused her gaze, and walked into the next casting room. She wasn't ready to be marooned just yet.

6

A Star is Tailor-Made

Rachel Zane was a ball buster. A ball buster to cast, a ball buster to play, and a ball buster even to name. Sexy but unapproachable, Rachel Zane was a character created as the love interest on a new show; so new they hadn't even worked out the title. Opinion was split. Some executives at USA Network, who were developing the show in 2010, went for *A Legal Mind*. Others thought the title *Suits* was tailor-made for a snappily dressed office full of sharp lawyers. *Suits* won out. That was just one of numerous daily battles to give the show a distinct identity. Casting and chemistry were critical to provide *Suits* with crackle and pop. Patrick J. Adams was perfect for the part of Mike Ross, the legal genius with an eidetic memory who couldn't afford law school because he was paying to keep his sick grandma in an upscale nursing home. The actor's eyes were the key to him winning the role: piercing blue, long-lashed. The rest of him was just average-looking boy next door. He combined a vibe of intelligence with just enough seediness to flesh out the part of the brilliant college dropout who made a living by taking law-school entry exams for other students.

After several weeks of casting, on 7 July 2010 they had signed up *The Others* star Gabriel Macht as top lawyer Harvey Reginald Specter, and cast Rick Hoffman as the duplicitous partner Louis Litt, as well as Gina Torres, who played the sharp-tongued founding partner Jessica Lourdes Pearson.

One part remained: the role of Rachel Zane. She was a paralegal who was smart, elegantly upper class, and so highly regarded at the fictional law firm that she had her own office, while several of the fictional lawyers still laboured on the main floor. She had to be sexy without being overtly so, secure in her own power as a woman, but with a certain vulnerability as shown by the fact that she was unable to pass the LSAT, the exam which determined eligibility for law school. The show's producers were looking for a woman who had toughness and attitude while still being engaging.

'The part was just a nightmare to cast,' recalls one studio executive. 'Then Meghan Markle came along.' Once told by famed casting director April Webster to use 'less make-up, more Meghan' when auditioning, Meghan had dressed sexy-professional-casual to screen-test for the role. Somewhat belatedly, she realized that the plum-coloured spaghetti-strap top, black jeans and high heels she was wearing were more single lady lawyer on the prowl than attractive paralegal with an encyclopaedic knowledge of the law. So, just before her audition, Meghan had run into an H&M store, picked out a simple black dress for $35 and raced back to the studio. She hadn't even had time to try it on for size. The producers of the then titled *A Legal Mind* asked her to change into the new garment before taking the screen test. It was the best $35 she had ever spent. As the show's creator Aaron Korsh told writer Sam Kashner: 'We all looked at each other [after the Meghan Markle screen test] like, "Wow, this is the one." I think it's because Meghan has the ability to be smart and sharp but without losing her sweetness.'

With the casting of Meghan Markle, the character of Rachel Zane was made flesh. Originally, the brainy and beautiful paralegal was named Rachel Lane, but the clearance department felt the name was too similar to that of a real person. Instead, they chose the surname of the show's casting director Bonnie Zane, an insider's compliment to the storied Hollywood professional for her work on the show.

It was not as if Meghan was a shoe-in for the role. Now thirty, on paper she was too old to play a young paralegal, and the multiracial Gina Torres, who played partner Jessica Lourdes Pearson, had already put a tick in the box marked 'ethnic diversity'.

Meghan's main rival was a younger, more experienced Canadian actor, blonde, blue-eyed Kim Shaw. By now Meghan had learned to manage her expectations and not take rejection too personally. She was too light, too dark, too skinny, too something or other for so many roles.

Meghan didn't feel great about her audition, and called her agent Nick Collins at the Gersh Agency from her car. She told him that she could not get her head around the lines. It was a mouthful, the worst audition of her life. 'I don't think I did a good job in that room, and I need to get back in there,' she wailed. 'I really want this part.' Her agent, as she later recounted to *Marie Claire* in 2013, had heard this before from many of his clients, and his answer was always the same: 'There's nothing I can do. Just focus on your next audition.' Once again she felt that moment of: 'Why am I subjecting myself to this torture?' She had a top degree, a sparkling résumé, great connections; she didn't have to put herself through the wringer every day. But there was an inevitability to it that Meghan found hard to resist. As she once said in an interview with Al Norton: 'If you grow up in a coal-mining town, you will probably become a coal miner. I grew up in the industry, and was always on set because of my dad, so it seems natural for me to be an actress.'

In spite of her considerable misgivings, she tried to stay optimistic, going to yoga classes and meditating to stay grounded. All the while she headed out to other auditions, though none of them inspired her as much as *A Legal Mind* aka *Suits*. In her heart, she felt the role would be perfect for her. And the fact that the character shared her first name, Rachel, added that extra something – it was kismet.

While Meghan felt she had blown the audition, unbeknown to her, behind the scenes the executives were busy drawing up the contract for the pilot if the network approved. As she recalls: 'We had no idea that they … loved my read. They loved my take on Rachel and they were putting together a deal for me. It was a really good lesson in perspective. I think we are always going to be our own worst critics.'

The head honchos at USA Network had chosen Markle over Shaw, formally casting her on 24 August 2010. As the then USA

Network co-president Jeff Wachtel explained: '[Shaw] was a little bit more traditional blonde girl next door; [the decision] was a tough one because they were both really good. Meghan had a certain type of sparkle and was a little more urbane, a little more worldly.'

The deciding factor was how they wanted the relationship between Rachel and Mike to play out. As Wachtel told *The Hollywood Reporter* in 2017: 'One of the things that we needed at the beginning with *Suits* was Patrick's character comes in as the hottest thing in town: he's brilliant, has a photographic memory and fakes his way into being a lawyer, and then he comes up against this girl who turns out to be the love of his life. We needed somebody who had a real authority to shut him down and still be the coolest thing around. And they had it right away. It was a lot of fun.'

Meghan was still taking other auditions when her mobile phone rang with a call from her agent, telling her she had been cast in the *Suits* series pilot and would begin filming in autumn in New York City. She was overjoyed but also wary. After all, she had gone down this road before, especially with *The Apostles*, which, at the time, she felt confident was going to be her big break. After eight years going from audition to audition, had she finally caught a break? Meghan's casting garnered a short article in *The Hollywood Reporter*, noting her uncredited role in the 2010 comedy, *Get Him to the Greek*.

When she began with a standard table-read of the script, it was obvious that Meghan and Patrick generated chemistry, this elusive quality the showbiz equivalent of lightning in a bottle. It was vital that they had a spark, as the ups and downs of their love story would be a narrative arc throughout the series – if the show was picked up by the network, that is.

In the autumn of 2010, Meghan flew to New York to shoot the ninety-minute series pilot. Since the elation of winning the part, reality had set in. She had already shot five pilots, including one for ABC with her current co-star, Patrick J. Adams, and none of them had got any further. Maybe he was her unlucky charmer. As she later observed: '[A pilot is] like your baby, then you wait and wait to see if it gets picked up and it's a hard thing to let go of. The one I had the most attachment to was one called *The Apostles*, which was my very first pilot. It's probably revisionist history, but I look back on it now and think: "That would have been amazing." But who knows?'

On her first day of the shoot, the normally nerveless Meghan was a little edgy. Though she had grown up on sets, and was no novice to TV productions, it was one thing sitting in the wings watching the action, or hovering on the edges as a bit part, but quite another to be centre stage. Nonetheless, all those hours after school on professional sound stages, observing the interaction of actors and crews, overhearing the snatches of conversation and gossip between production assistants, and hanging around the craft service table, had taught her how to behave on set. She was charming to everyone, from grips to the lighting director. There was a degree of self-interest at work, Meghan having learned from her father that the placement of a light could enhance or slightly deform a pretty face, and that some of the placement depended on goodwill.

Meghan was remembered as bubbly and warm, chatty but a good listener who didn't dominate on-set conversations. She was a team player who radiated a sweet intelligence, saving her sterner, more ambitious self for those important on-set interactions with Patrick J. Adams.

In a show that became known as much for its fashion as its plot line, costume designer Jolie Andreatta's vision of Meghan's on-screen look was crucial. She later recalled: 'Rachel is classic, to the word, with a hint of rebellion thrown in. Her style is understated and her cute figure pulls it off perfectly.'

On Meghan's return from New York, Trevor took her to a beach resort in the Central American country of Belize for a vacation. It was there, amid the tropical greenery and the soothing waves, that he asked his girlfriend of six years to be his bride, slipping a princess-cut diamond solitaire onto her finger. Meghan was thrilled. 'They were both googly-eyed for one another,' recalls a friend. 'They were very much in love.'

Meghan was engaged to her long-time boyfriend and was in a pilot for which the omens looked good. There was serious talk of a TV series. At long last her Hollywood dream was coming true.

As her half-brother Tom Junior told me: 'Meg was on her way up, marrying a guy with a production company and now making good money.'

All those on-set rumours turned into a joyous reality when, in January 2011, USA Network gave the green light for the first series. Shooting would begin on 25 April in Toronto. Finally, after years of auditions that went nowhere, roles that ended up on the cutting-room floor and, most dishearteningly, pilots that never got picked up, Meghan had a series. The only downside was that she would have to take a five-hour flight if she was to see her Hollywood-based fiancé. But since she and Trevor caught planes like others hailed taxis, the sacrifice was going to be worth it. They were both ambitious young people; if anything, Trevor was more driven than Meghan. He understood that this was an opportunity that she could not miss.

Her joy, however, was tempered with sorrow. While she was preparing for the series, her mother phoned to tell her that Alvin Ragland, her eighty-two-year-old grandfather, had tripped and fallen as a result of getting tangled up in a dog lead while out walking his dog. He had hit his head on the pavement and died of his injuries on 12 March. Meghan remembered Alvin as a real character, appreciating his knowledge of antiques, an enthusiasm that inspired her own fascination with the finer things in life.

In the family reorganization following his death, Doria inherited his single-storey green stucco house in what is known as the 'black Beverly Hills'. It was close to the University of Southern California where, in the late spring, Doria, now a mature student, would complete her Master's degree in social work. Her daughter was ecstatic, probably more effusive than her mother. She watched proudly as Doria collected her degree on a makeshift stage at one of the many June graduation ceremonies taking place on the extensive campus. Given the difficulties of her mother's background, the trouble at her high school following the 1971 San Fernando earthquake and the casual jobs she had taken on to make ends meet, her achievement was a genuine personal triumph, an indication of her smarts and her determination.

✳

The first episode of *Suits* aired on 23 June 2011 to generally favourable reviews and, more importantly, an enthusiastic audience. Cast, crew and the money men at the network were ecstatic, the producers thrilled that their gamble to cast Meghan opposite Patrick had paid off big time, the show's fans buzzing about the couple's on-screen chemistry.

Their off-screen chemistry was equally noticeable, almost uncomfortably so, according to guests at Meghan and Trevor's wedding, which took place in Jamaica in September 2011. The two actors had clearly developed a bond of familiarity that is invariably the corollary of working up close and personal for so long and so intensely. Patrick J. Adams has a different take on their interaction at that time. He later told writer Lesley Goldberg: 'In some ways, Meghan and I were the closest because we were the youngest people in the cast and both came in with the least experience. We grew up together over the course of the show.'

He might have kept his distance if he had known that she had been cast to play a calculating serial killer in an episode of the quirky crime show *Castle*, entitled 'Once Upon a Crime', which she filmed while *Suits* was on hiatus. As Princess Sleeping Beauty, Meghan's character plotted a complex series of murders with fairy-tale themes, having been cast for the part by her champion, Donna Rosenstein.

For Meghan, shooting her first series of *Suits* turned out to be more stressful than organizing her wedding. They had chosen the storied Jamaica Inn in Ocho Rios, an idyllic spot with balconies overlooking the sea. Famous as the honeymoon destination for playwright Arthur Miller and screen goddess Marilyn Monroe, Meghan said on the invitation that if it was good enough for the most glamorous couple of their generation 'it's good enough for us'. The full invitation read: 'Cheers to love, cheers to laughter, cheers to happily ever after.' Though she had delegated on the ground organization to an in-house wedding coordinator, Meghan insisted that she ran every decision big or small by the bride-to-be. Given the hectic lives that she and Trevor were leading, to be able to rely on such expert help was a lifesaver. It seemed that all she had to worry about was the guest list, choosing the flowers, agreeing to the menu – and packing a bikini or two. Oh, and her strapless white wedding dress. Of course, that overlooked the endless back and forth between the wedding planner and Meghan. Even though she was in a different country and time zone, she took charge from afar. As her father Tom Senior, who was praised in the wedding literature for his 'incredible generosity', later recalled: 'Meghan planned everything down to the tiniest detail. She micromanaged everything.' Even down to a 'baggie' of weed, which was given to every guest when they arrived at the resort.

Three weeks before their wedding, Trevor made an obscure podcast where he talked about his career with two old friends, Kristian Harloff and Mark Ellis. His breezy, self-deprecating manner – he told a story about how he was chastised by a senior agent at Endeavor for standing too far away from the urinal because he was afraid of getting 'splash-back' on his favourite Italian Canali 'hero suit' – was very different to his bride-to-be who, as her former colleagues on *Deal or No Deal* observed, was always very self-contained and considered. *The Schmoes Know* podcast was live-streamed, meaning that Trevor could be seen on camera swigging from an engraved hip flask – a gift from Meghan – during the show. She texted him to 'put that flask down, it looks incredibly unprofessional'. When one of the Schmoes suggested that they have Meghan on the show, Trevor interjected: 'She's a big deal, fuck off.' The podcast hinted at their personality differences: Trevor was loose-lipped, unconcerned and carefree; a striking counterpoint to Meghan, who was archly protective of Brand Meghan and always keen to project an air of sophistication and style.

She may have felt that at times Trevor was too brashly laid-back for comfort, especially now that her star was rising, *Suits* having been picked up for a second season. It was a cause for celebration but also uncertainty as, once more, the couple would be long-distance commuters, seeing each other every two or three weeks, depending on whether Trevor had meetings or had arranged to see his family, who lived on Long Island in New York State. Their wedding would be a rare opportunity to let their hair down, and they were determined to enjoy a long weekend of parties, including beach Olympics, culminating with the twelve-minute wedding ceremony, which made the 'Hitched, Hatched, Hired' column of *The Hollywood Reporter*.

With the ocean providing the backdrop, Meghan was walked down the 'aisle' by her mother and father before the couple recited loving vows that they had written themselves. One of Meghan's bridesmaids later recalled: 'It was such a moving wedding. I started crying the moment I saw her in her dress.' Though the pair had officially married in Los Angeles in a brief civil ceremony, this was the real celebration for family and friends, complete with a rousing chorus of the traditional Jewish 'Hava Nagila', which was sung while the bride and groom were hoisted up in chairs held above their guests' heads.

On returning from their Jamaican celebration, Trevor and Meghan were able to spend more time with one another before shooting was due to begin once more in Toronto. It was just as well that she was enjoying a brief break, as her father was in need of her support. For the last few months, he had been caring for his increasingly frail mother Doris, whom he had flown from her home in Florida to his residence in Los Feliz. As his house was close by the ABC TV studios where he worked, he was able to visit during the day to check that she was OK. Sadly, as her chronic forgetfulness slipped into dementia, that was no longer a practical option. The last straw was when she absent-mindedly left a pan on the stove, causing a small kitchen fire. He arrived home to find the fire department and paramedics at the scene.

The only option was to place her in a specialist facility, moving her into Broadview Residential Care Center, an affordable nursing home in Glendale, Los Angeles. Once the first season of *Suits* had wrapped up, Meghan and Trevor visited her grandmother as much as they could, making the 12-mile drive from their cosy house on Hilldale in West Hollywood to see her. Meghan read to her, brushed her hair, and did simple arts and crafts with her. As she slipped deeper into the gloaming of dementia, Doris no longer recognized Trevor, nor her son Tom Senior, nor her grandson Tom Junior. Yet her eyes would light up when she heard Meghan's voice and felt her comforting touch. 'With her dementia, Grandmother got weird about me and Dad, but was always OK with Meg,' recalls Tom Junior. 'I saw the private side of Meghan, a genuinely caring, loving person. She had an amazing relationship with Doris, even though she didn't know her that well.'

In October, Meghan and Trevor walked the red carpet at the Anti-Defamation League Entertainment Industry Awards dinner at the Beverly Hilton Hotel, the most high-level event she had ever attended. More importantly, she was Master of Ceremonies for the evening. She dressed for the part in a simple Stella McCartney velvet cocktail dress, while Trevor, beaming with pride, looked his usual slightly rumpled self. They mingled with other celebrities, and Meghan glowed. She was on her way.

Meghan continued to visit her ailing grandmother at the nursing home. Her father and half-brother could only be there on weekends, but Meghan came frequently during the week. With Doris fading fast, Tom Senior flew his brothers in to say their last goodbyes. She died on 25 November 2011. When Trevor and Meghan attended her funeral, it was the first time that most of the Markles had met the TV producer. Tom Junior remarked, 'She was completely head over heels and seemed really happy when I saw them together, despite the sad circumstances. They seemed extremely happy together.'

These family reunions were few and far between. The last time Meghan had seen her half-sister Yvonne, who had re-christened herself Samantha, was when she and Tom Senior made the trip to Albuquerque for the eldest Markle daughter's college graduation. 'She was lovely, very polite and sweet,' Tom Senior's first wife Roslyn told me about Meghan's visit. During the graduation ceremony, Meghan sat next to Samantha's pre-teen daughter Noel and made small talk with the girl, then posed for photos, smiling and trying to make everyone feel at ease.

It was the last time that Meghan would see her Markle relations, the actor also leaving Trevor behind when she flew to Toronto to settle back into her new life, filming for nine months on the show's successful second season. Of course the couple used

Skype and FaceTime, but it was wearing being apart, especially during the long, grey, Canadian winter. She did her best to get the Californian vibe going in her rented house in Summerhill, lightening the wall colours and trying to convey a bright and airy feel amid the chilly gloom. Candles, leafy plants and, of course, white hotel-style bedsheets with a high thread count helped to bring a touch of Hollywood to Toronto.

It might have been cold outside, but it was hot on set, the budding if often-thwarted romance between Rachel Zane and Mike Ross fuelling *Suits'* growing success as much as the Machiavellian plot twists about a law firm and its clients. On screen, sparks flew between Rachel and Mike, enthralling viewers, especially after the second-season finale, which climaxed with their characters having heated sex in the fictional law firm's file room. Fans had become really invested in the fictional couple. Patrick J. Adams recalls a chance encounter with a Swedish hiker who had twisted his ankle on a backpacking trail in New Zealand. When Patrick, who was on holiday, went to help, the young man forgot his injuries and told the actor how badly he wanted Mike and Rachel to 'figure things out'.

Their on-screen intimacy led to speculation that the pair had fallen into the trap of many co-stars – Elizabeth Taylor and Richard Burton, Angelina Jolie and Brad Pitt, Daniel Craig and Rachel Weisz – and fallen for one another. In fact, the Canadian-born actor only had eyes for an earlier female lead, Troian Bellisario – the daughter of producers Deborah Pratt and Donald P. Bellisario – who in 2009 had played opposite him in the play *Equivocation*. They had dated but broke up after a year, Bellisario going on to win a role in the first season of *Pretty Little Liars*. In a move that his *Suits* character Mike Ross would have approved of, Patrick devised a cute way of winning back the showbiz heiress. He quietly took a bit part on *Pretty Little Liars* and then joined his surprised ex-girlfriend on set at the table-read. His ploy worked, the couple reuniting and eventually becoming engaged in 2014 before marrying in 2016.

While the on-screen 'will they, won't they' romance between Rachel and Mike gave the show its sexual tension, it was the other man in Rachel's life, her father, a powerful rival lawyer played by African-American actor Wendell Pierce, who really caught the attention of some of the show's 4-million-strong audience.

As the story develops, we learn that Rachel, much to the disappointment of her successful and wealthy father, is stuck as a paralegal because she just can't pass the law exam, the LSAT. While her character has some daddy issues, it was Rachel Zane's dual heritage that stirred controversy, with both African-American and white viewers confused that a girl who looked so white could have had a black father. One fan asked if she was adopted, while others were more hostile about the fictional paralegal's origins. Even though the then American president himself was of dual heritage, the decision by the show's producers to cast a woman of mixed ethnicity as a modern-day equivalent of a conventional upper-class white woman helped to move the dial a little with regard to racial stereotypes and traditional images of beauty.

Though TV executives viewed *Suits* as a mid-ranking show on their roster, gradually its popularity began to grow. With the head honchos now taking notice, Meghan and her colleagues were asked to establish a following using social media in order to help with ratings. Even though she had never heard of Instagram, she found herself opening an account and posting photographs from her private life. What began as a chore turned into an enjoyable and highly addictive daily habit, the actor building up more than a million followers by the time she closed the account. Her first image on 24 May 2012 showed her *Suits* script from the episode 'Break Point', a copy of the American business magazine *Forbes*, as well as liberal TV commentator Rachel Maddow's first book *Drift: The Unmooring of American Military Power*, about the rise of presidential authority and the diminution of Congress. With her Instagram debut, Meghan was demonstrating that here was an actor with brains as well as beauty, who was involved and engaged with the world around her. Subsequent posts would be less forthright, featuring her favourite food, charming selfies, travels abroad and images of Toronto. It was a curated, very considered vision of her private world.

Her involvement in the outside world was not just through the distorting prism of Instagram. In February 2012, Meghan took part in a USA Network campaign against racism, appearing on screen in *Characters Unite*, an award-winning public-service programme created to address social injustices and cultural divides. Wearing a T-shirt with the words 'I won't stand for racism' printed on it, she encouraged people to stand together against prejudice, while sharing her experiences of being a fly on the wall as white people told black jokes or made bigoted remarks.

Closer to home, the actor volunteered to help at a local Toronto soup kitchen for the homeless, the St Felix Centre, which was founded by the Felician Sisters. She also asked the *Suits* producers if, at the end of a day of filming, they would donate any leftover food from the craft service, the daily unlimited buffet of snacks designed to fuel the actors and crew through the shoots. They were happy to agree to her request, the *Suits* family also making a substantial cash donation to the homeless charity. The actor, who held morning prayer meetings on the sound stage, found herself landed with a new moniker: 'Meghan gets shit done.'

The cast and crew were also encouraged to bond, to be a family. It helped all round. A happy set was a productive set. The result was a tight-knit group, bicycling places and going out for drinks or dinner, playing board games and drinking whisky, as one cast member recalled, 'into the wee hours'. The cast also holidayed together over Canadian Thanksgiving, Meghan bringing her Vitamix super-blender to whip up soups and cocktails for the group. It was during one of these group get-togethers that Meghan was inspired to take what turned out to be one of her favourite-ever holidays. During a casual conversation with Meghan's co-star Gabriel Macht, he told her that he and his wife loved campervan vacations. After listening to him wax lyrical about a trip to New Zealand, Meghan decided to follow suit. She and Trevor also hired a campervan and spent two weeks driving around New Zealand's sparsely populated South Island. They went hiking over glaciers, visited wineries in Marlborough, and rented a beach house for a few days.

She vividly remembers the extraordinary night they pulled up at a campsite in Akaroa, a small town surrounded by a dead volcano. As she later recalled when she talked to ZM radio in New Zealand: 'I was washing my hair and I hear something and I open the shower curtain and there is this thirteen-year-old boy who had crawled under the stall and was trying to steal my underwear. I grabbed my towel and I had shampoo in my hair and I yelled: "Where is your mother?!" I found his parents and they were mortified, of course. And to this day, oh my God, that kid will be sitting at home going "That's the girl from *Suits*, I saw her naked!"' Now, though, he will be able to boast that he saw a Hollywood princess in the buff. In spite of her encounter with this junior Peeping Tom, she voted the holiday one of the best trips of her life.

When she returned home, she discussed with Trevor the prospect of adding to their family. She wanted a dog. So, just before Christmas, she and Trevor found themselves gazing at a pair of six-week-old puppies at a pet adoption agency in Los Angeles. The pups had only recently been rescued from being put down at a dog shelter. One of the Labrador mixes was black, the other golden. As luck would have it, David Branson Smith, the screenwriter son of Sally Bedell Smith, who has written biographies of Princess Diana and Prince Charles, adopted the black puppy, whom he called Otto; Meghan took the golden puppy, whom she named Bogart. She had talk-show host and comedian Ellen DeGeneres and her wife, Portia de Rossi, to thank for the final decision. As Meghan was communing with the tiny pooch, Ellen tapped on the glass of the viewing area and yelled, 'Take the dog!' As Meghan explains: 'So I brought him home because Ellen told me to.' Soon the adorable Bogart had ousted pictures of herself and her husband on her Instagram feed, the puppy overrunning the joint social media feed.

In February 2013, Meghan emailed David Branson Smith to say that she and Trevor 'always wondered if [Bogart] and his brother would recognize each other ... Kind of a sweet thought.' Diaries were consulted and the two brothers had a reunion on the beach at Malibu. As Sally Bedell Smith revealed in the London *Sunday Times*: 'Otto bounded out of David's car straight towards

Bogart. For the next hour they romped around like, well, long-lost brothers.' Meghan filmed and posted the reunion like a social media pro, exclaiming, 'Oh my God, how sweet, they're really the same size!' It was to be the dogs' only meeting, but two years later, in 2015, Bogart was joined by another rescue dog, a beagle mix that Meghan named Guy.

By then the other 'guy' in her life was long gone. Even though Trevor had opened an office in New York – only an hour's flight to Toronto – to expand his business and to be nearer to Meghan and his family, cracks had begun to appear in their marriage. What once endeared now irritated. Meghan, a self-confessed perfectionist who was as fastidious as she was controlling, had tolerated Trevor's scattered approach to life for years. He was notorious for arriving late, his clothes rumpled, his hair dishevelled, and often as not with a new stain on his seersucker jacket. 'Sorry bro' was a constant refrain as he hurtled from meeting to meeting, always just behind the clock.

Meghan's house in Summerhill was a vision of order and crisply ironed perfection. When she flew back to their Los Angeles home after Trevor had been in solo residence for a few weeks, the sight that greeted her increasingly rankled. Though Trevor would consistently visit her in Toronto, he often felt like an outsider, his presence an irritating distraction.

Whether she wanted to admit it to herself or not, Meghan, who once said that she couldn't imagine life without Trevor by her side, was now building a new world for herself. As Toronto was becoming more her home than Los Angeles, the dynamics in their relationship subtly altered. She was her own woman now, earning a steady income, making new friends on set and off, no longer dependent on her husband's connections.

A $500 Vitamix blender symbolized the growing divide. She insisted that her favourite kitchen appliance from their West Hollywood residence come with her to Toronto, packing it into the back seat of her car that was being moved by truck to Canada, even though it would have been just as easy to buy a new one. It sat on the kitchen counter in the Toronto house, a material reminder that her home was no longer in Los Angeles.

While Meghan saw her star rising, her husband's career was treading water. During this time he produced *Amber Alert*, a low-budget thriller about a pair of reality-show contestants who spot a car containing a kidnapped child. Though it was an intriguing premise, the movie did little box-office business and garnered even fewer favourable reviews. With no new projects in sight and with *Suits* on hiatus, Trevor took Meghan on a cycling vacation to Vietnam. It didn't help that he became sick with food poisoning as a result of Meghan sampling obscure local dishes like a female version of the TV globetrotter Anthony Bourdain. Their escape to exotic locales, which once provided a backdrop for their love, only served to highlight the distance between them.

He was not the only one experiencing the Meghan chill. Her friends in Los Angeles noticed the change in her now that she was on the way up. She no longer had the time for friends she had known for years, cancelling lunches at short notice or expecting them to rework their own schedules to accommodate the busy life of the rising star. A networker to her fingertips, she seemed to be carefully recalibrating her life, forging new friendships with those who could burnish and develop her career. New people like talented fashion stylist Jessica Mulroney, who worked with Sophie Trudeau, wife of the Canadian Prime Minister Justin Trudeau, and her TV-personality husband Ben, the son of the former Canadian Prime Minister Brian Mulroney, now came into her orbit, as Meghan would see them regularly at the newly opened Soho House in Toronto. As she was expanding her social horizons, her LA circle felt they were being left behind. While she might have been getting above herself, everyone expected Trevor to keep her feet planted on the ground.

Without anyone really noticing it, the couple were going their separate ways. In February 2013, Trevor went to the Oscars without Meghan, who had dreamed of attending the starry event ever since she was a little girl. Trevor's older brother Drew laconically wrote on his Facebook page: 'My brother at the Oscars tonight proving that they'll let in just about any hobo off the street.' It seems that Meghan was too busy filming to join him. At least that was the story.

A few weeks later, on 8 April 2013, Meghan fully embraced her part-time home when she went to watch the Toronto Maple Leafs beat the New York Rangers at the Air Canada Centre. Not only was she watching the ice hockey game, she was there to support her friend Michael Del Zotto, nine years her junior, skate as a defenceman for the Rangers. Del Zotto played hard, incurring a two-minute time-out for high-sticking rival Nazem Kadri.

Two weeks later, on 21 April, Meghan was at Madison Square Garden to watch Del Zotto and his fellow Rangers defeat the New Jersey Devils, and was captured by photographer James Devaney casually dressed in jeans and grey scarf, sitting alone. In a series of posts on Instagram, Meghan documented her hockey adventures, on one occasion posing with Del Zotto and her *Suits* co-star Rick Hoffman. A year later, Del Zotto made headlines regarding his relationship with porn star Lisa Ann, best known for her parodies of former presidential candidate Sarah Palin. Lisa Ann publicly dressed him down, according to the *Toronto Star*, for pestering her to set him up on dates with other women while he was on the road. She outed his behaviour in a series of Twitter posts.

Whatever the nature of their friendship – representatives for both Meghan and Del Zotto emphatically denied to the *Sun* newspaper that they were in a relationship – by then the marriage of Trevor and Meghan was over. The sad news, in the summer of 2013, came as a bolt from the blue. Everyone in their circle was genuinely shocked, none more so than Trevor's parents David and Leslie, who had embraced her like a daughter.

As her maid of honour Ninaki Priddy told writer Rebecca Hardy: 'I knew they fought sometimes, but it wasn't anything huge. The only obstacle was the distance, because she was living in Toronto and Trevor was based in LA. But I thought they were manoeuvring through it. Trevor would take his work to Canada to be with her and run his office remotely.'

It was such a surprise for Trevor that, even five years later, he could barely contain his anger. During a brief interview with me in 2018, the normally affable, laid-back New Yorker instantly switched gear from his usual 'Hi bro, how's it going?' to a cold fury when her name entered the conversation. 'I have zero to say about her' was his firm response to my questions. Trevor went from cherishing Meghan to, as one relative told me, 'feeling like he was a piece of something stuck to the bottom of her shoe'. A wealthy entrepreneur friend claimed that the marriage ended so abruptly that Meghan sent Trevor her diamond wedding and engagement rings back to him by registered mail. Another confirmed that the decision to end the marriage was made by Meghan and that it had come 'totally out of the blue'. His family and friends reject the notion that Trevor was jealous of his wife's accomplishments, his uncle Mickey-Miles Felton later commenting: 'He was just happy for her success. Just thrilled.'

There were other consequences. The break-up also fractured her thirty-odd-year friendship with jewellery designer Ninaki Priddy. After listening to Trevor's side of the story, she decided she no longer wished to associate herself with Meghan. Exactly why is a closely kept secret. As she told the *Daily Mail*: 'All I can say now is that I think Meghan was calculated, very calculated, in the way she handled people and relationships. She is very strategic in the way she cultivates circles of friends. Once she decides you're not part of her life, she can be very cold. It's this shutdown mechanism she has. There's nothing to negotiate, she's made her decision, and that's it … The way she handled it, Trevor definitely had the rug pulled out from under him. He was hurt.'

Actor Abby Wathen, who had starred with Meghan in the low-budget movie *Random Encounters* in her pre-*Suits* days, had a different perspective on Meghan's break-up. As she explained in the ITV documentary *Prince Harry and Meghan: Truly, Madly, Deeply*, 'We both went through divorce, so we bonded on that too. I was destroyed, but she was empowered. She took her power back. It wasn't the right relationship for her, so she moved on.'

Now footloose and fancy-free, Meghan spent more time exploring downtown Toronto. She could often be found, glass of wine in hand, at Bar Isabel, the tapas bar where the grilled octopus and garlicky roast potatoes threw her into a 'carb coma'. She also went into raptures about the pasta at Terroni's, the local high-end

Italian deli chain, and enjoyed poutine, a dish that originated in Quebec in the 1950s, comprised of fries covered in gravy and cheese curds. According to Meghan, the best poutine squeaks when bitten into. On nights when she stayed at home, Meghan, who loves to cook, made vegetable soup in her beloved Vitamix or threw courgettes into the slow cooker with a little water and bouillon until it became what she called 'a filthy, sexy mush' that she would toss with pasta.

It was her fascination with food that got her a gig with *Men's Health* magazine. In 2013 they filmed an interview for their website, asking Meghan to give them the secret to a great burger and steak. It was sweet, unpolished and very natural; as a California girl, she said, she preferred fish tacos, but for a quick meal 'for her man', she would throw a steak on the grill. She also agreed to film a racier version of the same shoot. This video, which appeared two years later, showed Meghan riffing on her role in *Suits*, her hair in a bun, wearing sunglasses, a short leather skirt and power blazer. She unbuttons her sheer black top to reveal a spotted bra. 'Grilling never looked so hot' screamed the film title. As the steak smouldered, so did Meghan. But there was a hesitancy in her eyes. She was playing up to the camera but she seemed uncomfortable, conscious that she was portraying herself as a sex object to be leered at by men. She thought she had left those days behind on the set of *Deal or No Deal*. As far as she was concerned, this wasn't a part she was going to play for much longer.

During the *Suits* break, Meghan took the female lead in a low-budget crime thriller called *Anti-Social*. The drama, which was based on a series of real-life robberies involving graffiti gangs, was filmed in Budapest and London. While the money men on the production were looking for nude scenes between Meghan and her co-star Gregg Sulkin, who is ten years her junior, writer-director Reg Traviss stuck to his guns and refused to exploit his star. He later explained, 'It wasn't needed for the story.'

Meghan's stock and standing were rising with each season of *Suits*, which was now the highest-rated American TV show in the demographic sweet spot: those aged between eighteen and forty-nine. In November 2013, she was invited to attend the red-carpet premiere of *The Hunger Games: Catching Fire*, in London's Leicester Square. Two days later, Meghan and male model Oliver Cheshire were hosting the high-profile Global Gift Foundation charity gala, which benefited the Eva Longoria Foundation and Caudwell Children charities. Not that she was a fan of the red carpet, finding the glamorous shuffle with other celebrities an ordeal. As she wrote in her Working Actress blog: 'I loathe walking the red carpet. It makes me nervous and itchy, and I don't know which way to look. I just revert to this nerdy child that I once was. I hate it. I get off the carpet and have to shake it off. Sounds dramatic, but it's really nerve-racking for me.' As far as she was concerned, she never wanted fame. Acting was the chance to make a 'great living' by playing 'dress up and working with awesome people'.

She had arrived in London hardly knowing a soul, so she was appreciative when model and TV personality Lizzie Cundy took her under her wing at the pre-dinner party held at the home of billionaire businessman John Caudwell and his wife Claire. The American actor confided that she would like to work in London and mentioned an ambition to take part in the reality show *Made in Chelsea*. Just three months out of her marriage, she was looking for a date and asked Cundy if she knew any famous guys. The name of footballer Ashley Cole cropped up – as he did in other conversations with her new best buddies in the media. Cundy told *Grazia* magazine that Meghan was a real 'girls' girl ... very friendly, great fun and with a big smile'. What attracted her to the capital was how friendly everyone was. 'I've never been called "love" or "darling" more in my life,' she told Cundy. 'So it makes me want to stick around for a while.'

Along with her charity turn, Meghan, the consummate networker, hoped to raise her public profile during her time in London by discussing the last six episodes of the second season of *Suits* with members of the press. *Mail on Sunday* reporter Katie Hind wasn't expecting much when she agreed to meet Meghan on a chilly November night, just another up-and-coming actress looking for a mention or two in the press. From what she had read,

Meghan's ambition was to become a politician and she had fallen into acting during a holiday from her work at the US embassy in Buenos Aires, Argentina.

As they drank a bottle of Prosecco at the rooftop bar of the Sanctum Soho Hotel, the conversation turned to men and particularly, as Hind put it, to 'her keen interest in British men of a certain, well, standing'. To the reporter's surprise, Meghan took out her iPhone and showed her a picture of a handsome man on her Twitter account. 'Do you know this guy, Ashley Cole? He follows me and he keeps trying to talk to me on Twitter. He's trying really hard.'

Katie kept her cool, replying, 'I bet.' Meghan continued to confide eagerly. 'He wants to go out on a date while I'm over here in London. What do you think? Do you know him?'

The reporter certainly knew of his reputation as both an England and Chelsea football player and the ex-husband of Girls Aloud singer Cheryl Cole; someone who had cheated on his wife with several women, who had in turn sold their stories to the tabloids. Once Hind had broken the bad news, the actor seemed somewhat deflated, possibly having anticipated that her visit to London might have spawned a new romance. 'Thanks, I appreciate it,' Meghan told the *Mail* reporter, adding, 'Some of my friends told me to stay away from him, too. I think I'll leave it.'

During the next three hours, Meghan continued to down glasses of the Italian sparkling wine as she and Katie, both thirty-two, discussed the difficulties of modern romance and of finding the right guy. Meghan admitted that she was newly divorced – her decree cited 'irreconcilable differences' – and was now single and ready to mingle.

The tipsy talk wound down and the two hugged goodbye, with Katie wishing Meghan good luck. 'Not that she'd need it,' the reporter commented wryly as she watched Meghan, who was unable to catch a cab, persuade the owner of the Sanctum Soho to drive her the couple of minutes through the rain to her hotel, the Dean Street Townhouse.

7

The 'Aha' Moment

Feeling bloated and puffy-skinned, her black leather trousers a little too tight, Meghan, who had just returned from a 'carb-heavy' holiday, was just a tad out of sorts as she sat alongside her *Suits* co-stars on the dais at the five-star Langham Hotel in Pasadena, California, in early 2014. She looked out at the sea of television critics in front of her and seemed rather glad that her colleagues were fielding the questions from the Television Critics Association in a long-planned January conference. So far she had sat silently watching the back and forth, the discussion moving on to the shifting time slot, as *Suits* was scheduled to move from 10 p.m. to 9 p.m. 'Will that affect the cursing?' asked one critic, referring to the show's liberal use of profanity.

Meghan popped alive and grabbed the question. She looked at the show's creator and executive producer, Aaron Korsh, and playfully rephrased the question: 'Is that going to change for us being at nine o'clock – the shits and the dammits?' 'Shit, no!' responded Korsh. The audience laughed. This was classic Meghan: the good sport, the slightly naughty girl next door, the guy's gal. Her intervention had won over the crowd. But it was no longer enough. She wanted to stretch her wings; she had things to say, points to make that went way beyond the question-and-answer format concerning all things *Suits*. She was a well-travelled young woman with an appreciation of different countries, cuisines and cultures. Meghan had a take on everything from Middle Eastern politics to make-up. Her role on *Suits* was, she felt, a launch pad to something more. She knew she was not yet exploiting her full potential. But in order to do that, she needed to wield more clout.

Her recent visit to London, for example, had yielded only a small mention in the *Daily Mail* and a photograph in the *Metro*, a giveaway morning daily. She had appeared on numerous red carpets since her work on the series began, but what started out as thrilling was now routine. She was still just a pretty face in the crowd.

Meghan realized that she had to do better, to expand her visibility. From the moment *Suits* became successful, she could see that her young audience, especially teenage girls, were listening to what she had to say. Her Instagram following was growing exponentially, but static pictures of her life, her food and her dogs didn't provide an outlet for her thoughts on the world at large. She had a genuine point of view about a kaleidoscope of topics; she just needed a vehicle to enable her to express herself.

Just a few days later, on 22 January, she attended the annual Elle's Women in Television Celebration, her third appearance since *Suits* had launched. Meghan felt that she had come home. She was inspired to be surrounded by so many creative and stimulating women, such as cooking and lifestyle celebrity Giada De Laurentiis and multi-award-winning actor Tracee Ellis Ross, who, like Meghan, was bi-racial. Unlike Meghan, Ross came from Hollywood royalty; her mother was Diana Ross and her father was the music manager and industry executive Robert Ellis Silberstein.

Ross's career included a stint as a model, including walking the runway for Thierry Mugler, contributing as an editor and writer for *Mirabella* and *New York* magazines, and as the star of *Girlfriends*, a long-running sitcom, for which she had won several NAACP Image Awards. Her new comedy, *black-ish*, in which she played a doctor and mother of four, was garnering rave reviews. Rubbing shoulders with Ross and others, listening to their can-do success stories, stirred the urge in Meghan to do more. The questions was: how to go about it?

The answer came indirectly and unexpectedly. In February 2014 DirecTV, the satellite TV company, celebrated the Super Bowl with a huge televised pre-game party that they held the day before the big game itself. The spirited match of celebrity flag football, called DirecTV Celebrity Beach Bowl, was held in a large heated tent at Pier 40 on the Hudson River in Lower Manhattan. For the event, they created the world's largest indoor beach, trucking in more than a million pounds of freshly poured sand.

The band Paramore was scheduled to entertain the crowd and Food Network star Andrew Zimmern would broadcast live during half-time. Ever the good sport, Meghan joined model Chrissy Teigen, a former colleague on *Deal or No Deal*, and other celebrities, including former pro-quarterback Joe Montana, comedians Tracy Morgan and Tom Arnold, and the celebrity chef Guy Fieri, in a beach game, which Meghan's team won.

After the show, Meghan won much more – a new, influential friend, tennis legend Serena Williams. At the time, Serena held seventeen Grand Slam singles titles and almost as many for winning doubles tournaments. More importantly, she had parlayed her fifteen-year career as a super-athlete into lucrative endorsements, including her own fashion line and even some acting gigs. 'We hit it off immediately, taking pictures, laughing through the flag football game we were both playing in, and chatting not about tennis or acting but about all the good old-fashioned girly stuff,' Meghan later wrote. 'So began our friendship.'

What also impressed Meghan was how Serena had used online platforms to keep connected with and expand her fan base. She had an online clothing label as well as Instagram, Snapchat and Reddit accounts, and a regular newsletter, all pulled together on the serenawilliams.com website.

This was the light-bulb moment. Meghan had been mulling over a website for some time, and seeing how someone as busy and successful as Serena controlled her own site gave her confidence that she too could follow suit. Her thinking was reinforced by an approach from an e-commerce company, which offered to create an all-singing, all-dancing site with her name front and centre. At first she was excited by the idea. 'It will be your name, meghanmarkle.com, and we can run it for you,' they told her. Essentially, her name would drive consumers to the site. While there would be some created content, the aim was to sell clothing from which Meghan would receive a percentage of sales. She pondered their offer, then stood back for a moment and took a breath. As tempting as it sounded, the more she thought about it, the less it felt right. 'There was so much more I wanted to share,' she explained to friends. Meghan was looking for a place where she could showcase her deeper self, where her voice would be heard and where, if there was e-commerce, it would be thoughtful and ethical rather than just marketing the latest fast fashion and trend. She wanted to stress the importance of giving back. Dumping a bucket of ice-cold water over herself on the Manhattan apartment roof of golfer buddy Rory McIlroy for the ALS Challenge and then posting the result on Instagram wasn't quite enough, though it did raise money for a good cause: research into motor neurone disease.

For now, she left the website idea percolating in the background. With *Suits* on a break in filming, she flew to Vancouver in western Canada to appear in a Hallmark Channel TV movie called *When Sparks Fly*, in which she played Amy, a plucky reporter sent back to her bucolic home town to write a human-interest piece about growing up as the daughter of fireworks' manufacturers. Her old boyfriend is about to marry her high-school best friend and suddenly Amy realizes that maybe the big city life isn't for her after all. It was a pleasing trifle and a pay cheque, but that was about it. The plot, concerning a difficult return home, was the polar opposite of her next excursion, a visit to her old college, Northwestern University.

If she needed any more proof that she had an audience that went beyond the confines of *Suits*, she only had to look at the line snaking around the Ryan Auditorium as 600 students shuffled forwards for a coveted seat to see Meghan and the rest of the *Suits* family.

Communication Studies freshman Nikita Kulkarni, who waited five hours for the event, was breathless with excitement. 'I didn't think it was real when people first told me about it. I thought people were messing with me. I was excited to have Meghan come!'

Meghan basked in the attention from the Northwestern students, comparing shared college experiences and discussing her character's development. She gave her adoring audience a tour of the mind of her alter ego, Rachel Zane. 'She's layered and humanized; even though she seems so confident, she really has all these insecurities and vulnerabilities, and I relate to that as a woman and I think the fans will, too.'

After the chat she posed for photos, signed posters, and later she and fellow star Rick Hoffman, who plays Louis Litt, recorded a promo video for the Northwestern University Dance Marathon, a charity fundraiser in which Meghan had participated as a freshman.

This was the fourth stop of seven for the *Suits* university tour, which included the Universities of California at Berkeley and Los Angeles, the University of Arizona, Boston University, Harvard and Columbia. It was a bid by the network and show's producers to reward their highly engaged collegiate audiences by treating them to a preview screening of the winter mid-season premiere.

Returning home, the website idea now moved to the front burner, as she contacted her friend, photographer Jake Rosenberg. A graduate of Ontario College of Art and Design, Rosenberg had started Coveteur.com six months after graduating with a degree in industrial design. While he loved photography, he was also enthusiastic about branding and design. During a photo shoot in 2011, he and fellow twenty-something stylist Stephanie Mark ended up creating a site devoted to snapshots of beautiful closets and snippets of subjects' houses. 'We thought it would be fun and interesting to see what it is really like in stylish people's homes and closets,' Mark told *Forbes* writer Susan Price. The pair did six photo shoots and posted them on their new site, which crashed due to the amount of traffic. They immediately realized they were on to something that might be profitable as well as fun.

'We would come back and talk about what we had seen, where this person we'd met was shopping, which restaurants and bars people were talking about,' says Mark. 'We realized we had all this content.' They expanded their coverage and, in 2013, redesigned the site to make space for advertising and advertorial, a blend of advertising and editorial. Rosenberg listened to Meghan's concerns about her proposed site. Over tapas and several glasses of wine, they discussed her vision for the site, which would essentially be an insider's guide to travel, food, fashion and make-up with a leavening of more serious op-ed articles dealing with women's issues. Essentially, it would be a dash of Gwyneth Paltrow's blog, GOOP, with a soupçon of *Marie Claire* seasoned with Meghan's own style and focus.

Now with a vision in place, Meghan turned down the original company's offer to create a commercial 'Meghan Markle' site and decided to have a go on her own. First she hired a website designer. When she showed the results to Rosenberg, his sharp and practised eye immediately told him that this could be a problem.

'I beg you, please don't go down this path; use our graphic designer from Coveteur,' he told his friend. The result was TheTig. com, which featured Meghan's own elegant handwriting, and a logo with a wine drop as the dot of the letter 'i'. Meghan had chosen the name, The Tig, from an Italian wine called Tignanello. It is a Sangiovese blend and the first Chianti made without white grapes – a wine born out of the vintner's desire to make his product stand out in a sea of reds. Meghan liked that idea. Standing out. She would drink to that.

For Meghan, Tignanello had a deeper meaning, representing that 'aha' moment when she finally understood what components went to make a good wine, to give it length, finish and legs. She wanted to carry that excitement of discovery into her website, writing: 'The Tig is a hub for the discerning palate – those with a hunger for food, travel, fashion and beauty. I wanted to create a space to share all of these loves – to invite friends to share theirs as well, and to be the breeding ground for ideas and excitement – for an inspired lifestyle.' Frothy, fizzy and fun, The Tig appealed to her fan base, who appreciated her elegant style and her classy persona. At the same time, she envisaged using The Tig to express her thoughts on more serious subjects, in particular giving attention to social and political issues that affected women.

Meghan, the aspirational girl next door, had created a site for other classy girls like her who wanted to join the party. With the help of Jake Rosenberg, fashion designer Wes Gordon, and Brett

Heyman, designer of the acrylic purse brand Edie Parker who created a resin clutch featuring the words 'Ms. Tig' for Meghan, the stage was set. Finally, she also followed the advice of her co-star Gina Torres, who had told her, using one of Meghan's long-time nicknames, 'Nutmeg, just leave room for magic.'

When filming started again, Meghan's busy days didn't leave a lot of time for magic. She would wake up at 4.15 a.m., down a cup of hot water with freshly squeezed lemon, and eat a bowl of oatmeal with sliced bananas and agave. Then she would let the dogs out in the backyard before driving her leased Audi SUV to the set, a maze-like replica of a law office, detailed down to the pink message pads and pens on secretaries' desks, with pivoting glass walls that allowed the cameras to shoot any angle without glare. The New York skyline was a backdrop, and the location scenes were shot in Toronto, with establishing shots from the B-roll of Manhattan to give a sense of place. After early-morning make-up and wardrobe, where clothes would be altered 'on the inhale' to give them their tightest, sleekest fit, Meghan would wait in her trailer for her scene to be ready.

With the birth of The Tig, Meghan had her hands full, making sure that the new arrival was fed, watered and coddled. It was a full-time occupation: staying awake until the early hours cruising Instagram for ideas about what was trending, interesting and timely; writing all the short, snappy content herself; and hustling anyone and everyone to get celebrities to answer the five questions that created the format for Tig Talk. Actor and singer Emmy Rossum got the ball rolling by saying that if she was down to her last $10 – one of the standard questions – she would sing in the street for money. Others, like fashion guru Joe Zee and model Jessica Stam, added their thoughts, while Meghan dragooned interior designer Natasha Baradaran to talk about her favourite city, Milan. She knew that big names drove traffic and would attract other celebrities to participate. One of the first people she wanted to have for Tig Talk was model-turned-entrepreneur Heidi Klum. Meghan contacted everyone she knew, hoping to get her email address or phone number, or that of her assistant. In the end, Heidi responded, as did 'the Queen', who informed the actor that everything tasted better with a slug of vodka. Of course, the Queen she was talking about was TV screen queen Elizabeth Hurley, who played the conniving and occasionally cruel Queen Helena in the E! show *The Royals*, a tongue-in-cheek take on the House of Windsor.

There were profiles of cool places to visit, interesting restaurants and innovative chefs. This last feature introduced her to a new love. For years she had been eating at The Harbord Room, a small restaurant in downtown Toronto that opened in 2007. It was run by handsome celebrity chef Cory Vitiello, who boasted that he cooked the best burger in town. The foodie in Meghan was intrigued.

Over the past seven years, Vitiello had made a name for himself both in and out of the kitchen. He had famously dated Canadian heiress and former politician Belinda Stronach, as well as *eTalk*'s talking head Tanya Kim, before turning his attention to Canadian TV gossip reporter Mary Kitchen. Now with The Tig, Meghan had a way to get to know him better. Much better. For Meghan, life was looking rosy, but things were about to take a nasty turn.

❈

One evening, Meghan was curled up with her laptop, a glass of wine in hand, preparing for an evening finding stories and people to populate The Tig. Her methodology was to delve into other lifestyle blogs and online news sites, follow links for inspiration and then maybe poke around on Instagram using hashtags to guide her to potential Tig tales. First, though, she wanted to peek at the *Suits* pages on Facebook, Twitter, Reddit and USANetwork.com. The latest episode had a storyline featuring Rachel Zane front and centre, and it was airing that night in America. She was curious to know the response to her character's dalliance with an old boyfriend. As Meghan took another sip of her red wine, she nearly choked as she scrolled through to the comments: 'You dirty bird!' 'I'm unfollowing you! How could you cheat on Mike?' 'Whore …' And it just got uglier as the episode hit different time zones and aired right across the country. Meghan deleted the worst of the comments from her own page and Twitter feed, and blocked the abusive users. As the night wore on, she was genuinely concerned, and not a little afraid, as more and more emojis of knives and guns appeared.

Fans weren't just angry at her character Rachel Zane for kissing her old boyfriend Logan Sanders, played by Brendan Hines; they were furious at Meghan Markle. They believed that the actor was responsible for the storyline, not the scriptwriters. As she pondered just how fans could become so invested in a story, which was, after all, make-believe, the comments kept heating up. Now there were death threats. 'Meghan Markle, I wanna kill you. You slut.' This was out of control, as she later told writer Vanessa Pascale of *Miami Living* magazine.

The next morning, she went to see *Suits* creator Aaron Korsh. 'This has to stop,' she told him, adding that they had to scale this back. The producers and writers had always been good to her, incorporating aspects of her own personality into Rachel's character, making Rachel a foodie because Meghan enjoyed cooking and making her bi-racial because of Meghan's own family background. This time the lines were becoming uncomfortably blurred, with fans unable to tell the real Meghan from the fantasy of Rachel. Besides, Meghan wasn't that kind of girl. The storyline going forward had Rachel more actively attempting to seduce her old boyfriend as she turned her back on Mike. That plot development didn't feel right to Meghan, not least because it presaged a possible exit for her character, something for which she wasn't yet prepared. As she later told *Miami Living*, she discussed her concerns about her character's change of direction with Aaron Korsh.

'I like Rachel, I like playing Rachel, I like what she stands for. And this feels really out of character,' she said earnestly. It was a bold move, telling Korsh that she didn't like the direction her character was going in. But she felt she owed it to the fans and to her own integrity to speak up. Plus, she had been frightened by the aggressive vitriol online and threats of violence.

Editor Angela Catanzaro, who had worked on the series since the beginning, agreed with Meghan, telling Korsh, 'I love Rachel, but if you put that scene on the air I would never like her again. That's not the kind of woman I would like working with my husband.'

Korsh saw the wisdom in their words and, within an episode, Mike Ross and Rachel Zane's romance was correcting itself and gearing up to be back on track. Panic over. At least for the time being.

※

Meghan stared at her phone in disbelief. The inbox of her email was filling up almost faster than she could read the subject lines. Her website, The Tig, was proving to be more popular than she had ever imagined. At this early stage every email went directly to her mobile phone and as Meghan quickly scrolled through the ever-expanding list, one sender jumped out at her: the United Nations. It might just be a fundraising appeal, but what the heck? Meghan opened the message and read the contents with growing surprise. The United Nations were asking her to consider becoming involved in their new gender-equality programme, HeForShe. When Meghan dialled the number given in the email, the contact person at UN Women explained that they had read her short essay in The Tig on women's independence, which Meghan had published to coincide with America's Independence Day. She had begun by writing: 'Raise a glass to yourself today – to the right to freedom, to the empowerment of the women (*and men*) who struggle to have it, and to knowing, embracing, honoring, educating and loving yourself. On this day, and beyond, celebrate your independence.' She then went on to showcase the thoughts of Nigerian writer Chimamanda Ngozi Adichie.

While she was honoured by the approach, she also wanted to get an idea of what the project was all about, rather than blindly saying 'yes'. 'I have a one-week break. Can I come and intern at the UN in New York?' she asked them, offering to bring them coffee and answer the phones. Within a few weeks, surprised UN officials found themselves inducting Meghan into the bustling corridors of the New York-based institution. In truth, it was rather more than making the coffee. She shadowed Elizabeth Nyamayaro, head of the UN HeForShe movement to encourage men to support women in the quest for gender equality, and Phumzile Mlambo-Ngcuka, executive director of UN Women. She also sat in on meetings at the World Bank, the Clinton Foundation and even the war room for the UN Secretary-General, Ban Ki-moon. As she later remarked, 'I don't just want to show up somewhere and wave my hand and feel like that's enough.'

At the campaign's public launch, she was assigned a seat on the front row, as Harry Potter actor and UN Goodwill Ambassador Emma Watson made a rousing speech for men as well as women to join the HeForShe campaign. Watson noted that at the present rate of progress it would be seventy-five years before women were paid the same as men for the same work and that it would take until 2086 before all teenage girls in rural Africa receive a secondary education. The HeForShe campaign even garnered royal approval. Prince Harry tweeted his support for the gender-equality programme, saying: 'This is not just about women, we men need to recognize the part we play, too. Real men treat women with dignity and give them the respect they deserve.' It was the first interaction, albeit distant, between the prince and the actor. The stars were moving into alignment.

During the launch of the campaign, Meghan experienced her very own 'Tig' moment when she watched a conversation between the former President of Finland Tarja Halonen and a UN staffer. 'Madam President, may I get you anything?' she asked. 'Would you like water or a pen?' Halonen smiled and replied, 'A lipstick.'

It was something that Meghan connected to. She saw no contradiction between a woman running a country and still wearing lipstick – she could be feminine and a feminist at the same time; as she later wrote, 'a breadwinner at work, and a bread baker with her kids at home'.

At that time, before Donald Trump had entered the race for the presidency, one of her other female idols was his daughter, businesswoman Ivanka Trump, who had her own jewellery and clothing line. She was thrilled when Ivanka agreed to fill in her simple questionnaire for Tig Talk. More thrilled when she accepted her invitation to meet for drinks and dinner the next time Meghan was in New York.

Meghan gushed in The Tig: 'Don't get me started on her jewellery collection: the late-night "window-shopping" I have done on my computer, snuggled up in my bed with a glass of wine, staring longingly at the beautiful designs. And there are the shoes, the home collection, the clothing, and the natural extension of her brand with a kids' collection – a smart choice given that she is now a proud mama ... When we have drinks, I will make sure I order whatever she does – because this woman seems to have the formula for success (and happiness) down pat.'

With well-known names like Ivanka Trump involved, Meghan's 'little engine that could' – her nickname for her website – was gaining a head of steam. She was justifiably proud when The Tig was named Best of the Web in both *Elle* magazine and *InStyle*.

She was, though, in need of help to stoke the boiler. Every post on The Tig had to be cross-posted to Instagram, Pinterest and Facebook to increase traffic; luckily, there was an app for that. Even better, there was now a person, Judy Meepos. Meepos, then the deputy editor of the 'Tech, Yeah!' section of *InStyle* magazine, had received a lot of internet air kisses from Meghan in August when she had written a breathless profile of Markle and The Tig. Meghan decided to hire her in October 2014.

She was not only responsible for social media but also, as she says, 'wrote and edited daily postings, initiated collaborations and partnerships, and served as a market editor for posts and television appearances'. The popularity of The Tig and Meghan's Instagram account meant that after just six months her 'little engine' was ready to earn its keep through e-commerce. She followed the lead of Jake Rosenberg and Coveteur in partnering with RewardStyle. com, an e-commerce site which, rather clunkily, billed itself as an 'invitation-only, end-to-end content monetization platform for top-tier digital style influencers and brands around the world'. Or, in plain English, a clever way of helping upmarket blogs make money.

The site RewardStyle was founded in 2011 by the then Amber Venz and future husband Baxter Box as a way for Amber to monetize her fashion blog. For a while their system worked like a dream. Bloggers created clickable links from their content that led directly to retailers and brands. If a reader clicked through and made a purchase, the blogger earned commission, creating a semi-passive income stream.

With The Tig in Meepos's capable hands, Meghan boarded a plane headed to Dublin where she had been asked to participate in the One Young World Summit, an international forum for young leaders of tomorrow. The biannual conference was the brainchild of two advertising executives, David Jones and Kate Robertson, the duo aiming to 'gather together the brightest young leaders from around the world, empowering them to make lasting connections to create positive change'. Robertson felt that Meghan had something to say and was popular with the student-aged audience. Not only would she be discussing global issues with young people, but she would be rubbing shoulders with humanitarian celebrities like Mary Robinson, Ireland's first woman president, Sir Bob Geldof, and Nobel Peace Prize winner Kofi Annan. For her forum on gender equality she was part of a high-powered panel that included lawyer Sabine Chalmers, General Electric Senior Vice President Beth Comstock, digital pioneer Michelle Phan and film director Maya Sanbar.

In the beginning, Robertson, who chaired the discussion, was worried as to whether Meghan would cope with a question-and-answer style forum. She came away pleasantly surprised at Meghan's eloquence, saying, 'It wasn't your average actress stepping up and talking about gender equality. It was the real deal – very forthright, very confident and very un-celebrity.' Others in the audience were also impressed by her grasp of human rights and gender issues, as well as her approachability and warmth. Human rights lawyer Phiwokuhle Nogwaza told *People* magazine: 'She is really soft and gentle. She is friendly and very warm and engaging. It didn't feel like I was speaking to someone from one of the biggest shows on TV. It was like talking to a regular girl. She knew the problems in detail, which I found incredible. She is humble and really down to earth.'

She had, too, a real knack of mixing the glamour of celebrity with the commitment to her humanitarian work, she and her chef boyfriend Cory Vitiello flying to Florida in early December for Miami Art Basel, an offshoot of the Swiss original. The now annual event, started in 2002, attracts 77,000 visitors a year, and the place to see and be seen was her usual stomping ground, Soho House.

Meghan was excited. While she wasn't that into art, preferring fashion, food and wine, she welcomed the opportunity to network with a wider range of members and guests who were arriving at the Soho Beach House, a repurposed vintage hotel on the sand. She tried not to gawk as rap mogul Russell Simmons and actor and activist Rosario Dawson strolled by, or to take too much interest when Goldie Hawn's daughter Kate Hudson waved at friends from a terrace. She felt she had truly arrived. She had worked hard, she was on a top-rated show, and her blog was considered one of the best on the web. Miami Art Week, or at least the Soho Beach House version of it, would be hers.

Her great friend Markus Anderson, Soho House membership director, casually dressed in flip-flops and shorts, wandered over to say 'Hello' and brief them on the next few days of dancing, cocktails and luxurious beauty treatments. This was the life. A Sapphire gin gift basket awaited Meghan and Cory in their room, along with a fully stocked drinks bar. The celebrity tent would have a full selection of tropically themed gin drinks. And then there were the sparkling wines and champagnes …

Markus Anderson is a great fixer and mixer. He has an instinct for putting strangers together who he thinks might gel. At lunch he placed Meghan next to Bahrain-born fashion designer Misha Nonoo. At the time she was an up-and-coming designer known as much for her marriage to art dealer Alexander Gilkes, friend of Princes William and Harry, as for her maverick designs. Meghan and Misha got along famously, lunchtime drinks extending into evening cocktails. During the course of the afternoon they got to talking about Misha's new collection, which was going to be unveiled at New York Fashion Week. Meghan would be on a break from *Suits*. She would be there.

✻

Hours later, Meghan was once again on a plane, this time headed for Spain, one of five countries she was due to visit on a whirlwind tour. This time there were no luxury hotels or smart cocktails. Instead, Meghan was taking part in the United Service Organization holiday tour, visiting American military bases in Spain, Italy, Turkey, Afghanistan and England. Joining Meghan were eight-time USO tour veteran and country star Kellie Pickler and her songwriter husband Kyle Jacobs, comedian Rob Riggle, *Glee* co-star Dianna Agron, former Chicago Bears linebacker Brian Urlacher, and Washington Nationals pitcher Doug Fister, as well as the chairman of the Joint Chiefs of Staff, Army General Martin E. Dempsey and his wife Deanie.

When the travelling troupe, who were joined by USO President J. D. Crouch and his wife Kristin, met at the Joint Base Andrews passenger terminal in Maryland on 5 December, Deanie Dempsey told the assorted celebrities, 'Embrace this experience. You will be so proud of our service members and their families.' Meghan was excited and a little apprehensive. Not only would she be flying aboard Air Force Two, specially commissioned for this tour, but she would also be meeting thousands of service members and their families during the trip. While she had done fan meet-and-greets before, it had never been on this scale or at this intensity.

After arriving in Rota, Spain, Meghan and her USO group toured the USS *Ross*, an Aegis missile-equipped destroyer. Then they performed before an audience of 2,000 service personnel and their families in a hangar on the base. Meghan, in a blue hard hat, posed with servicemen before going into her routine. She knew that she, Kellie Pickler and Dianna Agron were carrying on a time-honoured tradition, following in the footsteps of stars like Marilyn Monroe, Bob Hope and Jayne Mansfield who had entertained the troops, providing a sweet taste of home, a reminder of why the troops did their jobs. Now things were rather different. There were women in the military and families on the bases, so goodbye cheesecake, hello folksy and funny. On stage she did one of her routines, giving a light-hearted talk about *Suits* before showing off her five-inch heels as Pickler and her band performed her signature song, 'Red High Heels'.

The USO tour group repeated their act in Vicenza, Italy, to soldiers of the 173rd Airborne Brigade and US Army Africa, before heading to the airbase at Incirlik, Turkey. Even though the base was several hundred miles from the battles raging in neighbouring Syria, the atmosphere was tenser, security tighter. Meghan smiled and tried to say more than 'thank you' as she passed out cupcakes to the several hundred who had gathered to watch Pickler and Jacobs perform country hits, and the troupe do various comedy sketches.

The next morning, the USO performers and their 'chaperones' gathered on the tarmac to head to their most challenging gig, Bagram airfield in Afghanistan. This was the most isolated outpost, home to 40,000 military personnel and service members. 'Bureaucrats, administrators, logisticians and thousands of International Security Assistance Force civilian contractors live at Bagram airbase,' said British photographer Edmund Clark. 'Unless you go out on patrol, you exist only on base.'

Surrounded by fencing and barbed wire, reinforced by sandbags, with ground-penetrating radar used to make sure enemy fighters don't use tunnels to break into the coalition base, Bagram was relatively safe. Except for the occasional Taliban rocket that made it over the walls.

Meghan and her fellow performers joined service members for a holiday meal before they took to the stage. Meghan turned her back to the audience and snapped a quick selfie with the uniformed military members, then went into her inspirational speech: 'I've never wanted to be a lady who lunches; I've always wanted to be a woman who works …'

Once again cupcakes were passed out, then, as fighter jets and C-130 transport planes taxied outside, Meghan and the others posed with groups of service members in front of a netting-draped wall. While the celebrities put on their practised smiles for the cameras, the troops could barely muster a grin between them. Unlike the stars who had swooped in for a couple of days, they had months more of mind-numbing boredom punctuated by bursts of frenzied action to look forward to. It was a poignant interaction.

Their final stop in Cambridge, England, was a perfect way to decompress. Before their final show, airmen at the base gave the USO troupe a tour of the military hardware at their command, including F-15E Strike Eagles and CV-22 Ospreys, a helicopter–plane hybrid. Meghan spent her time chatting with families, paying special attention to the children. That evening, the Dempseys hosted a thank-you gathering for the USO performers at a Cambridge pub, The Anchor, with the performers in turn warmly thanking the Dempseys and the USO for the privilege of being able to entertain the troops. Before the evening ended, the chairman of the Joint Chiefs of Staff serenaded the group. 'If only we could have gotten him to do that in Bagram!' someone joked.

That was to be Meghan's first and last USO tour. She expressed her feelings in an Instagram post, where she showed a picture from the tour and then a heartfelt caption: 'In gratitude to our troops, and the opportunity to thank them personally for their sacrifice and service. Such an honor and feeling very, very blessed.'

That Christmas it seemed that she too was blessed. She spent time during the festive season with Cory and his family who were all very fond of the American actor. His mother Joanne was convinced that one day soon she would be wearing Cory's ring on her finger. After all, Meghan was all about commitment – in life and in romance.

8

Seeing Both Sides Now

She had her passport. Check. Her bag of homeopathic remedies.
Check. Her vaccines, including hepatitis A and B, typhoid,
rabies and tetanus, were up to date. Check. She had super-strength
mosquito repellent. Check. A bag of long-sleeved light clothes.
Check. Her go-to tea-tree oil for soothing insect bites and skin
blemishes. Check. Meghan was ready for a very grown-up journey,
embarking on her first-ever fact-finding mission on behalf of the
United Nations. Though her visit to Rwanda in the heart of Africa
was to focus on issues surrounding gender equality, it was also a
chance for United Nations officials to run the rule over the *Suits*
star, to see if she was able and willing to make the commitment as
a Goodwill Ambassador for the international organization. A UN
official pointed out that Meghan's involvement as a gender-equality
advocate was at the level of an informal collaboration. That is to say,
was she the right fit for this prestigious if bureaucratic organization?

In early January 2015, when she landed in Kigali, the Rwandan
capital, her first stop was to be introduced to the nation's female
parliamentarians. Almost a week of meetings had been scheduled
to discuss the role of women in the nation's democracy and the
challenges facing Rwanda going forward. Time and again the point
was made that only when women were treated equally, in the home,
at school and in the workplace, could they enjoy rich, fulfilling
lives and give back to the community. The under-representation
of women in the top jobs, a feature of life not just in developing
countries but across the world, was an issue that always concerned
her. At the time, the UN was celebrating the fact that Rwanda was

the first, and at the time the only, country to have a female majority in the nation's parliament, with almost two-thirds of the seats taken by women.

It was a great step forward, Meghan complimenting Rwandan President Paul Kagame. 'We need more men like that,' she said.

Though Kagame has his critics, this was a truly remarkable turnaround for a country which, just twenty years earlier, had suffered an appalling genocide. The figures were astonishing, with approximately 1 million people killed, most brutally hacked to death with machetes, and 2 million displaced into refugee camps. Meghan travelled to see the other side of Rwanda herself, the actor and her UN team travelling by van to Gihembe refugee camp, the sprawling collection of huts studded into the lush green hillside now home to 17,000 people who had fled the violence in the neighbouring war-torn Democratic Republic of Congo. She wanted to speak to the women at grass-roots level, find out how they coped with a life that was meant to be temporary but had become permanent. Inevitably, every visit by a celebrity, even if the local population has no clue who they are, attracts a crowd, Meghan posing happily with dozens of curious and excited local children.

As she travelled back over the bumpy dirt road, past the grazing goats and the verdant fields, she idly checked her emails, amazed that the signal was better there than in some parts of Toronto and Los Angeles. While she bounced along the track she learned that she had been invited as a guest to the BAFTAs, the British Academy Film Awards, which take place a few weeks before the Oscars.

Her management company told her that she would be sponsored by a high-end jewellery company that would fly her directly from Kigali to London, where she would be whisked into hair and make-up before being poured into a gown. 'No,' screamed her gut. It had always been a dream to attend the BAFTAs, but she couldn't shift emotional gears that quickly, from the purpose-driven work she had been doing all week in Rwanda to the polished glamour of an awards show. There would be other BAFTAs, other red carpets. But for now there was only Rwanda. As she later wrote: 'This type of work is what feeds my soul.'

This topsy-turvy shot of Meghan when she was modelling in New York City in 2015 symbolizes her hectic and controversial life. Descended from slaves, she became the first dual-heritage member of the House of Windsor, her arrival helping to reshape the institution. Here she poses for photographer Tommy Mendes for the now defunct fashion website, The Aesthete.

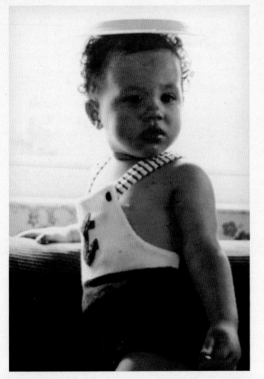

ABOVE: **On 23 December 1979, African-American Democrat Doria Ragland married Pennsylvania-born Republican Thomas Markle Senior at the Self-Realization Fellowship Temple in Hollywood.**

LEFT: Meghan, then a two-year-old toddler, was photographed endlessly by her doting father. Sadly, soon after this picture was taken, Doria and Tom went their separate ways.

ABOVE: Meghan's grandfather Alvin Ragland, standing next to her Aunt Saundra, holds a smiling Meghan at a family gathering while her half-brother Tom Markle Junior holds her ponytail. Seated are her mother Doria (left) and grandmother Jeanette (right).

LEFT: Meghan, aged about ten, with her Uncle Fred Markle (left), now presiding bishop of the Eastern Orthodox Catholic Church in America, with her father Tom and grandmother Doris. Meghan was devoted to Doris and was a regular visitor to her Glendale nursing home.

RIGHT: **A prescient photograph of Meghan and her best friend Ninaki Priddy outside Buckingham Palace in 1996 during their summer trip to Europe.**

BELOW LEFT: **Meghan with her father Tom after her graduation ceremony at Northwestern University, one of the highest ranking and most expensive colleges in the country. During her time there she studied English, international relations and theatre arts.**

BELOW RIGHT: **Meghan backstage on *Deal or No Deal* in one of the show's less revealing and more comfortable costumes. For a while, she became briefcase girl number 24, the long periods between filming giving her time to look for more serious acting jobs.**

ABOVE: Meghan and her mother Doria in Jamaica during Meghan's destination wedding weekend in 2011. Both of her parents walked her down the 'aisle', a corridor of sand on the beach.

RIGHT: Meghan and her first husband Trevor Engelson, an ambitious and successful film and TV producer. Shortly before they married, Meghan began shooting the legal drama *Suits* in Toronto, which meant a five-hour plane journey if she wanted to see her Los Angeles-based fiancé.

LEFT: In 2008, when Meghan appeared as junior FBI agent Amy Jessup in director J. J. Abrams' sci-fi drama *Fringe*, she hoped to have a lasting role. That she appeared in only two episodes came as a disappointment, one of the many she faced as an aspiring actor.

BELOW: *Suits* producers cast Gina Torres (left) as a founding partner of the fictional law firm, Rick Hoffman as her devious colleague Louis Litt, Meghan Markle as the sophisticated paralegal Rachel Zane, Gabriel Macht as hot-shot lawyer Harvey Specter, and Patrick J. Adams as brilliant lawyer Mike Ross, who became Rachel's love interest.

LEFT: Meghan takes calls at a fundraiser for the 2013 annual Charity Day, hosted by brokers Cantor Fitzgerald and held each year to commemorate their friends and colleagues who perished in the 9/11 terrorist attack.

BELOW: Meghan at the sprawling Bagram airfield in Afghanistan during her 2014 United States Organizations tour. From left to right: Washington Nationals pitcher Doug Fister, Meghan Markle, comedian Rob Riggle, country music performer Kellie Pickler, actor Dianna Agron and retired Chicago Bears linebacker Brian Urlacher (far right).

Meghan with Misha Nonoo at the Twelfth Annual CFDA/Vogue Fashion Fund Awards, 2 November 2015, in New York City. Meghan is wearing a dress from the designer's collection.

Of course she was not the first, nor will she be the last, celebrity to struggle to reconcile the air-kissing superficiality of Hollywood with the stark reality of life for so many in the developing world. Oscar-winning actor and UNHCR special envoy Angelina Jolie is a vivid example of a star who manages to straddle both worlds. The more she became involved with her humanitarian mission, the more she had to learn to switch off and switch on. Just like acting. But in real life.

Shortly after her return from Rwanda, Meghan was front and centre for New York Fashion Week in February. She was now on the front row, watching the models at the show of her fashion mentor Wes Gordon, but she was also photographed reviewing Misha Nonoo's stylish collection. The theme was Meghan's *cri de coeur*: the empowerment of women. Nonoo had the models do their hair themselves, pulling it back into ponytails using the minimum amount of product and as many bobby pins as they liked. 'It just set the tone,' Meghan enthused.

She was still raving about the collection when she appeared on Joe Zee's streaming fashion programme on Yahoo! Style. The duo went back years, from the time they first met in 2011, drinking and shooting the breeze until late into the night. What Joe liked about Meghan was that she was decidedly un-Hollywood; she appreciated people other than herself.

✳

In between the glitz and the glamour, her advocacy for UN Women continued, and she undertook further meetings at the World Bank and the Clinton Foundation, learning more about the facts and figures of gender bias in the developing world and, for that matter, her own country. While she had always had a thoughtful side, these days her friends noticed that she seemed more considered, more seasoned and more appreciative too of the advantages she had been given and the opportunity she had to make a difference. In the days when she was scrabbling to gain a foothold on the slippery ladder of success, her time was taken up not with causes but with endless auditions, simply trying to make a living. Such ambitions had seemingly been left behind when she graduated from Northwestern. But now, her acting success coupled with her voice on The Tig had opened up doors and brought back memories of the little girl who had written letters of complaint about sexist advertising and a young woman who had aimed for a job in the State Department.

She travelled to London to support Emma Watson in her HeForShe initiative, the Harry Potter actor holding a live Facebook event to engage her fans in the campaign. Then, back in New York, it was Meghan's turn to take centre stage in front of a friendly but awe-inspiring audience. Meghan took a deep breath and focused. She was about to hit a personal milestone. Her mother and friends were there to support her in front of global luminaries like United Nations Secretary-General Ban Ki-moon, UN Women Executive Director Phumzile Mlambo-Ngcuka, actor Patricia Arquette, her own mentor at the UN Elizabeth Nyamayaro, as well as former US Secretary of State Hillary Clinton. (Ironically, the same day, Clinton overshadowed Meghan's appearance with her comments about her controversial use of a private email server during her tenure in the Cabinet of the United States.)

On 8 March 2015, a day that she will always remember, Meghan was about to speak before the United Nations as the newly appointed UN Women's Advocate for Women's Leadership and Political Participation.

Understandably, Meghan's voice sounded a little higher when the normally nerveless actor opened her speech: 'I am proud to be a woman and a feminist, and this evening I am extremely proud to stand before you on this significant day, which serves as a reminder to all of us of how far we've come, but also amid celebration a reminder of the road ahead …'

She told her story of the LA riots, her schoolroom, Ivory dishwashing liquid, and the chauvinist little boys at her school; of how she wrote to Procter & Gamble, women's rights lawyer Gloria Allred, journalist Linda Ellerbee, and the then First Lady, Hillary Clinton. The putative presidential candidate smiled at that. Meghan spoke inspiringly of how her letter made a difference and how she felt that she had helped, in her small way, to make the change.

She took aim at the weak representation of women in the world's parliaments, citing data showing that the number of women lawmakers had increased by only 11 per cent since 1995. 'Eleven per cent in twenty years. Come on. This has to change,' she said to applause.

As Meghan concluded, UN Secretary-General Ban Ki-moon led the standing ovation. It was quite the accolade, one that would resonate as her speech was played in numerous classrooms around America and the world, inspiring and provoking a new generation of young girls to make a difference.

'Meghan Markle has helped raise global attention to gender-equality issues,' said a spokeswoman for UN Women. 'UN Women trusts and hopes that in her new and important public role she will continue to use her visibility and voice to support the advancement of gender equality.'

She appeared to have it all; she was a young, articulate campaigner with a tasteful, on-trend website and a successful TV career. Curiously, her speech to UN Women seemed to be the high-water mark of her involvement with the international organization. Once they had officially appointed her as an advocate, it seems that her charity work on their behalf tapered off considerably.

Nonetheless, the invitations to represent the issues she cared about, or to discuss them on chat shows, now started to come in thick and fast. And so it was only natural for her to be asked to host the Women in Cable Telecommunications 2015 signature luncheon. Maria E. Brennan, WICT's chief executive, explained the choice, saying: 'Meghan is a sterling example of someone who not only plays a strong female character, she is one in real life.'

Chat-show host Larry King invited her back on his show – previously she had talked *Suits* with Patrick J. Adams – to discuss her role as a women's rights advocate. Meghan was proving her skills at diplomacy, deftly deflecting King's question about which country had the worst record on gender equality by saying that we have to take into account cultural context.

Hand in hand with her humanitarian work were the undoubted perks of being a glamorous TV star. As her celebrity status rose, so did her price tag. She was learning that she could charge a fee just for turning up. Turbocharging these opportunities for her was Kruger Cowne, a speaking, branding and hosting agency with headquarters in Chelsea in central London and offices in Santa Monica.

The agency, founded in 1999, represents a whole range of celebrities such as Virgin boss Richard Branson, Cher and Sir Bob Geldof, as well as charities like One Young World, which Meghan had represented. The skincare line Clarins and the Pakistani poet Fatima Bhutto were also clients who were frequently namechecked by the actor. Meghan's rate? Ten thousand dollars and upwards per appearance.

She had entered a glorious, gilded world, Meghan previously writing about her rapidly shifting day-to-day existence in her anonymous blog, Working Actress. 'I work long hours, I travel for press. My mind memorizes. My mind spins. My days blur. My nights are restless. My hair is primped, my face is painted, my name is recognized, my star meter is rising, my life is changing.'

In March, just before her speech to the United Nations, she found herself on the island of Malta in the Mediterranean. The visit, sponsored by *Elle* magazine, was a chance for her to discover a bit about her roots – and to enjoy some of the island's fabulous but oft-neglected cuisine. Malta held a special place in her heart; her paternal great-great-grandmother Mary Merrill, the daughter of Mary Bird – a former housemaid to the British Royal Family – and a British soldier, had been born here and she was eager to know more.

She went by ferry to the tiny island of Gozo, tasted the famous Gozo cheeselet (a traditional filled flatbread and pastry dish), then, after returning to the main island, she explored the Casa Rocca Piccola in Valletta and viewed the Caravaggio paintings at St John's Co-Cathedral. During her week-long stay, she fell in love with Maltese cuisine. Meghan threw herself into her cooking lesson with chef Pippa Mattei, Malta's equivalent to Martha Stewart, at her home in Attard. Given that Meghan liked to emphasize that, as a California girl, her experience with farm-to-table cuisine was hardwired, here was an opportunity to see the Maltese version.

Mattei took her shopping for produce in the local fish market, then gave her a lesson in pasta and pastizzi-making, followed by a meal in Mattei's garden.

For the girl who conjured The Tig from her favourite tipple, no visit to Malta would have been complete without a comprehensive wine tasting, the actor visiting the Meridiana Wine Estate for a leisurely afternoon exploring fruity reds and tasty whites. As Maltese wines rarely, if ever, reach the shores of America, this was a real treat. She didn't discover much more about her Maltese ancestry – but at least her taste buds had a holiday to remember.

Her visit to Malta was a solo trip, even though her chef boyfriend would have been inspired by the variety and distinctiveness of the local cuisine. Like Meghan, he was being kept busy, on the verge of starting a new venture, FLOCK Rotisserie and Greens, a restaurant specializing in roast chicken and salad. The chef admitted that he had been testing a fair bit of roast chicken on Meghan, Cory working virtually round the clock running three restaurants.

He had been in front of the camera, too, taping episodes of *Chef in Your Ear* for Food Network Canada. Taking a leaf out of Meghan's philanthropy playbook, he also volunteered for Kids Cook to Care, a programme for youngsters who were taught how to make home-cooked meals by celebrity chefs. The idea was to ignite their understanding of proper cooking techniques and the importance of serving the community.

With his filming and restaurant commitments, Cory was unable to join Meghan on her next exotic jaunt – to Istanbul, where she, together with actor Eddie Redmayne, 'Fifty Shades' actor Jamie Dornan and singer Paloma Faith were on hand to celebrate the opening of the latest enclave of Soho House.

It was another glamorous interlude in her busiest and most successful year to date. The profile high of her UN speech was matched by an invitation to become the face of one of Canada's oldest and most respected retailers, Reitmans. What was more, the ninety-year-old store chain wanted her to curate her own clothing line. Not only was her face going to be on billboards and on TV all over Canada, she was going to influence how women dressed.

It was a marvellous opportunity, though when she first mentioned the overture to savvy friends they scoffed at the idea of involving herself with a retail brand that was so fuddy-duddy. 'Oh, that's where my mom would buy her jeans in the eighties,' they chorused. Meghan was not so sure. As she was American she didn't have the same knee-jerk reaction towards this venerable retailer as her Canadian friends. At meetings with store executives, Meghan brought a fresh eye. 'There are pieces here that are so cool that if you're going to re-energize it, I'd be happy to be a part of that,' she told fashion writer Jeanne Beker. They planned an advertising campaign starring Meghan wearing trimmer, slimmer, hipper Reitmans clothing. In one commercial, Meghan is filmed walking into an elegant restaurant where two ladies who lunch eagerly give the TV star the once-over. One exclaims, 'So stylish,' while the other asks what she is wearing. They then try to crawl over the back of the booth to get a closer look at the label in her shirt. Catching them in the act, Meghan smiles and says, 'Ladies, it's Reitmans.' Another showed Meghan, all crisp business, slick high heels and tight jeans, speaking on her mobile as she strides out into the street. As the camera follows her down the street, she notices herself in the store's glass window. Her cute alter ego in the reflection preens and wiggles for the camera before blowing her other half a kiss. Cue her slogan for the brand: 'Reitmans. Really.'

Not only was she the brand ambassador; she worked hard on a capsule collection to be launched in spring 2016. Meghan was thrilled, reflecting on the days when she was a little girl and how she had sat with her mother at her clothing store, A Change of a Dress, on N. La Brea Avenue in Los Angeles. In those far-off days, Doria had taken her daughter to fabric warehouses where she had walked along the aisles of fabrics. Now she had the opportunity to create her own fashion line. Meghan and the design team sketched out ideas, played with swatches, examined the zippers and fit of sample pieces. As she later remarked: 'I'm super-involved with the design process, and I'm sure that it drives them crazy. But how could I not? It has my name on it.'

First off the runway in the Meghan Markle Collection were four distinct dresses: the Soirée, Date Night, the Sunset maxi-dress and 'a little white dress', the Terrace. Once she had approved the designs it was a fingers-and-toes-crossed moment for the actor, anxious that her fans and the wider public should appreciate her efforts. As she wrote in her blog: 'I toiled over design and print, I shared my thoughts on everything and I ended up with a limited collection of pieces that reflect facets of my personal style that I think you'll love.'

All the dresses sold for under $100 each, revealing the budget-conscious nature of the creator, who boasted that she was the one who shopped on the sale rack. 'I've always been the girl flipping through the hangers trying to find the best deal.'

Of course, that's not quite true. When her designer friend Misha Nonoo invited Meghan to join her at the 2015 CFDA/Vogue Fashion Fund Awards in New York in early November, she was thrilled to wear one of the pieces from her collection. It was a short liquid-metal dress that combined with a plunging deep V-neck to make it a showstopper, photographers clamouring for a snap of the TV star.

On top of all of this, Ms Markle was also now the central character in a chick-lit novel, *What Pretty Girls Are Made Of*, written by her 'bestie from the westie' Lindsay Jill Roth, who was such a frequent visitor to her Toronto home that the spare bedroom was christened 'Lindsay's Room'. It had taken Lindsay five years, and copious glasses of wine, to craft the jaunty novel based on the exploits of her heroine, Alison Kraft. From when she had been a little girl, all Alison had ever dreamed of was being an actor. Too bad that after years of auditions she doesn't have the stellar career she envisioned. After some soul-searching she looks for other jobs and ends up working for a make-up guru.

It was, of course, a thinly disguised portrait of Meghan during her lean years in the noughties. Lindsay had all the research material she needed, not just from Meghan's lips but from the Working Actress blog, about the ups and downs of life for a struggling wannabe, which Meghan had written between 2010 and 2012. Meghan loved the book, posting effusive Instagrams touting the fluffy tome. Naturally, she was at the summer launch party, afterwards taking her pal to an ice hockey game. Not only did Lindsay give her actor friend a shout-out for helping her to explore 'what "pretty" is', but she also sent a copy of her amusing trifle to the Duchess of Cambridge at Kensington Palace, her accompanying card informing Kate that in her eyes she was the definition of 'prettiness'.

Lindsay then proudly posted the pro-forma thank-you note from the duchess's office online. She never for a second contemplated meeting the future queen at Windsor Castle after her best friend married Prince Harry. If she had suggested that plot to her publisher they would have laughed her out of their New York offices.

In actual fact Meghan *was* about to get married, but neither to Prince Harry nor to her boyfriend Cory Vitiello. She was due to walk down the aisle with badass lawyer Mike Ross in the climax to season five of *Suits*. Filming was scheduled for 13 November before the show wrapped up for the Christmas break. As she read the script, Meghan thought that if she was getting married, at the very least she – or Rachel – wanted a say in the style of the wedding dress. As she later told *Glamour* magazine, she contacted *Suits* costumier Jolie Andreatta and her friend, wedding stylist Jessica Mulroney, for inspiration. The three women met at the Toronto outpost of New York-based bridal store Kleinfeld. The store, which boasts 30,000 square feet of bridalwear in Manhattan, and even has its own show on TV, *Say Yes to the Dress*, has a much smaller outlet at The Bay. 'I need something that will be comfortable and won't wrinkle, that's classic and sort of fairy tale,' explained Meghan. Jessica pulled out an Anne Barge full-skirted V-neck with Swiss dot netting. Meghan tried it on. 'It screams Rachel!' she exclaimed.

'We need the dress in two days,' said Jolie. 'Can we do this?' In the original script, Mike and Rachel were finally going to get hitched. However, after producer Gabriel Macht and series creator Aaron Korsh reviewed the scenario, they decided it would be more plausible if Mike went to jail and told Meghan's character, a sobbing

Rachel Zane, that he could not marry her – at least not yet. This was the cliffhanger for the series five finale, which was broadcast in March 2016.

After filming her emotional scenes, Meghan flew to a location about as cold, if not colder, than Toronto. The California girl headed to Iceland to see the Northern Lights, along the way discovering Hafnarfjörður, a place known locally as the 'Town of Elves', where she couldn't resist posting a photograph on her Instagram site. From admittedly knowing little about the inner workings of the web, Meghan was now a social media junkie, posting cute selfies, wry observations – New Year's resolutions were to run a marathon, stop biting my nails, stop swearing and relearn French – and intelligent essays on her burgeoning social media accounts.

In the eighteen months since it had launched, Meghan had assiduously used The Tig to promote what she felt was important and beautiful: a charming photograph of Doria on Mother's Day, a recipe for beet pasta with arugula pesto, suggested reading lists, her favourite picture by artist Gray Malin, or a shot of her eating a raw urchin as she stood in the warm Caribbean surf. Meghan was relentless, diligent and disciplined about creating daily content. She brought in guest writers like PR guru Lucy Meadmore to write about a trip to Costa Rica, her yoga coach Duncan Parviainen and her *Suits* co-star Abigail Spencer. There was, though, a serious underpinning to all this gauze; in an essay entitled 'Champions of Change', Meghan wrote passionately about race relations, retelling the family story about the prejudice they suffered during a road trip from Ohio to California. 'It reminds me of how young our country is,' she told her readers. With its mix of serious and frivolous, girly and gritty, The Tig had the feel of an upmarket woman's magazine, but in Meghan's distinctive voice. As she said, 'It's my outlet to say my own words and to share all these things that I find inspiring and exciting, but also attainable.' It was bringing home a little bacon, too. Through her online shopping link and the promotion of brands such as Birchbox, a subscription beauty-box brand, she was now making money off the venture. 'I would never take ads,' she said. 'Or sell a $100 candle. Obnoxious.'

There were times she had to remind herself not to give in to compulsion to photograph and share every last detail of her life. She had to remember to enjoy real life as it happened. As Warren Beatty said of his then girlfriend Madonna, when she was making the documentary *Truth or Dare*, 'She doesn't want to live off-camera, much less talk.' He made that withering remark in the days before social media ran rampant. Now Meghan was one of a generation who, if they were not careful, would only define their existence through social media.

The real world, though, kept intruding. In February 2016, the actor flew to Kigali in Rwanda once again to undertake charity work.

Before she left she celebrated Valentine's Day; not with Cory, but with friends in New York's West Village. It had become a pattern, both of them being ambitious people, and neither willing to give the time – or effort – to nurture a meaningful relationship. He was immersed in his restaurant chain and television career as a celebrity chef, Meghan in her world as an actor, humanitarian and fashion personality. By the time Meghan boarded the plane to Kigali, it was clear that the writing was on the wall for their two-year relationship.

This time, her visit to Africa was arranged not by the United Nations but by World Vision Canada, an Evangelical Christian humanitarian aid charity. Their sister organization, World Vision, based in the United States, had hit the headlines the previous year with their decision not to hire Christians in same-sex marriages. It was a policy position quickly disavowed by their independent Canadian neighbour. The charity's mission statement reads: 'Motivated by our faith in Jesus Christ, World Vision serves alongside the poor and oppressed as a demonstration of God's unconditional love for all people. World Vision serves all people, regardless of religion, race, ethnicity or gender.'

On the surface it was an odd choice, especially as Meghan had rather trodden water with UN Women and had nothing in the diary in relation to her role as United Nations advocate. However, World Vision Canada were eager to harness her celebrity to promote their work in the developing world, notably bringing clean water to rural villages. Whatever misgivings she may have had, she accepted their invitation to see their work in Rwanda. It was an enthusiastic meeting of minds, recalled Lara Dewar, WVC Chief Marketing Officer. 'She's remarkably approachable. She was very open to a conversation about the kinds of causes that moved her and that she would like to learn more about.'

This was a very different kind of visit to her UN-sponsored trip where she met female parliamentarians and discussed how they could best promote women's issues in a mainly rural nation. Her tour this time was much more traditional, top-down benevolence, Meghan watching a well being completed in a village and then helping to turn on the mechanism that drew the water to the surface. All the while her friend, fashion photographer Gabor Jurina, captured the scenes.

Though her visit did not directly focus on gender equality, Meghan quickly grasped the concept that a community's access to clean water keeps young girls in school because they aren't walking hours each day to find water for their families.

Later, after taking part in a dance lesson, she visited a school in the Gasabo region and met twenty-five students whose access to a clean-water pipeline, installed by World Vision Canada, had transformed their lives. She sat with the children as they painted with watercolours using water drawn from the well, their paint-dipped fingers creating images of their dreams and futures.

When she returned to Toronto she staged a charity art sale, using the children's art as a basis for what she named The Watercolour Project. The invitation-only function, held on 22 March 2016 at the LUMAS gallery in downtown Toronto, was hosted by Meghan and raised more than $15,000, enough to bring clean water to an entire rural community. Applauded as World Vision's newly minted global ambassador, she told the sixty-strong audience, 'Access to clean water allows women to invest in their own businesses and community. It promotes grass-roots leadership, and, of course, it reinforces the health and wellness of children and adults. Every single piece of it is so interconnected, and clean water, this one life source, is the key to it all.'

Meghan was now the official face of the organization, short snappy videos of her appearing on the charity's website, on their financial statement, their promotional material and their online profile. Unlike the United Nations, where Meghan was one of many celebrities working to promote important issues within the organization, here Meghan was the figurehead of this Christian charity, one of Canada's largest.

✳

Meghan spun and posed in front of the white backdrop as her friend Gabor Jurina snapped away. Video was also rolling, capturing behind-the-scenes action as Meghan modelled the four dresses in her first capsule collection for Reitmans. Then she dashed home to write copy about the collection for The Tig.

She waxed rapturous over the Los Angeles-inspired maxi-dress, trilled over the Rachel Zane-esque little white dress, and gushed about the white flouncy dress with an asymmetrical hem. The maroon Date Night dress made Meghan feel 'fashion-y and Frenchie'. The day before the 27 April launch of her collection, Meghan hastened to New York to the taping of the finale of Fashion Fund, a *Vogue*-sponsored event where designers battle it out to win sponsorship and funding for their line. She was mixing and matching with fashion luminaries, the perfect lead into the launch of her collection. Meghan was also travelling alone. In news that shocked none of her friends, she and Cory had decided to go their separate ways. Nonetheless, the break-up still had an effect, a friend of Meghan's remarking that she felt down, vulnerable and hurt by the split. Though there were hints that Cory was seeing other women, the root of the issue was the plain fact that neither side was prepared to make any commitment. 'It wasn't a happy time for her,' commented a friend.

No matter. The next day she put on a brave face and enjoyed a glass of champagne as she attended the unveiling of her first-ever fashion collection at Reitmans' flagship store in Toronto. It was an immediate hit.

The collection virtually sold out on day one. Eat your heart out, Kate Moss. Meghan was thrilled, especially as the company was so enthused about sales that her second capsule collection, to be released in the autumn of 2016, was a done deal.

The actor barely had time to finish her glass of bubbly before she was one of the celebrity guests at a luncheon to honour ten game-changing women under the age of twenty-five. Meghan, along with Olympic athletes and successful internet start-up founders, was designated a mentor for the finalists at the fifty-ninth anniversary of the College Women of the Year. Now a grizzled veteran, Meghan was asked about the most common misconception about college girls. 'You realize there is so much depth, there is so much incredible inspiration, and that young women are thinking outside of the box in a way that we haven't seen before. It is the biggest sign that we are in good hands, that our world is going to be just fine, and that these are the women who are going to be the players changing the game.'

She wasn't so confident of the future a couple of weeks later, when she agreed to appear on Comedy Central and join a panel discussion on Larry Wilmore's *The Nightly Show*.

With the presidential election just six months away and Republican candidates dropping like flies, Donald Trump looked like the front runner. On the night she appeared, his endless attacks on Fox News anchor Megyn Kelly, calling her 'sick' and 'overrated', had finally engendered a response from the Republican-leaning channel. In a statement backing Kelly they said, 'Donald Trump's vitriolic attacks against Megyn Kelly and his extreme, sick obsession with her is beneath the dignity of a presidential candidate who wants to occupy the highest office in the land.'

Wilmore asked his guests, 'Do you think the momentum surrounding Mr Trump could be stopped?' Meghan joined in the banter with the host and his correspondents, laughing wryly, 'It's really the moment that I go; we film *Suits* in Toronto and I might just stay in Canada. I mean, come on, if that's the reality we are talking about, come on, that is a game changer in terms of how we move in the world here.'

A few minutes later she jumped in to make other points, 'Yes, of course Trump is divisive. Think about just female voters alone. I think it was in 2012, the Republican Party lost the female vote by twelve points. That's a huge number.' She went on to label Trump a 'misogynist' and suggested that voting for Hillary Clinton was the better option because of the moral fibre of the man she was up against. 'Trump has made it easy to see that you don't really want that kind of world that he's painting,' she argued.

It would not be long before Trump's long shadow would affect her life in ways that she could never have contemplated.

9

When Harry Met Meghan

Sometimes timing is everything. If Meghan Markle had met the man standing before her, casually dressed, hand outstretched in greeting, a couple of years earlier she would have likely smiled, made friendly small talk and moved on. Prince Harry would not have impressed – except as an anecdote to tell her friends.

Of course she would have noticed his ginger hair and beard – her father, half-brother and former husband Trevor Engelson are all strawberry blonds – and that at six foot one inch he is not far off her father's height, although skinnier and fitter with the rangy, loping gait of a young man who's spent a lot of time in the great outdoors. But Meghan would have found the early Harry hard work, something of a lost soul.

Looking back, Harry would be the first to admit that, during his twenties, his life had descended into 'total chaos', the prince struggling to process the black cloud of grief that had enveloped his life since the moment he was awakened from his slumbers in Balmoral in the summer of 1997 and told that his mother, Diana, Princess of Wales, had died in a car accident.

Though millions of tears had been shed as people around the globe watched the prince, then only twelve, walk behind his mother's coffin during the televised funeral, only he had been left to pick up the pieces of his life. Not even his brother Prince William, sober, pragmatic and sensible, had been able to reach him at times. In large gatherings, such as an indoor reception, he would suffer panic attacks. Even before leaving the house he would break into a sweat, his heart pounding. 'The people, the cameras, the attention, he had just let it get to him,' said a royal aide. 'He was always on edge.' Hardly a suitable mindset for a young man whose ultimate role in life was to fulfil the expectation that he would be on hand to steady and support his brother William when he became king. At least that's what Diana had envisaged, pigeonholing Harry as a 'back-up' in the years to come.

Without a mum, without a steadying, nurturing influence in his life, Harry had gone off the rails. He became notorious as an angry drunk who lurched out of London nightclubs, ready to lash out at the loathsome paparazzi who dogged his every footstep. For years he was carefully protected by highly paid public relations professionals who smoothed over his public escapades. So when, in February 2004, Harry was branded a 'national disgrace' and a 'horrible young man' by influential columnist Carol Sarler over his late-night shenanigans, Prince Charles's communications director Paddy Harverson swung into action.

Harry flew to Lesotho and was photographed with a little orphan called Mutsu Potsane, Harry speaking of his deep shock about the impact of AIDS on the country. The trip was followed up by royal aides helpfully releasing a letter he wrote to patients in a hospital unit dealing with the victims of rape and abuse. It was a classic public-relations exercise, utilizing Harry's evident personal qualities – an easy-going manner, fundamental decency and a sense of fun – together with his mother's humanitarian legacy to project a different narrative about a young man best known for his nightclubbing.

For many years this was the go-to template for the prince, any night-time indiscretions more than compensated for by his charity work and his life as a professional soldier, serving for a time in Afghanistan before training to fly Apache helicopters. In Prince Harry's world there has always been someone to do the sweeping-up. When he put on a Nazi uniform for a Colonials and Natives fancy-dress party shortly before Holocaust Memorial Day in 2005, his minders accepted that it was a 'poor choice of costume' but insisted that there was no malice in his decision. Similarly, when he was caught on video referring to a fellow officer cadet at Sandhurst as 'our little Paki friend' and another as looking like a 'raghead' (a pejorative term for an Arab), once again his PR minder Paddy Harverson came to the rescue.

If Meghan had been in his life at that time, she would not have been impressed by his casual racism. Nor were others. 'He was a very lost young man,' a former royal official told me. 'Harry was deeply troubled, unhappy and immature, imbued with the slanted, quietly racist views of those from his class and background.'

Perhaps the low point in Harry's party lifestyle came in 2012, when he was pictured cavorting naked in a Las Vegas hotel room during a game of strip billiards with a bunch of strangers, some of whom had camera phones and helpfully uploaded his antics for the startled world to watch. 'Too much Army and not enough prince,' was his rueful response.

In spite of the uproar, by and large the prince retained the affection of the public, who instinctively sympathized with the emotional difficulties he and his brother had gone through with their parents' bitter divorce and their mother's untimely death. The difference between them was William's more grounded temperament and, later on, his having the support of a sensible and stable wife to see him through the dark nights of the soul. The younger brother found a curious respite from his demons and developed a sense of purpose during his time in the Army. He is not the first, nor will he be the last, young person who has been given direction and discipline by the military. Harry also found that taking up boxing helped him to cope with his bouts of rage.

There was one episode in particular that had a profound impact on the course of his life. At the end of his first tour of duty in 2008, on a flight home from Afghanistan he travelled with the coffin of a dead Danish soldier, which had been loaded on board by the young man's friends, as well as three seriously injured British servicemen with missing limbs, all in induced comas who were wrapped in plastic. That flight set him on the trajectory that would culminate in the Invictus Games.

'The way I viewed service and sacrifice changed forever,' he recalled in his speech to open the 2017 Invictus Games. 'I knew that it was my responsibility to use the great platform that I have to help the world understand and be inspired by the spirit of those who wear the uniform.'

The prince's idea was to combine his royal connections, his lifelong interest in the armed forces and his passion for humanitarian causes into one focused event. The Invictus Games are an international multi-sport jamboree in which sick, wounded or injured servicemen and women compete in a variety of sports, such as indoor rowing and wheelchair basketball. In September 2014, after a year of planning and meetings, the first Games, which involved 300 Army personnel from around the world, were held in London. The event was a triumph, giving the prince, who was due to leave the Army in 2015, new focus and impetus. He was fully committed to using his unique position to help and encourage those who were at the sharp end of modern warfare, veterans who had been damaged and injured but who were prepared to fight on, albeit on a basketball or tennis court. The Invictus Games were the making of Harry. 'Since then he has become the man he is today,' observes a former royal courtier. 'It has not been an easy process. He has become more open and developed into someone who genuinely cares about social issues.'

The experience opened up something in Harry and, increasingly, he became happy to express his personal hopes and dreams, too. His conversations, public and private, were peppered with talk of the princely problem of finding a partner, of settling down and raising a family. It was clear that he had reached a crossroads in his life and that his days of sowing wild oats were coming to an end. As the rest of his friends were settling down and starting families, it seemed that Prince Harry was in danger of becoming the last man standing. He had seen his brother enjoying the simple joys of family life and wanted that experience for himself.

At a birthday party in February 2016, he told TV presenter Denise van Outen, 'I'm not dating and for the first time ever I want to find a wife.' It became a familiar refrain. Three months later, when he was in Orlando, Florida, for the Invictus Games, he again brought up the subject of love and marriage during an interview with the *Sunday Times*. 'At the moment my focus is very much on work, but if someone slips into my life then that's absolutely fantastic. I am not putting work before the idea of family and marriage. I just haven't had that many opportunities to get out there and meet people.'

The difficulty of finding someone 'willing to take me on' was an issue that was always at the back of his mind every time he met someone new. Were they attracted to him for his personality or his title? As one of his friends pointed out: 'You have to be a very special kind of girl to want to be a princess.'

※

In June 2016, as Meghan Markle nestled back in her seat in preparation for landing at Heathrow Airport, she had love and marriage on her mind. The actor was returning from a long weekend on the Greek island of Hydra, once home to the lugubrious poet and singer Leonard Cohen. It had been several days of wine, red mullet, hummus and incredible yoga moves as Meghan, her best friend from college, Lindsay Jill Roth, and Lindsay's bridesmaids discussed wedding dresses, veils, flowers, the past and the future. Meghan's relationship with celebrity chef Cory Vitiello had ended recently, withered on the vine as both their lives had become busier and busier, and Meghan relished time away from Toronto and the house they had shared there.

As maid of honour to Lindsay, who since leaving Northwestern had embarked on a career as a TV producer and novelist, Meghan had taken her role very seriously, organizing the bachelorette party in this beautiful Greek resort rather than some raucous downtown club. 'There is something wholly cathartic about being able to turn it all off – to sunbathe with no one watching, swim, eat copious amounts and toast to the day,' she wrote in her blog, The Tig. The mini-vacation was a triumph, as was her earlier surprise invitation asking Lindsay to Toronto, where she had arranged a wedding-dress fitting at the upmarket Kleinfeld Hudson's Bay bridal boutique (where she had previously shopped for Rachel Zane's wedding dress) with the help of another of her great friends, Jessica

Mulroney, who worked in public relations for the bridal shop. Lindsay, who was marrying a British actuary, ended up falling for a wedding gown from fashionable Lebanese designer Zuhair Murad, who has dressed many of Hollywood's elite, including Taylor Swift, Beyoncé and Katy Perry.

Having executed her duties as the impeccable maid of honour, Meghan arrived in London looking for a little self-promotion – and a few fun days socializing. This time it would not be just *Suits* she was endorsing but herself. She had recently signed up to a London talent and New York literary agency with the goal of producing a television and book version of The Tig, focusing primarily on cooking. Meghan would be filmed criss-crossing the globe to bring to her audience the unusual, the fresh and the sustainable into their kitchens. She also had other fish to fry.

With more than 6 million Twitter followers, a morning breakfast show and a plethora of high-profile celebrity friendships, media royalty Piers Morgan was a fabulous catch for an up-and-coming soap actor seeking her name in the headlines. After all, her week-long visit to London during the Wimbledon Championships was to gain column inches and to dress to impress in the fashions of her sponsor Ralph Lauren, who held (centre) court at the tennis tournament.

With the two of them already Twitter buddies, Meghan contacted Piers on 29 June while she was seated in the Wimbledon stands watching her friend, tennis legend Serena Williams. She called and suggested they meet. They arranged an early-evening drink at his local pub, the Scarsdale Tavern in Kensington. Piers was a *Suits* aficionado, but this was the first time he had met 'Rachel Zane' in the flesh. He revealed in the *Mail* Online: 'She looked every inch the Hollywood superstar – very slim, very leggy, very elegant and impossibly glamorous.' Or as the landlord put it, 'a stunner'.

As she sipped a dirty Martini, they chatted about *Suits*, her background, her days as a briefcase girl on *Deal or No Deal*, gun control in America, her passion for calligraphy, women's rights and her current ambition to be a TV presenter. And men. During their conversation, Meghan received a flurry of texts, the actor explaining to the married TV host that she was trying to fend off 'persistent' men. She was, she told Piers, recently single and 'out of practice' with the dating scene. (Unbeknownst to Meghan, though, her well-connected friends had other ideas for both the solitary actor and a certain lonely prince.)

As their two-hour meeting wound down, Piers was duly flattered and impressed by the Californian actor. 'Fabulous, warm, funny, intelligent and highly entertaining,' he later recalled. 'She seemed real, too; not one of those phony actress types so prevalent in California.' His influential opinion, which helped to shape the national narrative towards Meghan and the Royal Family, would be pivotal in the coming months.

At eight o'clock, she said her goodbyes and headed off to her dinner date at the private members' club, 5 Hertford Street. It was a meeting that Piers later incorrectly suggested was with Prince Harry. She was in fact meeting her photographer friend, Misan Harriman.

❋

The next day, 30 June, she was in full promotion mode, working with Violet von Westenholz, a senior Ralph Lauren media relations executive, who had organized her marketing efforts on behalf of the RL brand. 'How much more could I adore this gem?' an effusive Ms Markle wrote of her new 'bestie'. Not only was Violet a well-connected fashion maven but her father, Baron Piers von Westenholz, an upmarket interior designer, was also a friend of Prince Charles. Moreover her sister Victoria was once seen as a possible match for Prince Harry. Violet along with designer Misha Nonoo, Nonoo's then husband Alexander Gilkes, who moved in the same circles as Prince Harry, and Soho House's Markus Anderson were later identified as the likely if unassuming quartet who organized the famous blind date between Meghan and Harry.

Their meeting was arranged for 1 July, the evening encounter timed to coincide with his return from a First World War commemoration in France. Before their date, Meghan confided her secret during a lunch meeting with her agent, Gina Nelthorpe-

Cowne. 'Do you know what you are letting yourself in for?' asked Gina. Meghan blithely replied that it was going to be an experience and a 'fun night'. Her agent was less sanguine. 'This could be crazy,' she cautioned. 'You will be the most wanted woman.'

When she returned to her suite in the Dean Street hotel to get ready for the evening ahead, Meghan was nervous but more worried about what she should wear than Googling her princely date. Eventually, she plumped for a blue sun dress – months later fabric from the outfit would be incorporated into her wedding dress – as well as a pair of heels. For his part, Harry had looked at a picture of Meghan wearing Nonoo's silver liquid-metal dress. He approved.

Meanwhile, Canadian-born Markus Anderson, the brand ambassador for the exclusive Soho House, who had just returned from a holiday in Madrid with Meghan, was on hand to rustle up a private room at the members-only club for an intimate evening away from prying eyes.

The scene was set, Cupid's arrow was aquiver, the stars, as Harry observed during his engagement interview, were aligned. Not that Meghan had much of an opinion about the man she was about to meet. In a series of quickfire questions during a 2015 interview with *Hello!* magazine, she appeared nonplussed when asked to choose between William and Harry, and the presenter had to encourage her to pick the prince who was still single. During the quiz, Meghan confessed that she preferred the actor Dennis Quaid.

And so it seemed that Harry would have his work cut out if he wanted to use his title to impress. That said, Meghan was meeting a very different Harry from the young man who had made a profession of falling out of bars and using his fists rather than his brains. Earlier on 1 July he had been in France, joining the then prime minister David Cameron, Prince Charles, the Duke and Duchess of Cambridge, and other dignitaries at a service to commemorate the hundredth anniversary of the start of the Battle of the Somme, the bloodiest day of warfare in British history. At an evening vigil for the fallen, Harry had read 'Before Action', a poem penned by Lieutenant W. N. Hodgson, who had died on the opening day of the battle. The event had been a sombre and moving reminder of the enormity of that day. And Harry returned in sober spirits.

Meghan was meeting a grown-up, a man with focus, resolve and a sense of who he was and what he could achieve. She had asked her friends before their meeting if he was kind and nice; the answer lay in his blue eyes. As they say in the movies, they had each other at 'hello'. She was immediately sensitive to him, aware that this was a man who, beneath the banter and the surface chatter, was looking for a safe harbour. The question she asked herself after that first intoxicating meeting was: could she provide it – and all that it would entail?

Although there were, according to author Omid Scobie, a small number of friends present to help break the ice, the couple, seated side by side on velvet chairs, were immediately mesmerized by one another. Harry was enthralled by her beauty, sophistication and her perceptiveness. The prince was clearly genuine in his enthusiasm for Meghan's rescue dogs when she showed him their pictures on her phone. For her part she understood him as a man, not a title. In that subtle one-upmanship of a first date he realized that, while his grandmother might be the Queen, Meghan had given a speech at a United Nations forum. As he subsequently confessed, he recognized that he would have to up his game. He was not the only one to have dedicated chunks of his life to service. Nor the only one who had lost a little of their heart when they first visited Africa, topics that formed the backbone of their conversation.

At the end of the date, they said their goodnights and went their separate ways, he to Nottingham Cottage at Kensington Palace, she to her hotel suite in Soho. Both were buzzing. As she relived that fateful evening in her mind, she perhaps wondered if she had been too eager in accepting his invitation to meet again the following day. Stay classy, Ms Markle. However, the text she received from him as she got ready for bed made her realize that the enthusiasm was not just on her side.

As Harry later confirmed, the couple enjoyed back-to-back dates, making every minute matter before she had to fly home to

Toronto on 5 July to continue promoting the new series of *Suits*. The venue for their second date came courtesy of Markus once again, who arranged a private dinner *à deux* at Dean Street Townhouse. It soon became clear to the couple that they both ticked each other's boxes and that this relationship might last beyond the stage of a brief summer fling. This feeling was further confirmed when Meghan visited Harry at Nottingham Cottage. The normally self-contained actor was smitten. Unable to keep her feelings in check, her Instagram account gave away just a little; on 3 July she posted a picture of two 'Love Hearts' sweets that bore the simple message: 'Kiss me.' Next to the photograph Meghan posted: 'Love Hearts in London.'

Her last full day in London was spent at Wimbledon, where she sat in the players' box along with *Vogue* editor Anna Wintour and her niece. As she watched her friend Serena Williams thrash Russian Svetlana Kuznetsova, it began to rain. Meghan was wearing a simple but expensive black suede Ralph Lauren dress, so Anna, ever the fashionista, offered the actor her woollen cardigan so that the suede would not be stained by the water while they waited for the roof to roll across. Once play resumed, Anna recovered her cardigan and Serena eased her way through to the quarter-finals.

Though she was nursing the biggest secret of her life, Meghan was focused on the action, standing to applaud her friend's outstanding play. However, courtside photographers were more focused on Anna Wintour and the Duchess of Cambridge's sister, Pippa Middleton, than Meghan. She was placed under the heading 'incidental people' by one photographic agency. Not for much longer.

'Gutted to be leaving London,' Meghan told her army of Instagram followers before she boarded her flight to Toronto. It would be some months before even her close friends realized exactly why the parting was so bitter-sweet. As she sipped a glass of champagne on board the flight, she would have had time to ponder the preposterous course her life had taken. But not that long. Hours after she had landed, her life continued its dizzying pace. She barely had time to make a fuss of her rescue dogs, Bogart and Guy, and check in with the design team at Reitmans about her upcoming winter capsule collection, before this one-woman perpetual-motion machine was on her travels again, flying to New York and Boston to continue the promotional tour for *Suits*.

In Boston she posed for pictures and made a video for *Good Housekeeping* magazine, while for NBC's *Today* show she discussed her recipe for a grilled Caesar salad before talking about the plot developments in the new series.

During her publicity tour she realized how little she knew of her boyfriend's home country. On 12 July she took part in a light-hearted quiz on the Dave TV channel. She had gamely tried, and failed, to answer a series of questions about Britain, looking perplexed when asked what 'apples and pears' meant in Cockney rhyming slang. (Answer: stairs.)

Meghan was also amazed by the national animals of England, Scotland and Wales, complaining, 'Am I supposed to know that?' She pointed out that even the British camerawoman did not know that a lion was the national animal of England. '*You* don't know that,' she remarked.

She was delighted to discover that the national animal of Scotland is a unicorn, saying, 'No! Really? It's a unicorn! We're all moving to Scotland.' When she realized that a dragon is the national animal of Wales, she asked, 'Are these real right now? It's a dragon. Lions and unicorns and dragons, oh my.'

On 4 August, she was in New York for her thirty-fifth birthday, where she stayed in the five-star St Regis Hotel in Midtown in preparation for her friend Lindsay Jill Roth's big day. 'Happy birthday to the most kind, generous, wickedly smart and gorgeous (inside and out) #maidofhonor a girl could have!' Lindsay posted on Instagram. Intriguingly, on her birthday a bouquet of peonies, her favourite flowers, were delivered to her hotel suite. A princely offering, perhaps?

Certainly, something was going on in Meghan's heart. 'I am feeling so incredibly joyful right now,' she wrote in The Tig. 'So grateful and content that all I could wish for is more of the same. More surprises, more adventure.' She found herself saying, 'Yes, please' when, just weeks after their first meeting, Harry invited her to join him on safari. Diaries were consulted, dates were agreed, plans were made. She had to pinch herself. Here she was, about to travel halfway round the world to spend five days in a tented camp in the middle of nowhere with a man she had met only twice. It was a side to herself that she was just discovering.

She was by no means short of adventures. In mid-August, after the Roth wedding, she left behind the elegant butler service at the storied St Regis in New York and flew to Rome, where she joined her friend Jessica Mulroney. They planned to embrace *la dolce vita* in some style, checking into the equally civilized Le Sirenuse Hotel on Italy's Amalfi Coast.

With breathtaking views of the Bay of Positano, it is hard not to feel that this is but an anteroom to paradise. Typically, Meghan publicized every detail of their four-day stay, even giving the holiday the hashtag #MJxItaly. They lounged around the pool, strolled into the market square and took pictures of their breakfast under the heading: 'Eat Pray Love'. Meghan, who had had a couple of weeks to ponder the impending safari with Prince Harry, gave an indication of her romantic feelings when she held up a red leather-bound volume, entitled *Amore Eterno* (Eternal Love), and photographed it under the light of a full moon. It was, she said, given to her by friends as a good omen.

At the end of their stay, they returned to Toronto where Meghan began packing for her safari holiday. Then she flew to London and spent the night at Nottingham Cottage before the couple quietly boarded the morning flight to Johannesburg.

※

There may have been a slight raising of eyebrows inside the royal palaces when the news percolated through that Prince Harry was taking yet another girlfriend on a safari holiday to Botswana.

Those who monitor these things would have noted that this was his seventh holiday in Botswana with the fourth female companion to join him for a few romantic nights under the stars in a southern African hideaway. The young man certainly had style.

And he was not the only prince of the realm to fall headlong in love with the delights of the African continent. Another Harry, his great uncle, the Duke of Gloucester, enjoyed a torrid affair with the famous and married aviatrix Beryl Markham during a visit to Kenya in 1928. The duke's elder brother, the Prince of Wales – later and briefly King Edward VIII – took his mistress, Lady Thelma Furness, on safari while her husband camped nearby. 'This was our Eden and we were alone in it,' she wrote breathlessly. 'His arms about me were the only reality, his words of love my only bridge to life.'

There is something about the vast plains, the never-ending skies, the daily struggle for existence, that seems to bring out the passionate and the spiritual in a prince. Prince Charles has passed on his more mystical appreciation of southern Africa to both of his sons. His message to William and Harry was that the exploration of the outer world allowed a deeper engagement with the inner world, a chance to seek truth in their surroundings.

Charles's own guide was the South African philosopher Laurens van der Post, who encouraged the future king to find peace in the vast featureless wilderness of the Kalahari Desert. During a visit in March 1987, Charles and Van der Post travelled to the desert by Land Rover, slept under canvas and chatted around a campfire, listening to the sounds of the desert while marvelling at the brilliant night sky. On the third day they came across a herd of zebras that stretched across the flat horizon. It was such a magnificent and imposing natural wonder that Charles found himself moved to tears. Nowhere else on the planet gives such a vivid reminder of the ineluctable rhythm of life – and of death – than the African plains.

Perhaps with these thoughts and reflections in mind, a little over ten years later Prince Charles invited Prince Harry to join him on a five-day visit to South Africa, Swaziland and Lesotho. It was just two months after Harry's mother had died in a Parisian underpass and he was still numb with grief, struggling to come to terms with her loss. His father thought that time away from England would help the healing process.

Accompanying Harry, who was then thirteen, was his 'surrogate mum', Tiggy Legge-Bourke, who had been an official companion to the boy during his parents' separation; also his schoolfriend Charlie Henderson and Mark Dyer, a former equerry to the Prince of Wales. While Harry's father undertook official engagements, the young prince was taken on his first South African safari. It was the beginning of a lifelong love affair.

After touring some of the battlegrounds, such as Rorke's Drift from the famous Anglo-Zulu War of 1879, the prince met South Africa's first black president, Nelson Mandela, as well as the Spice Girls, who were then at the height of their popularity and had travelled to South Africa to perform in a charity concert.

It was six years before Harry enjoyed a return visit, the nineteen-year-old prince spending two months of his school gap year in the impoverished kingdom of Lesotho, the landlocked country which suffered from one of the highest HIV-AIDS infection rates in the world. Initially it was seen by many as a cynical public-relations exercise to restore the prince's stained reputation. Not as far as Harry was concerned. Moved by the plight of the children and with his mother's memory clearly in mind, Harry joined forces with the country's Prince Seeiso, who had also lost his own mother. In 2006, they set up the Sentebale charity to help children suffering from AIDS to lead fulfilling and productive lives. The charity – its name means 'forget-me-not' in the Sesotho language – was so popular and, thanks to the prince's involvement, became so well known outside the nation's boundaries that it expanded into neighbouring Botswana. Harry has energetically supported it ever since. In 2008, he recruited his brother to take part in a 1,000-mile, cross-country motorbike trek across South Africa's Eastern Cape to raise money for Sentebale and other charities supporting disadvantaged children. 'It's not just a bimble across the countryside; we're expecting to fall off many a time,' Harry told the BBC before they set off.

Alongside his visits to help conservation projects as well as his charity work for Sentebale and official duties, Harry made Africa his favourite holiday destination – especially when trying to impress a girlfriend. Before Meghan, he had taken TV sports presenter Natalie Pinkham, Zimbabwean-born Chelsy Davy and actor Cressida Bonas on safari. Botswana was the preferred destination. As his biographer Penny Junor observed: 'Africa is the one place on earth where Prince Harry can be truly himself. He describes Botswana as his "second home". He is not a prince under African skies. He is just Harry.'

The problem with these romances was that once he arrived back in Britain, the HRH tag got in the way of building an honest, workable commitment. Harry's previous serious relationships with Chelsy Davy and Cressida Bonas floundered because the women couldn't cope with being in the spotlight. His first serious girlfriend, Chelsy, bore the unwelcome media attention for seven years before she got sick and tired of the circus. During their on–off relationship, which lasted from 2004 to 2011, the feisty blonde was often described as the love of his life.

She became part of the royal set, and was invited to the weddings of Prince William and Kate Middleton, and of Princess Anne's daughter Zara Phillips and rugby player Mike Tindall. The trainee lawyer admitted that she found it difficult to deal with the pressure. 'It was so full on – crazy, scary and uncomfortable,' she later revealed at the launch of a jewellery range in June 2016. 'It was tough being chased down the road by photographers. I was trying to be a normal kid and it was horrible.' These days, she enjoys a 'calm' life making jewellery.

Cressida Bonas told a similar story. She put her career on hold during her two-year romance with the prince. Though nervous of the paparazzi, she did agree to join him at a public charity event at Wembley Arena in North London. In a telling exchange, she felt that as an actor she was being defined by a 'famous man' rather than by what she had achieved herself. 'Yeah, I think it's that thing of being pigeonholed,' she complained during an interview on Radio Four's *Woman's Hour*. 'Especially in this country [Britain] I find people are very quick to put you in a box or put you in a corner.'

Other girlfriends, such as lingerie model Florence 'Flea' Brudenell-Bruce, former girlfriend of Formula One racing champion Jenson Button, seemed to enjoy the limelight – but not Harry's roving eye. For his part he complained, as have princes down the ages, about the difficulty of finding a partner who wanted him for himself. As one of his friends observed in the *Sunday Times*: 'He's always wary in case women throw themselves at him to make a name for themselves. And often the sincere ones who love him for who he is don't want to live in the goldfish bowl that is the Royal Family for the next fifty years.'

But despite the obstacles, it doesn't appear to have been too much of a hardship, the prince enjoying romances, confirmed or suspected, with a veritable galaxy of beautiful, successful women, among them actors Sienna Miller and Margot Robbie, TV presenter Poppy James, Brazilian socialite Antonia Packard and German model Anastasia Guseva. The list is by no means exhaustive. Just a few weeks before he met Meghan for the first time, he was seen 'dirty dancing' with a pair of brunettes and downing shots at Jak's bar in West London. A mature young man but with an undeniable streak of mischief.

10

Into Africa

In August 2016, as far as the public and media were concerned Harry was taking yet another trip to Africa. The prince was scheduled to spend several weeks in Malawi, helping to protect elephants from poaching, before travelling to Botswana to work on measures to save the dwindling rhino population. He had taken part in a similar effort the previous year in Namibia. As well as his charity work, on 6 August he was to be a guest at the wedding of his cousin George McCorquodale to Bianca Moore at Netherwood, a wedding venue in KwaZulu-Natal, South Africa. Unfortunately, the social occasion ended up eclipsing his good works, *The Sun* newspaper describing how the prince and his friends, all the worse for wear, were said to have stripped a younger cousin naked during a drunken late-night session of high jinks. Under the headline 'Jäger Lout Harry Strips Wed Guest', a fellow reveller was quoted as saying: 'Harry was on his best behaviour during the wedding, but afterwards he went pretty wild. Everyone was laughing, having a good time.' The story was typical of the media narrative that cast the prince as a hard-drinking young man on the lookout for some fun.

For all the banter and horseplay, Harry had something more meaningful on his mind – his upcoming safari vacation with Meghan. After they flew from London to Johannesburg, they took a further flight to Maun Airport in northern Botswana. The final leg of their journey was a bouncy ride along a series of dirt roads in a rugged four-by-four off-roader. At a roadblock, the couple had to get out of their vehicle and walk across a disinfectant mat, a precaution to prevent diseases from the outside world getting into the vast game reserve. When they arrived at the exclusive tented camp known as Meno a Kwena, or 'teeth of the crocodile', they were greeted by breathtaking views across the dark-blue waters of the nearby Boteti River, meandering along the valley below them. It was a magnificent natural paradise, with herds of elephants, zebras and wildebeest cooling off in the waters. A casual visitor would never have known that for nearly twenty years the river had been dry and had only come back to life in 2008, when millions of gallons of water came gushing through from the Okavango Delta due to a shift in the tectonic plates.

Situated halfway between the delta and the spectacular Central Kalahari Game Reserve, the camp has nine luxurious guest tents, all with en-suite bathrooms equipped with solar-powered, hot-and-cold-running showers.

It is run by conservationist David Dugmore, an old friend not just of Harry but also of his brother and father. He and his brother Roger, who organizes mobile safaris, were guests at William and Kate's wedding in 2011. At the forefront of dealing with the conflict between wildlife and cattle farming, Dugmore's views have helped to shape the princes' thinking towards conservation. He has a radical plan to make Botswana the biggest conservation project in the world by creating a trans-frontier park in which animals can freely migrate between the Okavango and the Kalahari. Doubtless he discussed the latest developments with the prince, while giving a conservation primer to Harry's American girlfriend.

However, the couple had not come thousands of miles to learn about conservation. Their days and nights under canvas in the middle of nowhere were a chance to get to know one another without any distractions. That meant, for once, the chattily effusive Ms Markle maintained radio silence on her social media accounts, the normally prolific web maven going dark between 21 and 28 August.

Conversationally, Harry, who has spoken about his ambition to be a safari guide, was on home turf, the old Africa hand well able to impress Meghan with his local knowledge of the bush and the dynamic relationship between indigenous tribes and the native flora and fauna. After all, what is there not to love about a man who spends his holidays saving elephants and rhinos? Even though she was a dedicated world traveller herself, Meghan was impressed by the vast beauty of the African bush. Her visits to Rwanda paled by comparison to this remote and uncomplicated vista. Sipping a glass of decent red wine by the pool at Le Sirenuse in Positano simply did not compare with watching the vast herds roaming the plains, a 'sundowner' cocktail in hand.

When the sun finally did go down, after a meal of chicken or game stew, they drank in the shimmering carapace of the stars above them. And when they retired for the night, they were lulled to sleep by the chirping of the yellow-throated sand grouse and the melancholy call of zebras at the water's edge. At dawn they were awoken by a chattering chorus of birds, noisier than usual as it was their mating season.

During the days, the couple were able to choose from walking tours or day-long safaris deep into the Kalahari Desert. Along the banks of the river, crocodiles are a common sight, while sharp-eyed visitors can occasionally see lions and cheetahs. After a dusty safari the couple could relax in the natural rock swimming pool overlooking the river – crocodiles excluded.

It was here, in this natural idyll, where the couple cemented their relationship, both of them realizing that they had found something special. As Harry later described: 'It was absolutely amazing to get to know her as quickly as I did.'

In spite of the looming difficulties of distance and busy diaries, by the end of those magical six days they knew that their blossoming love affair was too precious to waste. As Meghan later told the BBC: 'I think that very early on, when we realized we were going to commit to each other, we knew we had to invest the time and the energy and whatever it took to make that happen.'

Luckily, they had a template in Meghan's friend, the recently married Lindsay Jill Roth, who had managed to juggle executive-producing *The Real Girl's Kitchen* for the Cooking Channel in New York while dating London-based Gavin Jordan, an actuary for

Ernst & Young. Their long-distance relationship had thrived and even ended in marriage – as had many others in Harry's circle.

However, with due respect to Harry's male friends, none of them would qualify for the position of one of the world's most eligible bachelors. While their relationship was as tricky as any other long-distance affair, they had other considerations to bear in mind. Paramount among them was secrecy. Meghan and Harry needed their romance to be private, at least long enough for them to decide honestly if their relationship was going to succeed in the long run – or whether it was a feverish summer fling that would not endure the winter chills and inevitable absences.

A very early experience of how different life was going to be if Meghan continued down this romantic road was in the everyday act of grocery shopping. On one of the first occasions that Meghan visited Harry at Kensington Palace, the couple went to a local supermarket. But this was food shopping with a difference. Once inside the store, they separated and pretended they didn't know one another. When they wanted an item, they would text each other. As they went up and down the aisles, Harry adopted his default incognito look: baseball cap pulled down low, no eye contact and an aggressive demeanour to deter those who may have recognized him. For Meghan, it was a somewhat unusual experience but curiously fun. It was an early indication that she would face obstacles that just don't occur in most relationships. As a result, it would not be long before Meghan had to ask herself if she was in love with the man or the position, and, if she loved the man, could she cope with the position? She might be a popular actor and used to being recognized in public, but that was nothing compared to the scrutiny she would be under should she choose to go the distance with Harry. Celebrity boyfriends like chef Cory Vitiello were one thing, but royalty was quite another. Could she take it? And, for that matter, could her family and friends?

As they became more and more consumed by their romantic dance, Harry realized that he had fallen for a (slightly) older, dual heritage divorcee from California. He didn't need any reminding of the chaos and bitterness caused by the last American to marry a member of the Royal Family. When King Edward VIII fell for Wallis Simpson, the twice-divorced woman from Baltimore, he abdicated the throne rather than give her up.

Long after Edward VIII had gone into self-imposed exile, divorce remained the great no-no inside the Royal Family. In the 1950s, the Queen's sister and Harry's great aunt, Princess Margaret, had agreed, after much pressure from the Church and politicians, to walk away from her relationship with another divorcee, the late king's equerry, Group Captain Peter Townsend. Her life was never really the same again.

Of course, his father Prince Charles had married his mistress Camilla Parker Bowles at Windsor in 2005 after leaving a decent interval following the death of Diana in 1997 and that of his disapproving grandmother, the Queen Mother, who died in 2002. That union signalled a permanent retreat from the moral position that the Royal Family had clung to during the bitter run-up to the 1936 abdication.

There was much history – far more than dragons, unicorns and lions – for Meghan to learn and absorb, if she was minded. Though he was instinctively protective towards her, Harry wanted Meghan to understand clearly what she was getting into and make her own choices. Hopefully in his favour. Though Meghan confessed herself 'spellbound' by the new man in her life, ironically Harry was much more the anxious supplicant, worried that the price of his fame could be his future happiness. Like clambering into the unheated plunge pool at the Meno a Kwena camp, it was best if her introduction into his world was *'pole, pole'* ('slowly, slowly' in Swahili). For her part, she wanted to learn about her man through her own first-hand observations, not the distorting lens of the tabloids or TMZ. In fact, she deliberately tuned out what she called 'the noise' surrounding her boyfriend and his family, pointedly ignoring the warnings of concerned friends about the attentions of the notorious British tabloids or Harry's controversial reputation. 'How bad could it be?' she reasoned of the British media. She would find out all too soon.

As far as she was concerned, at this stage in their relationship it was the practical issue of actually seeing one another that bothered her most. Many long-distance couples apply the twenty-one-day survival rule – to make sure that they see one another at least every three weeks. Harry and Meghan managed every fourteen days. Jet lag – not the paparazzi – became their main enemy. Meghan would often arrive in Toronto and go straight to the set of *Suits* and start filming. As she later recalled during the couple's engagement interview: 'I think we were able to really have so much time just to connect and we never went longer than two weeks without seeing each other, even though we were obviously doing a long-distance relationship … we made it work.'

When they compared diaries before they parted it was clear that, if anything, Meghan was the busier of the pair in the autumn of 2016, what with her TV filming commitments, promoting her new fashion collection on behalf of Reitmans, her blog and humanitarian work. Even before Harry came into her life she was often up till the wee small hours, scouring the internet for inspiration for The Tig. Now she was going to be stretched even further.

Upon his return to London, Harry was soon back in the royal routine. After celebrating his thirty-second birthday on 15 September on the Queen's Balmoral estate in the Scottish Highlands, he undertook engagements in Aberdeen on behalf of The Diana, Princess of Wales Memorial Fund, the charity set up in his mother's name which recognizes young people who have made a difference to their communities.

Meanwhile, in the last weekend in September, Meghan travelled to Ottawa, the Canadian capital, to attend her second One Young World Summit. The non-profit organization had Meghan's resounding endorsement: 'They are delegates who are speaking out against human rights violations, environmental crises, gender-equality issues, discrimination and injustice. They are the change.' Meghan, who had already spoken at the Dublin conference in 2014, joined other inspirational counsellors, notably the former Irish President Mary Robinson, Canadian Prime Minister Justin Trudeau, as well as actor Emma Watson and fellow Kruger Cowne clients, including former UN Secretary-General Kofi Annan, poet and activist Fatima Bhutto, and singer Cher. As a sign of her standing, Meghan was asked by *Vanity Fair* photographer Jason Schmidt to pose alongside Mary Robinson, Fatima Bhutto and Saudi activist Loujain al-Hathloul, with the Ottawa Parliament building as a backdrop.

Inside the conference centre, Meghan, speaking without notes, told a women's equality forum about the time she had confronted the creator of the *Suits* TV show concerning the fact that the scriptwriters were sketching too many scenes that opened with her character, Rachel Zane, emerging naked from a shower dressed only in a towel. It was sexist, it was unnecessary, it was stopped. Her complaint came years before the rebellion about the way women were treated by Hollywood, in the light of the Harvey Weinstein scandal, and the subsequent #MeToo campaign. For all her own professional difficulties, she admitted to feeling humbled, nervous and rather emotional when she introduced activist Luwam Estifanos, who had bravely escaped a life of slavery in Eritrea and now works to end that government-sponsored practice in her home country.

Meghan's exposure at the conference was a reminder to Harry, if any were needed, that he was dating a very special woman. A keeper, as they say.

She arrived in London shortly afterwards for a reunion with the prince. As the watchword was privacy, they stayed at his modest grace-and-favour home Nottingham Cottage, in the grounds of Kensington Palace. Best remembered now as the place where thousands of people laid flowers in the summer of 1997 in memory of Diana, Princess of Wales, the palace is probably the most exclusive village in Britain, home to an assortment of royals, including the Duke and Duchess of Cambridge and their children, courtiers and retired staff. Like any village, it feeds on a diet of gossip and rumour, but for the most part what happens inside Kensington Palace stays inside Kensington Palace.

If Meghan was expecting to be sleeping in a palace, she was sadly disappointed; Harry's home was smaller than her own place in Toronto – and with lower ceilings. Prince William and Kate had lived there while their capacious apartment 1a Clock Court, the former residence of the late Princess Margaret, was being renovated. Cosy and neat, the cottage, known as 'Notts Cott' by residents, boasts two bedrooms, two bathrooms, two reception rooms and a small garden. In summer it has the feel of being in the heart of an English country village, which perhaps explains why the first thing Harry did when he moved in was to install a hammock in the garden.

It had the virtue, also, of being private and secure, the exits and entrances watched twenty-four hours a day by armed police. It is here, as schedules permitted, where they began living together, quietly, secretly, unobtrusively. Meghan recalled: 'I don't think that I would call it a whirlwind in terms of our relationship. Obviously there have been layers attached to how public it has become after we had a good five, six months almost with just privacy, which was amazing.'

Fortunately for Meghan, the palace is also in the centre of an extensive park which meant the actor was able to go jogging – mobile meditation as she calls it – along the tree-lined avenues or stroll on Kensington High Street to go shopping. It will doubtless have given her a kick to know that when she went into Whole Foods Market, the American-owned supermarket, which shares a building with journalists from the *Mail* newspaper group, she was operating under the radar.

Not that Kensington Palace was a home away from home. It was a culture shock. Not just the security but the rather utilitarian way the royals live. Take, for example, food. As a rule the Royal Family eat to live rather than live to eat, watching their diets so that they remain the same shape and weight. 'Bloody organic,' said Prince Philip to palace chef Darren O'Grady one day, when confronted with a basket of his eldest son's home-grown produce.

When Harry was growing up, it was a treat to be taken to McDonald's by his mother for a hamburger. For the most part, he was brought up on institutional food at his boarding schools and then, during his Army career, fed with whatever was available, especially when he was based in Afghanistan. He was raised in a family where, traditionally, everyone stopped eating once the Queen had finished. When she put down her cutlery it was a signal for all the plates to be cleared away. Hardly the recipe for a calm digestion.

Though all members of the Royal Family have their dietary quirks, none seemingly enjoys the act of cooking – though Prince Philip used to like a barbecue when at Balmoral. Meghan, though, comes from the other end of the foodie chain; she loves cooking, exploring new foods and experimenting with fresh flavours. Indeed, she was in the process of selling a cookery book idea when she first met Harry. During the first few months of their romance, Meghan's blog, The Tig, enthused over recipes for pumpkin fondue, spiced broccoli and hempseed stew, poached pear in orange, spelt Anzac biscuits, and red wine hot chocolate. As she likes to sample her recommendations, Harry will have been the royal guinea pig.

Meghan also extolled the virtues of a 'holistic, plant-based, food-delivery service', complete with brand ambassadors who were 'experts, influencers and leaders in the wellness world'. Maybe it was wise to have kept Prince Philip out of the loop on that one.

Just as Meghan encouraged a helping of culinary adventure, so she dramatically changed the contents of Harry's fridge. Meghan never leaves home unless she has hummus, carrots, green juice, almonds and chia-seed pudding in the fridge. When California met Kensington there was only going to be one victor in the dietary smack-down. As one female American writer noted: 'American women like to change their men in many small ways.'

They were, however, hardly prisoners of the palace. As Harry doubtless told himself, if his mother could keep her long-time romance with heart surgeon Hasnat Khan a secret, then he could do the same with Meghan. They enjoyed a quiet trip to see the musical The Lion King and visited Princess Eugenie, the Duchess of York's daughter, and her soon-to-be fiancé Jack Brooksbank at her apartment at St James's Palace. This was an important meeting as Harry trusted Eugenie implicitly and used her as a sounding board to assess the women in his life. Meghan passed this critical test, Eugenie describing the American actor as 'just the tonic' for her cousin.

'Eugenie and Meghan have become firm friends, bonding over a shared love of art, dogs and late-night macaroni-cheese suppers,' one friend of the couple later revealed. 'Eugenie loves Meghan to bits and believes she is perfect for Harry.' The prince also carefully introduced her to his closest friends, notably Hugh van Cutsem and Rose Astor, and his schoolfriend Tom 'Skippy' Inskip and his wife, flame-haired Lara Hughes-Young.

They also visited the gastropub The Sands End, in south-west London, which is owned by Harry's 'second dad' and mentor Mark Dyer. Dyer was utterly delighted that Harry had found a 'good sort' after so many years of drift and occasional debauch. It probably helped that Mark is married to Texan heiress Amanda Kline, who was able to give Meghan recommendations for mundane but vital matters for an actress, such as hairdressers, nail bars and beauty salons.

'Meghan loved her from the start,' observed a friend of the Dyers. 'She is a compatriot and terribly kind and jolly – and Harry trusts the Dyers implicitly.'

On several occasions Harry and Meghan headed to the Cotswolds, where they stayed at the Oxfordshire farmhouse run by Soho House. They would also take a suite at its companion site, Babington House, in Somerset. These club houses are seriously stylish hang-outs for metropolitan hipsters who want to road-test their designer wellies. Every night at Soho Farmhouse a cocktail cart visits the various rooms and wooden cabins, dispensing Martinis and, in Harry's case, aged Scotch whisky. During one of their stays there, the club's founder Nick Jones introduced Meghan to musician Richard Jones, husband of singer Sophie Ellis-Bextor, whom Meghan had met at the opening of Soho House in Istanbul in 2015. A keen amateur pilot, Richard said to Meghan, 'Let me show you how to fly a plane.' As he later told the *Daily Mail*: 'She jumped at it. I took her up with me and she loved it. She was great, a natural, and we flew over the Cotswolds.'

On 11 October, she boarded a rather larger conveyance than Richard Jones's single prop and flew from London to Atlanta, Georgia, where she was guest speaker at a blogging conference aimed specifically at millennial women who want to network and learn how best to use digital space. In a thirty-five-minute discussion on stage with Create and Cultivate founder Jaclyn Johnson, she passed on her own pearls of internet wisdom and made it clear that she planned to expand The Tig. By now her baby brand, which she described as 'aspirational girl next door', had grown into a toddler that needed constant feeding. At the same time as she was trying to come to terms with the insatiable demands of her blog, she was juggling her complex private life. There was no simple solution. This was the downside of dating a prince.

During the course of the conversation, she gave her adoring audience a window into the whirlwind that was her world, admitting that she had arrived from London the previous night and, after the conference, was flying to Toronto to film three episodes of *Suits* for the show's sixth season. Though there was no hint of her royal boyfriend, her talk left the audience impressed by her candour and smarts. 'Charming, intelligent and unafraid to let her guard down, Meghan is the definition of the modern woman,' noted Jaclyn Johnson.

Once Meghan had finished filming it was Harry's turn to join her in Toronto, visiting Canada three times between August and October. When Meghan travelled she was comfortably camera-ready, quietly sitting in business class in her jeans or chinos and black tailored blazer, a cashmere scarf on her shoulders, reading *The Economist* while listening to Petit Biscuit or Christine and the Queens on her designer headphones. By contrast Harry is more aggressively private. He is the boy in a beanie, travelling head down, avoiding eye contact. Fortunately for the royal lovebirds, unlike London, Paris and New York, there is no paparazzi culture in the Ontario capital, so life was more relaxed for the couple. Once again they were able to continue with their relationship outside of public or media scrutiny.

Less so in West Hollywood, where that autumn they spent a few days at the Hollywood home of Harry's friend, Arthur Landon. Here the paparazzi stalk the streets of nearby Sunset Strip hoping to snag a celebrity. It was, however, worth taking the risk as it gave

Meghan the opportunity to introduce her mother to the man in her life. Though she found the experience somewhat surreal, Doria realized that Harry was a genuine suitor, a kind man who had genuinely lost his heart to her daughter. At some point, too, via mobile phone she introduced Harry to her father, who lived in a village near the Mexican border. As Tom Markle Senior later recalled on *Good Morning Britain*: 'I eventually spoke to him and he was a very nice man, a gentleman, very likeable.' As a code name, Tom and Meghan called him 'H' in private father-daughter conversations.

The West Hollywood jaunt was a one-off. For the most part they lived a quiet life in Meghan's Toronto house, which was situated on a tree-lined street in the affluent neighbourhood of Seaton Village. Apart from an SUV containing plain-clothes police, there was no obvious sign that a member of the British Royal Family had come to visit.

With its wooden floors and light painted walls, Meghan's open-plan property had the feel of Southern California, a hard trick to pull off on a dull October afternoon in Toronto. By contrast with Harry's bachelor pad at Kensington Palace, Meghan's rented property was luxurious, the three-bedroom home featuring a cinema room, a high-spec kitchen-diner and two bathrooms. Her rescue dogs, Bogart and Guy, had the run of the house and, despite having a kennel outside, the pair often slept on Meghan's king-sized bed. When Harry came to stay, she dressed them in the dog-sized Union Flag jumpers she had bought to amuse her boyfriend.

Meghan would also throw barbecue parties for friends who were in the know, such as stylist Jessica and TV presenter Ben Mulroney and their children, twins Brian and John, and daughter Ivy. If they ventured out, usually they would go to Soho House for drinks. Housed in an elegant Georgian building in the west of the city on Adelaide Street, the club provided cosy corners and intimate bars. Here they could enjoy the Italian-style cuisine or venture onto the rooftop terrace for panoramic views of the downtown skyline. For much of the time they just hung out, Meghan cooking dishes fit for a prince, mainly pasta and her signature roast chicken, which also happened to be Harry's favourite.

At Halloween, the eve of Meghan's collection for Reitmans hitting the stores, they met Princess Eugenie and Jack Brooksbank, who were over in Canada on holiday, at Soho House for supper. Then Harry donned a mask and went trick-or-treating with his girlfriend. It turned out to be a fun and carefree evening, the last they would enjoy for some time. Unbeknownst to them, their days of secrecy and privacy were coming to an end. Meghan and Harry were about to be unmasked.

11

A Very Public Affair

On a briskly chilly but blue-skied day at the end of October 2016, Camilla Tominey, the royal editor of the *Sunday Express*, was cheering on her young son Harry in a Sunday league soccer match. Much to Camilla's delight, her six-year-old had made it onto the score sheet.

Some hours earlier his mother had scored, too, breaking the biggest royal story of her career. Under the headline HARRY'S SECRET ROMANCE WITH A TV STAR, and billed as a Royal World Exclusive, she told her readers that Prince Harry was 'secretly dating a stunning US actress, model and human rights campaigner'. Her story went on to detail the romance between the Queen's grandson and *Suits* actress Meghan Markle. It quoted a source as saying that Harry was the happiest he had been in years.

Her editor, Martin Townsend, was equally happy, so thrilled with the royal exclusive that he shared it with the *Daily Star Sunday*, sister paper to the *Sunday Express*.

The story was gold dust. And Camilla was absolutely confident of her source. For once the newspaper decided against placing a courtesy call into the press office at Kensington Palace. The fear was that the palace would put out a statement, thus spoiling their scoop.

It was just like the old days of Fleet Street, the one-time newspaper capital of Britain. Normally, Sunday newspapers have a gentleman's agreement whereby they swap their first editions so that if a rival has missed a story, they have a chance to catch up for later editions. Not this night. Townsend decided to deliberately delay printing the first edition of the paper so that none of his rivals was in a position to match their scoop. Late on Saturday night, frantic calls from journalists were being made to Kensington Palace when word spread that the *Express* had landed 'a big one'. Camilla's agitated competitors were met with 'No comment' by the duty press officer. Off the record, Prince Harry's communications secretary Jason Knauf, an aggressive American, was reluctantly admitting that the article had a ring of truth about it.

Within minutes of the *Sunday Express* story breaking, social media went into meltdown as bloggers, royal enthusiasts, *Suits* fans and online newspapers worldwide spread the news. Overnight Meghan Markle went from being a moderately well-known actor to one of the most famous people on the planet.

When the story became public, Harry was staying with Meghan in Toronto. After he took a call from Knauf, informing him that their cover had been blown, he and Meghan poured themselves a glass of wine and toasted each other. But the celebration came with a sober warning, Harry telling Meghan: 'Our lives will never be the same again.' They decided to ride out the storm at the home of their friends, Jessica and Ben Mulroney. It would give them breathing room before the world's media descended on Meghan's Seaton Village home.

In some ways the public unveiling of their relationship was something of a relief. At least they no longer had to hide from the world. Nor was the actor going to lose her mischievous sense of humour over this dramatic development in her life. Just hours after the story broke, she posted a cryptic photo on her Instagram site of two bananas cuddling, with the caption 'Sleep tight xx'. The photograph, which showed the bananas 'spooning' – lying next to each other like a pair of spoons – attracted thousands of 'likes' from her followers, who quickly realized what she was alluding to. One user posted 'Princess Meghan Markle', while another wrote: 'Is this a message for your red-haired Prince?'

Equally tongue-in-cheek was another photo she posted, featuring a cup of English breakfast tea and a jigsaw, perhaps indicating how the couple were spending their time indoors. But their light-hearted attitude did not last long. Meghan had to return to her home and face the media music.

※

There is a famous scene in the movie *Notting Hill* where Julia Roberts, who plays a glamorous American actress, opens the front door of the home of her bookseller boyfriend, played by Hugh Grant, to be confronted by a baying pack of photographers and reporters. Roberts promptly slams the door and heads inside. That's probably how Meghan felt when, dressed in a long coat, a beanie hat and dark glasses, she finally ventured out of her front door and made her way through the mob of media into a waiting Dodge van, which then whisked her to work on the set of *Suits*. Harry had made his escape earlier, catching a flight back to London.

Meghan might have been a veteran of promotional panels, forums and podiums, but nothing could have prepared her for the sonic boom, the shock wave of publicity that hit her.

Within the space of a few days, much of the print and digital media had painted her as a 'gold-digger' whose 'torrid sex scenes' from *Suits* were featured on porn sites. One story suggested that Prince Harry was responsible for breaking up Meghan's relationship with chef Cory Vitiello; another that the prince had inundated her with texts until she agreed to meet for a date.

Under the headline 'Harry Girl's on Pornhub', one tabloid helpfully reported that she featured on the adult site, where she could be seen 'stripping off and groaning', straddling her co-star Patrick J. Adams in an office, as well as mounting him on a sofa. 'It also includes close-ups of her crotch and her lacy bra – and has been viewed more than 40,600 times.' Another porn site superimposed Meghan's head onto the body of a glamour model. Meghan and her advisers were helpless to stop this grotesque sexual caricature. She felt sick to her stomach, the actor in tears as she became swamped in a tsunami of speculation.

Commentators too had a field day. Columnist Rachel Johnson, sister of British Prime Minister Boris Johnson, described Meghan's mother Doria as a 'dreadlocked African-American lady from the wrong side of the tracks'. Regarding Meghan, she continued, 'If there is issue from her alleged union with Prince Harry, the Windsors will thicken their watery, thin blue blood and Spencer pale skin and ginger hair with some rich and exotic DNA.' The online *Daily Star* claimed: 'Prince Harry could marry into gangster royalty – his new love is from a crime-ridden Los Angeles neighbourhood.' The story suggested that Meghan's mother lived in a high-crime locality surrounded by 'bloodbath robberies and drug-induced violence'.

The stories acted as the call of a hunting horn for a torrent of racist abuse from online trolls. In a matter of days, Meghan had experienced racism and sexism on a level beyond any she had endured before. While she had been discussing and writing about such issues for the last few years, nothing came close to this onslaught. It was neither pleasant nor accurate, Meghan the campaigner, the humanitarian and the woman being reduced to a two-dimensional caricature. As biographer Sam Kashner wrote: 'Criticism of Markle has been snob-ridden, racist and uninformed.'

It was reminiscent of the gleeful horror that greeted Prince Andrew's romance with American actor Kathleen 'Koo' Stark in 1982, when it was revealed that she had starred in a mildly erotic rite-of-passage movie called *Emily*, her role involving brief nudity and a tender lesbian shower scene. But back then there was no internet. This time around the ubiquitous nature of social media gave the whole world and its nasty brother (and sister) the opportunity to 'join the conversation'.

While a teary Meghan was sympathizing with her mother, who found herself accosted by photographers every time she went out, as well as by confused friends wondering what they should say to the media, other members of her own family added to the tumult.

Her half-sister Samantha (previously named Yvonne) appeared particularly keen to share the limelight. Describing Meghan, whom she had not seen for years, as 'selfish', Samantha accused her of being a shallow social climber with a 'soft spot for gingers'. Samantha, who suffers from multiple sclerosis and uses a wheelchair, went on to say in an interview with *The Sun* that her half-sister's behaviour was 'not befitting of a Royal Family member', berating her for shunning her family after she became famous on TV. She revealed that she would be writing a book about Meghan and her family entitled *The Diary of Princess Pushy's Sister*.

Then Meghan's young half-nephew Tyler Dooley, the son of Tom Markle Junior, weighed in, announcing that Meghan was blissfully happy and that the actor was 'hurt' and 'stung' by his aunt's accusations. If nothing else, these scattered comments gave a sense of the dysfunction at the heart of Meghan's family.

The coverage was Harry's worst nightmare come true. Meghan had made the mistake of falling in love with him. Now she, her family and her friends were destined to suffer. Through it all, neither Harry nor Meghan had made any statement. Kensington Palace also remained tight-lipped. But the media bedlam could not continue for much longer. The association with Meghan's appearances on *Suits* and the porn site Pornhub, as well as the lascivious headline 'Fancy a Quick Puck Meg', which suggested that Meghan's marriage to Trevor Engelson had collapsed because she had become close to Canadian ice hockey star Michael Del Zotto, proved to be the last straws. While Del Zotto and his agent categorically denied the suggestion, Harry decided to act. He contacted his brother, who had faced similar hysterical coverage during his courtship with Kate Middleton. They chewed over the problem and though William was cautious about issuing a statement, especially as it would confirm Meghan was Harry's girlfriend, he felt that matters had gone too far to remain silent. Unlike their father, William and Harry are not of the old royal school whose motto is: 'Never complain, never explain'. They have a track record of aggressively using the law to seek redress against intrusive photographers and other media outlets that invade their privacy. William, for instance, successfully sued a celebrity magazine and two photographers for publishing topless photos of his wife while they were sunbathing at a private chateau during a holiday in France. This time around Harry went so far as to suggest hiring a retired Scotland Yard protection officer to watch over Meghan, who thought the idea 'charming but unnecessary'. That didn't stop the *Suits* producers from employing their own heavies to protect their valuable asset, increasing security on set and accompanying her to and from work.

Amid these media histrionics, Harry's communications secretary Jason Knauf drafted a lengthy statement that addressed the prince's concerns and complaints. There was no hiding the anger and distress that suffused the bulletin, the voice of a young man trying to protect the woman he loved – and preserve their future together. He was desperately worried that she might cut and run. The coverage was his worst nightmare – far more explicit than with his previous girlfriends. Prince Charles, who was on a tour of the Gulf at the time, was given only twenty minutes' notice before the official communiqué was issued, the Prince of Wales reluctantly accepting that the timing would totally overshadow this important overseas visit.

On 8 November, Kensington Palace formally released the extraordinary statement. It acknowledged that there would be curiosity about the prince's private life, but the past week 'has seen a line crossed'.

His girlfriend, Meghan Markle, has been subject to a wave of abuse and harassment. Some of this has been very public – the smear on the front page of a national newspaper; the racial undertones of comment pieces; and the outright sexism and racism of social media trolls and web article comments.

Some of it has been hidden from the public – the nightly legal battles to keep defamatory stories out of papers; her mother having to struggle past photographers in order to get to her front door; the attempts of reporters and photographers to gain illegal entry to her home and the calls to police that followed; the substantial bribes offered by papers to her ex-boyfriend; the bombardment of nearly every friend, co-worker and loved one in her life.

Prince Harry is worried about Ms Markle's safety and is deeply disappointed that he has not been able to protect her. It is not right that a few months into a relationship with him that Ms Markle should be subjected to such a storm. He knows commentators will say this is 'the price she has to pay' and that 'this is all part of the game'. He strongly disagrees. This is not a game – it is her life and his.

While the prince's statement helped to calm the hysteria, his formal confirmation that Meghan was indeed his girlfriend meant that all media outlets, not just the British tabloids, now saw Meghan as a possible royal bride. Picture editors around the world scoured their back catalogues for shots of the latest royal-in-waiting. A photograph of her modelling a wedding dress for a scene from *Suits* was manna from heaven.

Her now official proximity to the Royal Family became the new agenda, several newspapers wrongly reporting that Meghan had helped Harry to celebrate his thirty-second birthday at Balmoral, and that during her time in the Scottish Highlands she had even met with Prince Charles, who found her 'charming'.

Though the story was incorrect, they were on the right scent. Meghan was indeed now an accepted part of the royal furniture – as senior journalist Richard Kay, who had been a close friend of Diana's, discovered when, on 10 November 2016, he popped out of his office to buy a sandwich for lunch.

As he strolled down a busy Kensington High Street, he could scarcely believe his eyes when he spotted Meghan walking along the road, holding two bags filled with produce from the Whole Foods Market store.

He followed her back to Kensington Palace and saw her waved through security into the grounds. It was an obvious sign that the relationship between the actor and the then fifth in line to the throne was 'serious'. Kay observed: 'The timing of Miss Markle's visit is hugely significant, not least because it appears she was in the UK when Harry publicly declared his love for her.'

What was even more telling was the fact that Meghan had spent only two days with Harry before flying back to Toronto to resume the filming of *Suits*. Now that *was* commitment, having taken the trouble to see her boyfriend before he embarked on an official two-week tour of the Caribbean.

On the tour, he would be representing the Queen at independence anniversary celebrations in Barbados, Guyana and Antigua. It was a test of his mettle – and he knew full well that his grandmother would be monitoring his progress, as it was one of his first overseas tours undertaken on her behalf. It would prove to be of more import than he realized at the time.

Among many other activities, he took an AIDS test with superstar Rihanna in Barbados, observed a minute's silence for Fidel Castro in St Vincent, and played cricket in St Lucia.

Harry managed to remain cool when, at a reception for 300 guests, Antiguan Prime Minister Gaston Browne suggested that he and Meghan should return to the island for their honeymoon. 'I believe we are expecting a new princess soon. I want you to know that you are very welcome to come on your honeymoon here,' he was reported to have said. Harry was later introduced to a group of scantily clad models with the words: 'Whatever is done here, stays here. So don't worry.' The prince said nothing, but afterwards told aides he found the incident 'pretty distasteful'.

Not that Meghan was worried. He was in constant touch with her via Skype, reporting back on the progress of his solo visit. He was given full marks by the trailing media, royal editor Camilla Tominey commenting: 'With his American girlfriend Meghan Markle putting a spring in his step, it's fair to say Prince Harry has rarely been on better form.

'Comfortable in his own skin and completely at ease with the spotlight being shone on his official duties as the Queen's representative overseas, he has truly come of age.'

Though the attendant media were assured that the prince was heading back to London, it was a red herring. Instead, Harry took a 1,700-mile detour to spend a few precious hours holed up in Meghan's rented house in Toronto. Her followers had the first clue that Harry was on his way when Meghan posted a picture of herself wearing a necklace featuring the letters 'M' and 'H', as well as a snap of her beagle, Guy, in his Union Flag jumper. For the first time, a grand royal passion was being played out before the eyes of the world on social media. Not that such access would last for long.

Within forty-eight hours the prince was flying back to London. He had just enough time to take a shower before he was on parade in the City of London, answering phones and joking with callers for an annual charity fundraiser, where his charity Sentebale was a recipient.

Harry then joined his friends for a shooting weekend at Oettingen Castle in Bavaria, Germany, before he was reunited with Meghan, who came for a week-long stay at Nottingham Cottage in early December.

They bought their first Christmas tree together, the staff at the Battersea garden centre, Pines and Needles, giving them a bunch of mistletoe for good luck. For the most part they managed to elude the watchful paparazzi, the couple wearing matching blue beanie hats to obscure their faces. They walked through the theatre district, where they saw the slapstick comedy *Peter Pan Goes Wrong* and sometime later the brilliantly staged *The Curious Incident of the Dog in the Night-Time*, based on Mark Haddon's novel.

Much as they would have liked to spend Christmas together, royal tradition put a stop to their plans. Every year the extended Royal Family gathers at Sandringham, the Queen's 20,000-acre estate in Norfolk. Girlfriends and boyfriends are excluded. By contrast, Meghan spent her holidays enjoying the warmer climes of Hollywood where she was reunited with her mother and enjoyed Christmas with her friend Benita Litt and her family.

The couple did, however, see in the New Year together at Nottingham Cottage, before flying on 2 January to the remote town of Tromsø in northern Norway, on the edge of the Arctic Circle, to see the dazzling and awe-inspiring aurora borealis, or Northern Lights. Her love of adventure, being happy to sleep under the stars, canvas or, this time, in a cabin with a wood-fired stove, delighted Harry, who was thrilled that he had at last found a mate who shared his love of the great outdoors.

On their return in early January, Meghan finally had the chance to meet with Kate at the Cambridges' apartment, 1a Clock Court at Kensington Palace. She was also introduced to three-year-old Prince George and Princess Charlotte, who was then twenty months old. During their brief encounter, she presented Kate, who had celebrated her thirty-fifth birthday the day before, on 9 January, with a small but thoughtful gift, a soft leather Smythson notebook. Meghan, who, according to biographer Omid Scobie, had previously met William for a cup of tea in early November 2016, days after their romance had hit the headlines, was assured by Kate that she was always ready to help and advise in this bizarre new world in which Meghan found herself. Harry was desperate for Meghan and his sister-in-law to bond, a tall order given their contrasting careers and social backgrounds. Like the Queen, Kate offered friendliness but not friendship. Her cool and somewhat reserved nature would have profound consequences. Even though Meghan was still on the periphery of the Royal Family, they and others had to anticipate the future. In his mind, *Suits* creator Aaron Korsh decided that Meghan's private life now overshadowed her character Rachel Zane. For her sake it was best to write her out of the hit series. As he later told the BBC: 'I had a decision to make because I didn't want to intrude and ask her: "Hey, what's going on and what are you going to do?" So, collectively with the writers, we decided to take a gamble that these two people were in love and it was going to work out.' As Harry's previous actor girlfriend Cressida Bonas had discovered, there was a high professional price to pay for dating a prince. If Harry and Meghan's relationship had petered out, Meghan would have been out of work. It was a high-stakes romance with many unintended consequences.

Indeed, for how much longer could a potential princess be seen cuddling up to her screen lover, Patrick J. Adams, her hand placed suggestively on his knee? When Patrick was asked by a fan what it was like 'making out on screen with a potential future English princess', he replied, deadpan, 'The same as it was before she was a potential future princess.'

That said, both Meghan and Patrick had by now appeared in more than a hundred episodes of the hit show. As far as he was concerned, it was time to hang up his role on *Suits*. Even if Meghan had felt the same way, her personal life took this professional decision out of her hands.

As Patrick later told *The Hollywood Reporter*: 'There was this natural sense that we both knew that the time had come for both of us. It went unspoken and we just enjoyed the hell out of the last few episodes that we got to shoot. We both knew that we wouldn't be coming back. It made every one of our scenes that much more special. We had a great time. We could laugh through it. Even the things that might have frustrated us about the show, they became things that we could have a good laugh about and compare notes on just how crazy this thing had become.'

For as long as she was in *Suits*, the producers were ready and willing to use her royal connections and new-found celebrity – in February 2017 she was ranked fourth in a list of the most eligible dinner guests by *Tatler* magazine – to boost ratings. One trailer promoted the characters as 'almost royalty', while another featured a scene of Meghan in a wedding dress from a previous season.

Others had the same idea. A gritty British crime movie *Anti-Social*, originally released in 2015, was repackaged as a 'special edition' and featured Meghan's name prominently in the publicity. In the movie she played fashion model Kirsten and was seen emerging from a shower dressed in a towel, drinking champagne and kissing an on-screen lover. A number of Trevor Engelson's friends, who knew that he had always been reluctant to cast Meghan in his productions, now teased him mercilessly, telling the Hollywood producer that he could have made a fortune repackaging his movies if Meghan had featured in the original. 'He got a lot of flak,' a friend told me.

Meghan herself had some serious commercial decisions to make. Her blog, The Tig, had meant the world to her. She had watched it grow from a modest one-woman show to a brand that represented her very civilized, refined, yet adventurous view of life. It was aspirational, frothily feminine, but always with a serious point, be it about gender equality or human rights. The Tig was, as she always said, the little engine that could. Now she realized that her blog couldn't go on as it had in the past as long as she remained within the royal orbit. Her pictures, comments, recommendations and thoughts would be taken out of context and associated with Prince Harry or the Royal Family or both. She was no longer Meghan the blogger, she was one-half of a partnership where the man she wanted to spend the rest of her life with was fifth (now sixth) in line to the throne. Different rules applied.

For all her possible protestations and doubts, she conceded that if she was going to go forward with the prince, she would have to severely modify the contents of The Tig. Or put the little engine permanently into the sidings.

This was to be her first major reality check. If matters became more formal, in the shape of an engagement ring, then she would have to rethink the entire existence of her online identity. A friend said, 'She's trying to figure out how to scale back what she puts out there about her life, including her social media and website. If she had to leave all that she's doing for the relationship to work, she would without hesitation.'

But it was much harder than it sounded. In January 2017, for instance, with her global ambassador hat on, she flew to India on behalf of World Vision Canada. The five-day visit was intended to focus on child poverty and specifically on why teenage girls from slum communities dropped out of school. The answer partly lay in the fact that when girls begin menstruating there are no facilities in the local schools to help them cope with this perfectly natural change in their bodies. Ashamed, they stay at home and miss out on their education. It is a hidden issue, one which Meghan felt could be easily solved with the proper use of resources. She felt comfortable taking on these issues, telling an audience in Atlanta before she left that humanitarian work made her life feel more 'balanced'. Her new-found international celebrity enabled her views to find a wider audience, her essay on her visit to Delhi and Mumbai to discover why periods affected the potential of millions of teenage girls appearing in the March edition of *Time* magazine.

Her humanitarian work, though, was a ticklish issue. While the palace may not have objected in principle to the causes she espoused, they were not undertaken under the umbrella of the Royal Family. In short, she was acting as a freelance operation within the corporate royal 'firm'. She had already articulated her vision of service in an article in The Tig, where she avowed: 'I've never wanted to be a lady who lunches – I've always wanted to be a woman who works. And this type of work is what feeds my soul and fuels my purpose.'

There was bound to be a conflict. In her own mind, Meghan had to square the intellectual and emotional circle. The Tig was designed to empower women and encourage gender equality. Yet she accepted that the mushrooming interest in her blog and Instagram had little to do with her work and was more due to the fact that she was dating a man who occupied a position of authority and influence simply by dint of birth. The irony was not lost on the actor, who realized that she was now a walking paradox. Her romance with the prince had given her a megaphone with which to articulate the issues she held dear.

As she pondered the future of her online community, Meghan was given a classic lesson about life in the royal goldfish bowl. In early March, the couple made their separate ways to Jamaica for the three-day wedding festivities of Harry's close friend Tom 'Skippy' Inskip and the Hon. Lara Hughes-Young.

Harry met Meghan at the airport and drove her to the exclusive Round Hill Hotel at Montego Bay, where they were booked into a $7,000-a-night villa. They changed into their swimwear, Harry in a pair of green swim trunks, Meghan into a dark-blue bikini topped off with her trademark white fedora, and kissed and cuddled as they paddled in the warm Caribbean water. Suddenly Harry's mood turned dark. It was nothing to do with Meghan. It was the presence of paparazzi photographers, their long lenses focused on the couple. Even Meghan's consoling arm around his shoulders did little to calm him down. In her eyes it wasn't the worst thing that could happen. Until recently photographers had been her friends. After all, it was a magazine shot of Meghan in the silver liquid-metal dress designed by Misha Nonoo that had first caught Harry's eye. The prince, however, saw things very differently.

He had and has a visceral loathing of photographers, particularly the freelance paparazzi whose behaviour in taking pictures of his mother as she lay dying in a Paris underpass he could never forgive nor forget. His policy is of total war, aggressively using the law of privacy to stop the publication of illicitly taken images. On this occasion he spoke to the palace and effectively ordered them to use every means possible to prevent publication. He gained a partial victory. Although the British media did not publish the offending pictures, several European magazines as well as websites had no such qualms. It was the first in a series of confrontations as the prince tried to protect both his privacy and that of his girlfriend.

The day after his media spat, Harry was one of fourteen ushers for the Hughes-Young–Inskip wedding in the Hopewell Baptist Church. He was in a jauntier mood while Meghan, who wore a $2,000 floral-patterned Erdem dress, was noticeably affectionate and loving throughout the ceremony.

Pastor Conrad Thomas, who conducted the service, said afterwards: 'Harry and Meghan held hands and I will never forget their radiant smiles. They looked so happy together. I told him, "It's your turn next, Sir."'

At the evening reception, guests, including the Duchess of York and her daughter Princess Eugenie, feasted on jerk chicken and lobster washed down with rum cocktails and champagne. Unfortunately, Harry knocked over some drinks as he did a 'Michael Jackson moonwalk' on the dance floor.

'He was going backwards as "Billie Jean" blared out when he banged into a waitress carrying a tray of drinks and sent them flying,' said an onlooker. 'Harry gasped, looked shocked and put his hands on the waitress's shoulders and apologized.'

It was a temporary blip in an evening of drink, dancing and jollity, Meghan and Harry on the dance floor or in each other's arms – or both. Love was definitely in the air.

After the raucous party, Harry took Meghan to the exclusive Caves Hotel in Negril for three precious days alone. Afterwards, their long-distance commute continued, Meghan flying back to Toronto but returning to London a week later. Her absences from Canada were now so frequent that she had to hire a dog-sitter to look after Bogart and Guy. In between *Suits*, The Tig, social media, a royal romance and charity work, something had to give. Her baby, The Tig, paid the price. In early April 2017, she said a sad farewell to her thousands of Tig followers: 'After close to three beautiful years on this adventure with you, it's time to say goodbye to The Tig,' she wrote. 'What began as a passion project (my little engine that could) evolved into an amazing community of inspiration, support, fun and frivolity. Keep finding those Tig moments of discovery, keep laughing and taking risks, and keep being "the change you wish to see in the world".'

Meghan's relationship with Harry was becoming all-consuming. No sooner had she shut down her blog than he arrived to spend Easter with her. He had other reasons for being in Toronto. In September, the Invictus Games were due to take place in the city, and he had many meetings to attend and numerous plans to go through. Top of the list on his personal agenda was a firm decision for Meghan to be by his side at some point during the Games.

Veteran reporter Phil Dampier quoted a royal source as saying: 'Harry wants everything out in the open and for the days of skulking around avoiding photographers to be over. He wants to show Meghan off as his future wife. The Games, which he has put his heart and soul into, will be the perfect platform to do that.' Dampier was on the money.

At long last their unconventional long-distance romance assumed familiar royal contours. Like so many girlfriends and wives in the lives of assorted princes, she ventured to watch Harry play polo, this time at Coworth Park in Berkshire on 6 May. It is something of a royal rite of passage. Some of the best – and most affectionate – photographs ever taken of Princess Diana were when she attended polo matches involving Prince Charles. Kate Middleton, too, was always keenly on point when Prince William got in the saddle. It was no different when Meghan, who was accompanied by Mark Dyer and his wife Amanda, arrived at the ground. She dutifully clapped and smiled as she followed the back and forth of this most un-spectator-friendly of sports. Fellow attendees at the charity match, which raised funds for Sentebale and another of Harry's charities, WellChild, included Oscar-winning actor Eddie Redmayne, former ballerina Darcey Bussell and actor Matt Smith, who played Prince Philip in the first two seasons of the hit Netflix series *The Crown*. The crowning joy, as far as the serried ranks of photographers were concerned, would be to see the prince kiss his girlfriend.

Harry made them all wait. It was the following day, after playing in a match with Prince William, when Harry gave the cameramen what they wanted – he kissed Meghan in the car park. Game on.

Once again Meghan flew home, only to return just a week later to attend Pippa Middleton's wedding to financier James Matthews on 20 May. So as not to overshadow the bride's big day, Meghan stayed away from the wedding ceremony at St Mark's Church in the village of Englefield, Berkshire. After the service, Harry picked her up from nearby lodgings that they had rented and then took her to the reception at the Middleton family home in the village of Bucklebury.

The evidence had been piling up all year and by now it was clear that it was only a matter of time before she was walking down the aisle herself. In fact, Harry was nursing a secret. Earlier in May, during a visit to Botswana as patron of the Rhino Conservation, he had picked out conflict-free diamonds for the engagement ring he had quietly helped to design.

While he kept his future plans close to his chest, the world could see which way the wind was blowing. When Meghan attended a *Suits* convention in Austin, Texas, she dodged questions about her future, but most of her fans reluctantly conceded that this season would probably be her last. She did admit, though, that the sex scenes she had done in the past now seemed 'weird'.

A couple of weeks later, in mid-July, Meghan opened the door of her Toronto home and greeted Sam Kashner, the bestselling biographer of *Furious Love* – his dissection of another power couple, actors Richard Burton and Elizabeth Taylor. From the moment he arrived at her front door, bookies no longer needed to take bets on a royal marriage. The bespectacled scribe was there on behalf of *Vanity Fair* magazine, not only to savour the pasta she had bought specially from the fashionable Italian deli Terroni's, but also to imbibe her life.

It was an extraordinary development. Traditionally, royal brides-to-be are Sphinx-like, blushing furiously, ducking away from photographers, smiling politely but not saying a word.

It is the uniting thread that links Lady Diana Spencer, Sarah Ferguson, Sophie Rhys-Jones and Kate Middleton. They know the consequences of opening their mouths. When Diana's sister Sarah was dating Prince Charles, she was cast into the outer darkness the moment she chatted to royal correspondent James Whitaker about her relationship.

For Meghan to be giving an interview before any engagement announcement was a royal first, all the more so as she would not have gone ahead without the agreement of Prince Harry, his private secretary Edward Lane Fox and his communications secretary Jason Knauf. Nor was she making anodyne remarks about fashion and *Suits* with the odd aside about her royal romance. No, Meghan was telling her true story – in her own words. She was emphatic, no dithering around the issue.

'We're a couple,' she told Kashner. 'We're in love. I'm sure that there will be a time when we will have to come forward and present ourselves and have stories to tell, but I hope what people will understand is that this is our time. This is for us.

'It's part of what makes it so special, that it's just ours. But we're happy – personally I love a great love story.'

Just so he got the point, she emphasized, 'We're two people who are really happy and in love.'

There was one troubling sentence amid the startlingly open declaration of love and commitment. 'I'm still the same person that I am and I've never defined myself by my relationship.' Perhaps not in the past. But certainly in her future. *Vanity Fair* would not have given her a prized front-cover photograph accompanied by the bold-face headline 'She's Just Wild About Harry!' if she had been simply an actor on a mid-range cable TV drama. The clue was in the title. His title. Whether or not she wanted to embrace the idea, in the future her considerable influence, her ability to make the change, would rest on something that goes against some of her core beliefs, namely women gaining power not through their own endeavours, but because of whom they marry.

The 'Meghan Paradox' was a conundrum to ponder for another day. For the moment she was going where the internet signal was weak, Botswana, as she and Harry celebrated her thirty-sixth birthday. The prince was so happy to be returning to his second home that he even gave a thumbs-up to waiting photographers when he was reunited with Meghan at the airport. His gesture sent the media rumour mill churning. As journalists did not know that Meghan and Harry had already visited Botswana, and as William had proposed to Kate in Kenya in 2010, the obvious conclusion was that, during this trip, Harry would get down on one knee. The holiday was romantic enough, the couple once again staying at the Meno a Kwena camp before driving their hire car on the eight-hour journey to Victoria Falls, one of the natural wonders of the world.

During their visit they stayed at the privately owned Tongabezi Lodge by the Zambezi River, where they were enticed with sunset cruises, romantic sampan (a flat-bottomed boat) dinners and early-morning game drives. They even had their own valet to cater for their every whim.

At the end of the holiday, though speculation was at fever pitch about a royal engagement, Meghan made herself scarce when Princes William and Harry, together with the Duchess of Cambridge, made an important pilgrimage. On 30 August, the day before the twentieth anniversary of their mother's fatal car crash in Paris, William, Harry and the Duchess of Cambridge marked the occasion with a visit to the White Garden at Kensington Palace, which had been specially planted with her favourite flowers. They then met representatives of charities supported by the late princess.

Amidst the growing drumbeat of marital speculation, other voices urged caution. His friend Tom 'Skippy' Inskip told him bluntly that it seemed he was rushing into marriage. 'Give it time,' was his refrain, a sentiment that found a significant chorus when his brother William chimed in. He had famously wooed and won his bride after a courtship lasting around eight years. He and Kate had lived together – with the Queen's implicit permission – before they had formally tied the knot. William knew Harry's character well, aware that he was instinctive, impatient and headstrong, being led by his heart rather than his head. These qualities, though they endeared him to the public, were not ideal when it came to choosing a royal bride, especially one who clearly had little basic understanding of the workings of the monarchy. Did she realize what she was letting herself in for? Did he?

William told him: 'Don't feel you have to rush this. Take as much time as you need to get to know this girl.' Those words 'this girl' rankled with Harry, who felt he was being patronized and that his girlfriend, who was on the verge of her thirty-sixth birthday, was being diminished. This conversation was pivotal in the brothers' relationship, William's words of caution interpreted by his younger sibling as snobbish and admonishing. As royal correspondent Emily Andrews noted: 'He (William) just wanted to stress that becoming part of the Royal Family is a massive undertaking, and the pressure and scrutiny is unrelenting. Was Meghan the right one?' After all, he argued, the family knew next to nothing about her background, her intentions or her character. The media criticism of Meghan by her half-sister and pictures of her now retired father, who seemed to be living as a recluse in the sleepy Mexican resort of Rosarito, hardly inspired confidence.

Sensitive to criticism or advice, Harry brooded. As far as he was concerned, he wanted endorsement and support from his brother – similar to that which he had offered during William's endless courtship with Kate Middleton. Harry had embraced Kate when she was on the outside looking in – now it was William's turn to repay that trust. That he failed to do so rankled with Harry. It was the beginning of a rift that would be characterized as the battle of the brothers. On the surface, though, the two princes presented a united front, as William, in spite of his misgivings, issued his own formal statement on 27 November 2016 where he stood four-square with Harry: 'The Duke of Cambridge absolutely understands the situation concerning privacy and supports the need for Prince Harry to support those closest to him.'

In any case, the marital train was about to leave the station. Harry had the ring prepared – all he had to do now was introduce his future bride formally to the world. What better occasion than the Invictus Games, which began in her adopted city, Toronto, on 23 September. Harry's own venture had grown into a mini-Olympics featuring 550 competitors from seventeen countries taking part in twelve sports. It was hardly surprising that he chose that week for Meghan to make her debut on the world stage as a potential royal bride.

Just before the Games began, Harry visited the set of *Suits* with Meghan, who introduced him to her co-stars, the scriptwriters and the crew. 'Meghan showed him around set. Everyone was so excited. He's incredibly supportive of her work,' a member of the cast was quoted as telling *Hello* magazine. During the run-up to the Games, he also took the time to visit the Toronto Centre for Addiction and Mental Health, which his mother had toured twenty-six years before when it was known as the Addiction Research Foundation.

At the opening ceremony in the Air Canada Centre, Harry sat with America's First Lady Melania Trump, Canadian Prime Minister Justin Trudeau and Ukraine's President Petro Poroshenko. As was widely anticipated, Meghan was in the crowd accompanied by her friend, Canadian-born Markus Anderson, who had previously been so instrumental in helping to arrange Meghan and Harry's first date. Wearing a carefully chosen midi dress by Aritzia and with a matching burgundy leather jacket by Mackage slung over her shoulders, Meghan seemed comfortable and relaxed. Though she was not in the VIP section, the presence of a Scotland Yard bodyguard sitting near her was a sign that her days on the outside were numbered.

She listened intently as Harry told the audience of competitors, their friends and families, 'You are all winners and don't forget that you are proving to the world that anything is possible.'

As Toronto sweltered in a heatwave with temperatures nudging 35°C (95°F), the burning question was: when would they be seen together?

Two days after the opening ceremony, a posse of photographers who were snapping the wheelchair tennis match between Australia and New Zealand were approached by a Kensington Palace press officer.

Without mentioning Harry or Meghan by name, she whispered to them, 'When they arrive, stay in your seats and don't move out of them. If you do they will leave.'

A few minutes later the waiting press pack watched with eyes bulging as, hand in hand, Meghan and Harry walked in to Nathan Phillips Square and sat down at the side of the court. In the choreography of their romance, this was a showstopper. They laughed and joked, stroked each other's arms, whispered sweet nothings, and chatted to the families and friends of the competitors. When Meghan was handed a bottle of water, Harry advised her to put it on the floor and not drink it in view of the cameras. Pictures of celebrities drinking can look awkward and clumsy.

Meghan had her own agenda. Instinctively attuned to the semiology of fashion, it was entirely deliberate that she teamed her ripped blue jeans with a loose-fitting shirt designed by her great friend Misha Nonoo called 'the husband shirt'. Naturally, the white shirt, which Meghan had once described on her blog as 'my very favourite button-down', sold out within minutes. That her handbag was made by the ethical brand Everlane also sent out a message: what she wore mattered.

The enthusiastic crowd enjoyed another sideshow with the arrival of former US President Barack Obama, along with his erstwhile Vice President (now President) Joe Biden and his wife Jill. The dignitaries were mobbed by cheering spectators as word spread of their arrival. Harry and his American guests looked totally relaxed as they cracked jokes and posed for selfies with members of the crowd.

During his whistle-stop visit to the city, Mr Obama joined Harry at a city-centre hotel where a suite of rooms had been rigged up into a makeshift radio studio. The prince conducted a twenty-minute interview with the former president about life after the White House, their relaxed chat becoming the centrepiece of Harry's debut as a guest presenter on BBC Radio Four's *Today* programme in late December.

As the event came to an end, Harry told the cheering crowd, 'You have delivered the biggest Invictus Games yet, with the most incredible atmosphere, making our competitors feel like the stars they are.'

At the closing ceremony, Harry gave Meghan a kiss on the cheek as they watched Kelly Clarkson, Bryan Adams and legendary rocker Bruce Springsteen play the Games out. Standing beside them in the VIP enclosure was Meghan's mother, Doria Ragland, who had flown in from Los Angeles to see her daughter and her boyfriend. Her presence was a further sign, if any were needed, that it was time to dust off the morning suit.

12

Tea With Her Majesty

It was the most important audition of Meghan's life. No rehearsal, no script, no second takes. This was live and improvised. When she was driven through the gates of Buckingham Palace on an overcast, drizzly Thursday in October 2017 in a black Ford Galaxy with darkened windows, the actor was about to give the performance of her career. Even though she has often said that she is not a woman who gets nervous, she could be forgiven for being a tad dry-mouthed. She was about to meet the Queen for afternoon tea. Gulp. Of course she had Prince Harry by her side, holding her hand, telling her it would be fine, just be yourself. Still, it was tea with the Queen of England.

There was a touch of cloak and dagger about the affair, which did little to quell the nerves. The Ford Galaxy nosed in so close to the palace's entrance that Harry, Meghan and their Scotland Yard bodyguard were able to slip inside unnoticed.

They were then escorted along the seeming miles of red carpet to the Queen's private sitting room that overlooks the palace gardens by Constitution Hill. So discreetly did they arrive and depart that even senior palace servants were unaware of their visit until a few days later.

If truth be told, Meghan had quietly anticipated this moment. A few months before she had taken a secret excursion to Rose Tree Cottage, a little slice of England nestling in Pasadena in the suburbs of Los Angeles. It sells a plethora of British goodies, but the centrepiece of the emporium, owned by Mary and Edmund Fry, is the serving of afternoon tea. Meghan had visited several times, not only to buy English gifts but also to take afternoon tea. Perhaps there had been just a little rehearsing, after all.

In truth, this was not the first time that she had seen the Monarch in person. She had enjoyed a brief and unexpected meeting at Royal Lodge, the Duke of York's home on the Windsor Great Park estate. She and Harry were visiting Princess Eugenie for lunch when the Queen decided to drop in after the morning church service. Over the years the Royal Lodge has seen some embarrassing encounters between the Sovereign and assorted boyfriends and girlfriends. On one occasion Princess Margaret's lover, Roddy Llewellyn, walked into the nursery dressed in just a shirt and underwear, looking for the nanny to sew a button on his shirt. Instead, he came face-to-face with the Queen. He apologized before making a rapid retreat. During his courtship with Princess Margaret, photographer Antony Armstrong-Jones would often hide away in a bedroom when her sister visited rather than endure a regal conversation. The previous American to capture a royal heart, Wallis Simpson, recalled that when she met the Duke and Duchess of York (the future King George VI and Queen Elizabeth), who were then living at Royal Lodge, the ducal couple were keen on the King's new American interest, a Buick estate wagon, but not his other American passion, that is to say herself.

Then there was the technical difficulty of the curtsy to negotiate. Prior to her first encounter with the future King Edward VIII during a weekend house party at Melton Mowbray in 1931, while nursing a heavy cold Wallis Simpson practised the respectful manoeuvre in a swaying rail coach on the way there by train. More than eighty-five years later, Meghan had a similar experience, this time learning the technique in the driveway outside the Royal Lodge. Initially, she was nonplussed when Harry had said she had to curtsy, in private and indoors. She simply thought that the act was a public event for the cameras, part of the arcane theatre of royalty. Fergie, the Duchess of York, quickly disavowed her of that notion as she quickly demonstrated the finer points of paying obeisance to the Queen. Meghan's acting smarts paid off, the future royal dropping a perfect deep curtsy before engaging the Queen in polite conversation for a few minutes.

Her second meeting was rather more important. She flew over from Toronto, where she was filming the final episodes of *Suits*, specially for the royal audience – and tea for three. The offering of thinly sliced sandwiches of cucumber and egg mayonnaise, the selection of small scones and cakes, and Her Majesty's own Queen Mary blend of tea, with the option of coffee for the American visitor, tells only part of the story.

Afternoon tea is a chance for the Queen to catch up on the Upstairs gossip from her ladies-in-waiting, the Downstairs chatter from her senior servants, and to see members of her family. In times past, Princess Diana – when she hadn't brought the boys with her, which wasn't often – used these informal occasions to tackle the Queen over her eldest son's affair with Camilla Parker Bowles. As she sipped her tea, the princess was looking for sympathy. Vainly, as it turned out. The topic was much too emotionally unsavoury for her regal mother-in-law, so the matter was dropped.

Though the encounter with Ms Markle and Prince Harry was much less fraught, there was still an initial air of tension about the occasion. This was perhaps inevitable. As fifth in line to the throne (he is now sixth), the prince, under the 2013 Succession to the Crown Act, had to obtain his grandmother's formal permission to marry.

For centuries the royal Houses of Europe have been defined by bloodline and breeding. In Queen Victoria's day, English princes and princesses could only marry their German counterparts. That changed during the First World War when, in 1917, George V not only changed the family name to Windsor, but also allowed his offspring to marry English aristocrats. Down the decades even this edict has been considerably diluted.

For the most part, the Queen's brood have married commoners. An Olympic horseman, an equerry, a photographer, the daughter of the royal polo manager and a public relations executive have all joined the Royal Family without a title between them. Only Lady Diana Spencer was from a traditionally aristocratic family. And look where that got them. The House of Windsor has been sustained by commoners – not by blue bloods. In fact the same could be said of most of the royal Houses of Europe. And while divorce had long been a sticking point for the royals, Harry's own father had knocked that particular issue on the head when he married Camilla Parker Bowles.

Any possible uncertainty about the outcome of this meeting lay not with Meghan, but with the man she wanted to marry. He was the one who had been, if not on trial, then under close scrutiny.

If he had come to see his granny a few years earlier, when he had an unenviable reputation as an angry drunk with poor judgement, it would have been doubtful that the Queen would have agreed to him marrying a divorced American actor. 'It would have been a grim, unhappy confrontation,' a former senior royal official told me. What a difference a decade makes. It seemed to the Sovereign and her advisers that Harry's common touch combined with his maturity had, alongside the popular union between Prince William and Kate Middleton, secured the future of the monarchy. Harry's impeccable behaviour in 2016, when he represented the Queen in the Caribbean, and his commitment to the Invictus Games had been shrewdly watched and assessed by the Sovereign. As a courtier told me: 'The Queen trusts her grandsons. She has confidence in them in a way that she never has had with her eldest son. They have really established themselves as being in touch with the public. William and Harry have star quality, believable and authentic heirs to the monarchy.'

The final seal of approval came from the Queen's dogs – Willow, her remaining corgi, and dorgis Vulcan and Candy. These normally irascible breeds were friendly and welcoming when Meghan entered the Queen's sitting room. As Prince Harry said, somewhat ruefully, 'I've spent the last thirty-three years being barked at; this one walks in, absolutely nothing.' They lay at her feet and wagged their tails. 'Very sweet,' Meghan later told interviewer Mishal Husain.

During their seventy-minute meeting, which overran by ten minutes, Meghan witnessed at first hand the genuine respect and love that Harry feels for his grandmother. 'She's an incredible woman,' she said afterwards. It was clear, too, that the Queen was delighted that her grandson, so often troubled and out of sorts with life, had found a mate who seemed to have grounded him.

Amid a flurry of barks and with a final curtsy, Harry and Meghan bade their farewells, swiftly leaving the palace before the royal gossip factory was able to get into gear. Job done.

Not quite. Meghan still had to speak to her elusive father and bring him up to speed. Since his retirement, Tom Senior had become more reclusive, heading to Mexico where he had bought an apartment in the popular beach town of Rosarito, 10 miles south of the American border. He changed his mobile phones frequently and even moved on from one apartment because the widow of the recently deceased owner was becoming 'too friendly'.

When she finally reached her father, she told him her news, warning him that the media would try to speak with him when the engagement was announced. He had already spoken with Prince Harry, so he knew what was on the horizon. At some point, Harry had asked the voice at the other end of the phone for permission to marry his daughter. Not quite as traditional as tea with the Queen had been, but then there was not much about this romance that conformed to the conventional royal playbook. As Tom Senior later told *Good Morning Britain*: 'I said, "You're a gentleman. Promise me you'll never raise your hand against my daughter and of course I give you my permission."'

❈

With both families alerted, it was time for the happy couple to take a public bow, their engagement announced at 10 a.m. on Monday 27 November 2017. The news was released from Clarence House, the home of Prince Charles and the Duchess of Cornwall, Harry's father expressing his 'delight' at the engagement. The bulletin continued: 'His Royal Highness and Ms Markle became engaged in London earlier this month. Prince Harry has informed Her Majesty the Queen and other close members of his family. Prince Harry has also sought and received the blessing of Ms Markle's parents.'

Within minutes, dozens of reporters, photographers and TV crews assembled outside Kensington Palace for a photocall at the

Sunken Garden. At two in the afternoon, on a bitterly cold, windy day, the happy couple emerged and walked arm in arm down to the side of the pond. Harry looked more nervous than his bride, Meghan stroking his arm reassuringly. They answered a couple of shouted questions, the prince telling the throng that he knew she was the one the first time they met and describing himself as 'thrilled, over the moon'. Meghan smiled and said they were 'so very happy'.

As they walked away, Meghan rubbed his back as if to say 'well done', the couple returning to the palace, arms linked, for a twenty-minute interview with BBC reporter and campaigner, Mishal Husain. The forty-four-year-old mother of three, who had been named Broadcaster of the Year at the 2015 London Press Club Awards, first caught Meghan's eye for her campaign to win equal pay for women working at the BBC, and she and Harry hand-picked her to undertake their engagement interview.

The televised conversation began with the couple describing the moment the prince proposed, saying that they were in Nottingham Cottage, roasting a chicken, his favourite dish, when he got down on one knee and asked her to marry him. 'Just an amazing surprise, it was so sweet and natural and very romantic,' said Meghan, who confessed that she said 'Yes' before he had finished the proposal. They recalled that they had met one another through a mutual friend on a blind date in July 2016, and after two back-to-back meetings Meghan had agreed to join him on a safari holiday in Botswana. At the time Harry had never heard of *Suits* or the Californian actor and she admitted that she didn't have much of an idea about Harry.

This had helped rather than hindered the development of their love affair. As Meghan observed: 'Everything that I've learned about him I learned through him as opposed to having grown up around different news stories or tabloids or whatever else. Anything I learned about him and his family was what he would share with me and vice versa. So for both of us it was just a really authentic and organic way to get to know each other.' It helped to cushion the shock they both experienced with the level of media interest once the romance became public.

Nurturing their relationship had been their priority, the couple describing how they had made a promise from the start to make their long-distance relationship work. 'It was just a choice, right,' said Meghan. 'I think that very early on, when we realized we were going to commit to each other, we knew we had to invest the time and the energy and whatever it took to make that happen.'

It helped to navigate the bumps in the road that virtually from the start the couple saw themselves as a 'team' with a shared vision of how they wanted to make a positive difference in society. Their mutual commitment was, Meghan observed, 'what got date two in the books'.

She recalled: 'One of the first things we started talking about when we met, just the different things that we wanted to do in the world and how passionate we were about seeing change.'

As with his brother's engagement interview, the spirit of their late mother hovered over the occasion. On that November day in 2010, the focus was on Diana's own engagement ring, which William had carefully carried with him before he proposed to Kate Middleton during a holiday in Kenya. This time, small diamonds from Diana's jewellery collection decorated Meghan's engagement ring, which was dominated by a conflict-free diamond from Botswana, the country where they fell in love. They were incorporated into Harry's design so that his mother would be there to 'join us on this crazy journey'.

Just as William had said in his own engagement interview, Harry too felt Diana's absence on these special days. The prince was clear about how she would have responded to her American daughter-in-law. 'They'd be thick as thieves, without question; I think she would be over the moon, jumping up and down – you know, so excited for me.'

Certainly there was a real sense of destiny for Harry about his romance with Meghan. As he admitted: 'The fact that I fell in love with Meghan so incredibly quickly was sort of confirmation to me that everything – all the stars were aligned – everything was just perfect. It was this beautiful woman just sort of literally tripped and fell into my life, I fell into her life.' Meghan's engagement interview was worlds away from the shy, blushing days of Lady Diana Spencer and Prince Charles, and his comment 'whatever loves means', which skewered his romantic reputation forever. Different, too, from the more formal and conventional affair when Prince William and Kate Middleton faced the cameras. Then a visibly, and understandably, nervous Kate deferred to William in her responses. Not this time. Meghan was warm, affectionate and supportive, more at ease with the media than her royal fiancé. 'A breath of fresh air' was a common view.

The rapturous reception of the news of the engagement suggested that this indeed was a popular match and that the country, beset by Brexit angst, still loved a fairy-tale royal romance. Naturally the Queen and Prince Philip were 'delighted', while the Duchess of Cornwall described Meghan as a 'star'. 'America's loss is our gain,' she said.

The then Prime Minister Theresa May commented that the engagement marked a 'time of huge celebration and excitement', while Barack and Michelle Obama wished them 'a lifetime of joy and happiness together'. Meghan's parents said they were 'incredibly happy' for their daughter, while her TV father from *Suits*, actor Wendell Pierce, gave Harry his blessing. The king of Twitter, President Trump, however, remained silent about the first American since 1937 to marry into the Royal Family.

As for her screen lover Patrick J. Adams, he joked on Twitter: 'She said she was just going out to get some milk.' He later added his genuine thoughts: 'Your Royal Highness, you are a lucky man and I know your long life together will be joyful, productive and hilarious.' There was one victim in a day of smiles and laughter. While Meghan had been able to bring Guy, her rescue beagle, to London to live with her, her second dog, Bogart, a Labrador mix, was deemed too old to travel. He had been sent off to spend his final days with Meghan's friends.

There were other forfeits, too. Following the public announcement, Meghan resigned from her position as global ambassador for World Vision Canada and stepped back from her involvement with gender equality and women's empowerment in organizations like the UN Women and One Young World. Now she was inside the palace walls she had to play by their rules.

Politics, in particular, was firmly out of bounds. Meghan had previously used her celebrity status to back Hillary Clinton, lament Brexit and attack Donald Trump as 'misogynistic' and 'divisive'. Such strident opinions were now muted by palace protocol that aims to prevent royals, not always successfully, from publicly expressing views on political figures, parties and issues.

The couple's communications secretary Jason Knauf told around a hundred journalists who had arrived for a briefing at Buckingham Palace that, after touring the country, Meghan's withdrawal from her existing humanitarian work would give her a 'clean slate' to judge where best to invest her time and talent. It was a struggle and a test for a woman who had grown used to a public platform. As a friend of Meghan's told me, presciently: 'She is going to bring a lot of diversity and new ideas, new ways of doing things. She is not just going to blend into the royals.'

It was like a rebirth: a new country, a new culture, a new language (sort of) and certainly a new career. In making a new beginning with the man she loved, Meghan was also giving up a great deal. She could never again wander down to the shops without a bodyguard, never take her dog Guy for a walk on her own, never tell the world about a passing thought or fancy on Twitter or Instagram. In short, her life would never be the same again.

Almost overnight she and Prince Harry were the most famous couple on the planet and 'Meghan Markle' became the most Googled name of 2017. She had been blessed with a gift, a gift that would challenge and fulfil her, giving her the kind of access and influence she had never dreamed of. Her next test would be how to use that gift wisely.

13

The Billion-Dollar Bride

The moment that Meghan Markle said 'Yes', you could almost hear the cash registers singing. Within minutes of committing to the Royal Family, the recently retired actor spawned a one-woman industry to rival any Hollywood blockbuster.

Everything from the coat, dress and boots she wore for her engagements, to her eye shadow, nail varnish, sweaters – even her cute turned-up nose – was copied, imitated, advertised and sold. She was big business, very big business, the fairy dust of royalty boosting fashion brands, tourism and even plastic surgery. The white wool coat by Canadian company Line the Label, which she famously wore on the day of her engagement announcement, sold out within minutes, leaving eager customers no option but to add their names to the 400-strong waiting list. It was relaunched the following spring when it had been renamed 'The Meghan'.

Meghan-mania gripped the nation, newspapers printing special supplements about the life and times of Britain's newest 'Mega Star', to steal *The Sun*'s headline. In a declining industry, the hope was that Meghan, like Diana before her, was the new golden goose who could lay profitable circulation eggs.

Step aside Kate Moss, there was a new queen of the High Street in town. Everything Meghan touched or wore transformed lives – and bottom lines. The niche sunglasses firm Finlay and Co. was able to open a shop in Soho, central London, on the back of a surge in sales after she wore their shades on her first public outing with Prince Harry in Nottingham. The company sold £20,000 worth of glasses within twenty-four hours thanks to Ms Markle's Midas touch.

Again, when she carried a £500 tote bag produced by a small Edinburgh-based company called Strathberry, stocks ran out within an hour. Strathberry co-founder Leeanne Hundleby couldn't believe her luck. A couple of weeks before, acting on impulse, she had sent Meghan a selection of handbags and was thrilled to see her product given the royal seal of approval. 'It's just amazing for us, it really is the greatest,' said a company spokesman. 'It was a fantastic surprise and we are really excited. We're suddenly incredibly busy.'

For Meghan, her induction into the Royal Family was an opportunity to influence her new army of fans by wearing the labels of ecologically and ethically minded designers, as well as companies that have a philanthropic element within their business ethos.

She previously used her blog The Tig to promote such brands as Conscious Step – a socks company that plants twenty trees for every pair sold – as well as The Neshama Project, a California-based jewellery business that donates a percentage of profits to Innovation: Africa.

Careful and considered, Meghan was aware that anything she wore, be it make-up, clothes, a new hairstyle or jewellery, had an impact. She had to think strategically, her approach guided by endless phone calls with her stylist and friend Jessica Mulroney, who lived in Toronto.

During her days on *Suits* she got used to being looked at and discussed. But this was a whole new level of scrutiny. She had the personality to cope, describing herself as someone who likes to consider things carefully, to pause before she jumps in. As she admitted: 'I give things a lot of thought and I try to be as sensitive and thoughtful as possible to how it'll make someone feel.'

For example, during the couple's visit to Cardiff in January 2018, she carried a bag by DeMellier, a British label that funds lifesaving vaccines through their sales, and wore a cruelty-free coat by Stella McCartney, an animal-rights activist as well as a top-line designer. She also exhibited spot-on sartorial diplomacy by sporting black jeans from the small Welsh brand Hiut Denim, the future royal raising some eyebrows when she described her husband-to-be as a 'feminist'. As Meghan once noted on her blog:

'It's good if you are fabulous, but great if you do something of value to the world.'

Not everyone was impressed. Newspaper columnist Amanda Platell snarked, 'There's a thin line between doing good and signalling how virtuous you are. We may live in an age of social media, but the Windsors are NOT the Kardashians.' In this pre-honeymoon era, hers was a lone voice. Most tabloid hacks went all misty-eyed about Meghan's performance. 'Centuries of royal tradition melted away as the American actress brought the warmth of modern celebrity to adoring crowds,' opined *The Sun*'s Jack Royston.

Whether she wanted to or not, Meghan became a one-woman walking, talking advertising board; everything she wore was examined and then sold online. Websites such as Meghan's Mirror were created expressly to cash in on the Markle sparkle. These sites were online stores devoted to all things Meghan, selling and shipping with just a few clicks. The editor of Meghan's Mirror, Christine Ross, believed that Meghan's popularity was because her style was relatable to the everyday woman.

This total head-to-foot commercialization of a future royal princess was a far cry from the days when a bored Buckingham Palace press officer would grudgingly hand out a piece of paper describing what the Princess of Wales was wearing that day – and, if you were lucky, giving the name of the designer. During the 1980s, Diana rarely wore High Street, preferring designers like Arabella Pollen, Victor Edelstein – who made the famous John Travolta dress – and later, in her years of independence, the unfussy creations of Catherine Walker. When she did occasionally step out in a High Street brand, such as an elephant-themed ensemble from the upmarket German fashion chain Escada, she faced criticism from the fashion elite.

Even if online shopping had been available in the Diana years, the cost and exclusivity of her clothing would have prevented her adoring female fans from dressing like the late princess. Of course, for years, copies of royal dresses have been run up cheaply and quickly. When Wallis Simpson was married in June 1937, for example, she was furious to learn that her carefully crafted wedding dress, by the American designer Mainbocher, was copied and on sale within hours of the wedding pictures being released. In those days 'cheap' was a relative term, and even the designer knock-offs were beyond most budgets.

In her own quiet way Kate Middleton began the fashion revolution in the House of Windsor by deliberately wearing accessible and affordable clothes, mixing these with high-end designer labels. The Reiss brand, for example, was a regular staple. She was the first proletarian princess – the palace and the High Street working in harmony, her styles and choices imitated from Maidenhead to Madison Avenue. 'Catherine is stylish in affordable clothes and accessories,' noted Reiss brand director Andy Rogers.

Meghan has taken it a stage further, using the semiology of fashion to focus on little-known ethical brands. It was an interest she had long before she met Prince Harry. At the 2014 One Young World Summit, for example, Meghan made a point of befriending Ali Hewson, wife of U2's Bono, because she wanted to learn more about her ethical clothing and make-up lines, Edun and Nude.

Ironically, when Meghan did dress like a princess, wearing a £56,000 gown by the London-based Ralph & Russo for her formal engagement portraits, she was criticized for her extravagance. First in line was her half-sister Samantha, who wondered how she could spend so much on a dress when her father Tom Senior was in need of a helping financial hand. Meghan was discovering, as Diana and Kate had before her, that whatever she chose to wear, someone would have a critical opinion. The stunning black-and-white photographs taken by fashion photographer Alexi Lubomirski for the engagement at Frogmore House – a country house within the grounds of Windsor's Home Park – were a reminder of the charm and appeal exerted by this couple. 'Meghan's sheer glamour marries Hollywood to the House of Windsor,' declared the normally sober London *Times*. As Lubomirski commented: 'I cannot help but smile when I look at the photos that we took of them, such was their happiness together.'

While the Royal Family were not manning the checkout tills, they had approved the sale, at gift shops in Kensington Palace, Sandringham and Buckingham Palace, of mugs, gold-plated spoons, bookmarks, notepads and postcards all adorned with the smiling image of Meghan and Harry, whose wedding was scheduled for 19 May at St George's Chapel in Windsor Castle. When about a thousand £20 ($27) ceramic mugs commemorating the engagement went on sale following the announcement, they had sold out within twenty-four hours. Every hotel and guest house in the vicinity of Windsor Castle was booked up long before the wedding day, while the English tourism board was expecting a huge influx of visitors – around 350,000 extra tourists came to Britain during the royal wedding of William and Kate. If visitors could not get a decent view of the happy couple, there were plenty of professional Harry and Meghan lookalikes to take their place, for a fee.

As for other happy couples, online wedding planner Bridebook reported that enquiries for castles and honeymoons in Botswana had risen dramatically, while sales of diamond engagement rings *à la* Markle had gone up by a third. Bridebook.com chief executive Hamish Shephard told IBTimes UK: 'Meghan and Harry's nuptials will boost both the wedding industry and the British economy. We're expecting a huge increase.'

Overall, the London *Times* reckoned that the Royal Family would contribute £1.8 billion to the British economy during 2018. Of that total, valuation consultancy Brand Finance estimated that the royal wedding could be worth £1 billion to the economy and, post-Brexit, help improve Britain's relationship with the United States. Chief Executive of Brand Finance, David Haigh, told Reuters: 'The last royal wedding had an electrifying effect on people's attitude to the monarchy and Britain, and this will impact even more because it has taken things to a global level with Harry marrying a glamorous American.'

❋

Away from these frothy financial figures, on 1 December, a week after the engagement announcement, Meghan had her first introduction to her new world when she travelled to Nottingham, meeting and greeting members of the public during an official royal engagement. It was just like walking along the red carpet, except colder, wetter and with no red carpet.

Unlike the Duchess of Cambridge, whose first engagement was christening an offshore lifeboat at a modest ceremony in Anglesey, North Wales, Meghan was thrown in at the deep end as thousands of people waited for hours under chill, leaden skies for a glimpse of the Hollywood princess. Though the focus was on a visit to a centre linked to the World AIDS Day charity, everyone wanted to see the bride-to-be. She looked a tad nervous, as well she might, and Harry frequently put his arm around her and whispered words of encouragement in her ear. Introducing herself as Meghan, she quickly got used to the English default conversation, chatting about the weather. (In LA it's the freeway traffic.) She thanked people for waiting in the cold, accepted sweets, hugs, kisses, comparisons to Princess Diana, and flowers, but declined selfies – the royal bride-in-waiting was learning fast.

Inside the AIDS centre they met with victims and organizers, Meghan impressing with her natural empathy. HIV sufferer Chris O'Hanlon of Positively UK, a charity which helps people recently diagnosed with the disease, found the couple easy to talk to, sincere and attentive. His verdict: 'Not only will she make a good addition to the Royal Family, she will make an excellent ambassador to any of the causes she puts her heart and mind to.'

The royal couple went on to watch a hip-hop opera, where Harry told a fellow ginger-haired man that being with Meghan was 'Great, unbelievable.' They left Nottingham folk all aquiver. Complimenting Meghan on her 'charm and ease', columnist Jan Moir cooed, 'What an impressive debut. Meghan Markle was not born to be a princess, but she moves with ease in her brave new world.' With internet searches for Meghan Markle outstripping those for the recently released iPhone 8, it seemed that everyone wanted to dial into the charismatic Ms Markle.

Just so the Queen and Prince Philip could understand what Harry saw in the American actor, the prince made an edited version of *Suits* for their private viewing pleasure. The Monarch was impressed enough to waive long-standing rules that only the Royal Family gather at Sandringham for Christmas. She extended an invitation for Harry's fiancée to join the clan. It was an acknowledgement of the changing times, as the couple had effectively been living together for more than a year. 'Queen Bends the Yules for Meghan' punned *The Sun* headline.

The first stage of Meghan's Christmas royal progress was to join the Queen and Prince Harry for the annual Christmas staff party at Windsor Castle. Hundreds of footmen, maids, butlers and gardeners jostled for position to snatch a brief chat with Meghan, who worked her way slowly around the room. One guest said, 'She asked everyone their name and what they did – she was a natural.'

No sooner had she met the staff than Harry was driving her to Buckingham Palace where, on 20 December, the extended Royal Family – all seventy of them – gather for lunch. Though it is a family affair, it is still a *royal* family affair and there is a whole hierarchy to follow of who bows to whom and who curtsies to whom. Meghan, for instance, had to curtsy to her future sister-in-law, the Duchess of Cambridge, and also to the Countess of Wessex because Prince Edward was in the room. (Interestingly, custom dictates that if he had been absent, Meghan would not have had to flex her knees.) Diana's brother Charles Spencer recalled that at one event at Buckingham Palace there was so much bowing and curtsying he ended up bowing to a bemedalled footman.

For a girl from California where casual is king and the average American bows to no man, this occasion must have been perplexing, not to say a little troubling. Here she was, a standard-bearer for gender equality, curtsying to all and sundry. Of course everyone was dying to meet the new arrival, so along with curtsying, it was also a frenzy of handshaking and brief introductions: 'How do you do?' and 'So pleased to meet you.'

When they were seated for lunch, Meghan found herself between her future father-in-law Prince Charles, and Peter Phillips, an events organizer and only son of Princess Anne. They pulled crackers together, then Meghan put on a paper crown and joined the others in reading out corny jokes as they tucked into turkey and all the trimmings.

A royal source was quoted in the *Daily Mail* as saying, 'She was obviously a bit nervous at first, but she soon relaxed with Prince Harry's help as he introduced her to everyone and then she really enjoyed it.'

The lunch, however, is destined to be remembered for all the wrong reasons, as Meghan's near-neighbour, Princess Michael of Kent, who lives at apartment 10 in Kensington Palace just across from Nottingham Cottage, arrived at Buckingham Palace sporting a blackamoor brooch, a piece of sixteenth-century Venetian jewellery that is now considered racist for its depiction of slaves and servants. As Meghan is of dual heritage and this was her first encounter with the wider Royal Family, Princess Michael's decision was considered particularly offensive, not just by Meghan but by the watching public. The seventy-three-year-old princess apologized profusely and promised not to wear the brooch again.

'The brooch was a gift and has been worn many times before,' a representative for Princess Michael said in a statement. 'Princess Michael is very sorry and distressed that it has caused offence.'

Princess Michael, whose husband is a cousin of the Queen and whose father was a member of Hitler's Nazi Party, was no stranger to racial controversy. When she was at a New York restaurant in 2004, she had a bust-up with a group of African-American diners, reportedly telling them to 'go back to the colonies'. In order to restore her reputation, she gave an extraordinary TV interview in which she described passing herself off as a 'half-caste African' in her youth to experience life among these 'adorable special people' as she travelled around South Africa and Mozambique.

But Meghan had more to worry about than her new neighbour's crass behaviour. Her beloved rescue dog Guy had broken both his back legs in an accident. Thankfully, the beagle mix was on the mend after receiving treatment from TV 'Supervet' Professor Noel Fitzpatrick at his Surrey clinic. Meghan was so grateful for his ministrations that he was one of the first to be invited to the royal wedding of the year.

Guy's injury did mean that he was left behind when, on Christmas Eve, she and Harry drove to Sandringham to spend Christmas with the Royal Family.

Though there were enough bedrooms in the majestic pile – Sandringham has 270 rooms – Meghan and Harry accepted William and Kate's invitation to stay with them at their newly renovated country home, Anmer Hall.

Though it was fresh and exciting for Meghan, Christmas at Sandringham has a regular soothing rhythm, like one of the many grandfather clocks that dominate the corridors. On Christmas Eve, following afternoon tea, the Royal Family open their presents, German style. Then it's church on Christmas Day morning and the main house for lunch. Afterwards everyone watches the Queen's Christmas broadcast. The day after Christmas, a Boxing Day pheasant shoot is held on the vast, flat estate.

✳

The opening of presents on Christmas Eve at six o'clock is a time of merriment and silliness as members of the Royal Family all race to rip off the wrapping paper. Gifts are laid out on cloth-covered trestle tables, with a name-card marking each person's pile of goodies.

Princess Margaret's ex-husband Lord Snowdon once described the scene as 'total uproar' as everyone tore open their gifts. The royal adults don't buy expensive things but rather joke items or whimsical presents. One year Harry received a 'grow-your-own-girlfriend' kit from Kate, while he gave the Queen a shower cap with the phrase 'Ain't life a bitch' printed on it. Another year he gave her a singing Big Mouth Billy Bass, which now has pride of place on the piano in her Balmoral study. In her day, Diana was once given a pair of false bosoms, while Princess Anne received a monogrammed doormat. One report suggested that Meghan had got into the zany spirit, giving the Queen a singing hamster and William a breakfast spoon inscribed 'Cereal Killer'

Once the merriment had subsided the family headed to their bedrooms to dress for dinner – long dresses for the ladies, black tie for the men. At eight o'clock on the dot the family gathers once more for pre-dinner drinks. The Queen arrives at 8.15 for her evening tipple, a dry Martini.

The Duchess of York once recalled: 'Christmas can be exhausting, not least because you sometimes change seven times in twenty-four hours. You never let the Queen beat you down for dinner, end of story – to come in any later would be unimaginably disrespectful.'

On Christmas Day, Meghan enjoyed a light breakfast with Harry, William and Kate at Anmer Hall as George and Charlotte excitedly opened their main presents.

Then it was over to the Big House for the walk to the nearby church of St Mary Magdalene. Warned beforehand about the biting Norfolk winds, Meghan dressed stylishly but warmly in a cream, baby alpaca wool wrap coat by Sentaler, suede boots and a brown beret-style hat. The 3,000-strong crowd, some of whom had been waiting in the freezing conditions for hours, cheered as Meghan, Harry, William and Kate walked by. Meghan smiled, waved and even playfully stuck her tongue out.

As luck would have it, the best photograph of the day was taken not by a professional cameraman, but by single mother Karen Anvil, whose picture of the royal quartet easily paid for her own Christmas.

When they came out of church, it was time for Meghan's first public curtsy as the Queen walked back into her chauffeur-driven Bentley.

For the first time, Meghan looked visibly nervous, clinging on to her fiancé's arm as she dropped a wobbly bob, a rictus grin on her face. A smiling Kate – a seasoned veteran of such occasions – showed how it should be done, dropping the perfect relaxed curtsy.

Then it was time to thank those who had waited for so long. The most that well-wishers could hope for was a handshake and a brief 'Happy Christmas'.

A few, though, went further to win a moment in the royal sun. Among the crowd were a large number of Americans, some from a nearby US Air Force base. Student Michael Metz from Wisconsin made the occasion extra special by proposing to his

Texan girlfriend Ashley Millican. When Harry and Meghan heard about their betrothal, they offered their congratulations. 'It was amazing, like a fairy tale,' said Michael.

Traditionally on Boxing Day, the royal men lead the guns out to the fields, where hundreds of pheasants, specifically reared for this sport, are slaughtered. William and Harry love shooting – Princess Diana called her boys 'the killer Wales' – and enjoy spending the day outdoors in field sports. Not this year. For the first time, Harry left his guns in their cases. His absence from the fields of Sandringham was noted widely among the press – 'Gunder the thumb already?' stated one headline, implying that Meghan was behind his non-appearance.

In fact, he had to be in London to prepare for his stint as the guest editor of the *Today* programme, the BBC's flagship morning radio show. He had been given a free hand and had decided to highlight causes close to his heart, notably youth violence, mental health, social media in society, the armed forces, conservation and the Commonwealth. He had lined up a number of big hitters, namely his father Prince Charles, who called Harry 'my darling boy' and discussed the 'untold horrors' caused by climate change, and the former American president Barack Obama, whom he had interviewed at the Invictus Games in September in the Fairmont Hotel, Toronto.

Before the interview began, a clearly relaxed Obama jokingly asked if he should speak with a British accent. He also wondered if he should talk faster than usual, because he was a 'slow speaker'.

The prince replied, 'No, no, not at all. But if you start using long pauses between the answers, you're probably going to get the face.'

When Mr Obama asked to see 'the face', Prince Harry gave him a stern look. 'I don't want to see that face!' retorted a laughing Obama.

The conversation covered topics including Obama's memories of the day he left office and his hopes for his post-presidential life, including his plans to focus on cultivating the next generation of leaders through the Obama Foundation. With an oblique swipe at the man who took his job, Mr Obama said that irresponsible use of social media was distorting the public's understanding of complex issues.

In a quick-fire round of questions he was asked which programme he preferred, *The Good Wife* or *Suits*. The ex-president replied, '*Suits*, obviously.'

A whimsical piece in *The Times* caught the mood of the broadcast. 'The man who was once naughty Harry, drunken Harry, Boujis Harry, has left behind the fleshpots. Now he is Saint Harry who spends his time toiling among the needy and making outreach radio in which he speaks to those others ignore. The injured. The depressed. The Prince of Wales.'

By great fortune, the Radio Four presenters had backed their way into a scoop, Harry's engagement having been announced long after they had arranged for his stint as a guest editor. The news angle was the upcoming nuptials.

Boxer Anthony Joshua, who was interviewed by the prince, offered to be his best man, while presenter Sarah Montague quizzed Harry about Meghan's first Christmas with 'the Firm'. 'It was fantastic, she really enjoyed it,' he said. 'We had great fun staying with my brother and sister-in-law and running around with the kids. I think we've got one of the biggest families that I know of, and every family is complex as well. She has done an absolutely amazing job.'

So far, so endearing. As the interview wound down he remarked, 'She's getting in there and I suppose it's the family she's never had.'

Cue foot in mouth. Prince Philip would be proud.

14

Invitation to a Wedding

Retired Army captain Prince Henry of Wales walked straight into a fusillade of criticism when he told the world that the Windsors were the family that Meghan Markle never had.

The Markles galloped straight into action, Meghan's half-sister Samantha leading the charge. 'Actually, she has a large family who were always there with her and for her,' she thundered. 'Our household was very normal, and when Dad and Doria divorced, we all made it so it was like she had two houses.'

For once Tom Junior, who generally had little time for his elder sister, went into battle on her side. 'My father will be extremely hurt. He dedicated the majority of his time and everything to her. He made sure that she had what she needed to be successful and get to where she's at today.'

As far as the pundits were concerned, Harry 'dropped a clanger' or a 'howler' by commenting on the family set-up of his future in-laws. In his defence, he was basing his account on that presented to him by his fiancée. When she was growing up, she felt little sense of family – after all, her parents separated when she was only two. That was her truth, no matter what others believed.

Within days the plotting and infighting among the Markle clan suggested a family at war. Samantha continued to tout her upcoming book, *The Diary of Princess Pushy's Sister*, although she subsequently appeared on TV to ask for Meghan's forgiveness and speak of her hope that she would receive an invitation to the wedding. She never did. Neither her nor any other member of the Markle clan. Only Meghan's parents were invited – as was the case when she married Trevor Engelson.

Samantha dismissed suggestions that her retiring father would not be speaking at the royal nuptials. 'He should not be deprived of the right that fathers have to give a proud speech at the wedding. A father speaking at a wedding is not patriarchy, it's poetic justice.'

Finally, the reclusive man at the centre of so much speculation, Tom Markle Senior, was tracked down to his Mexican hideaway by an enterprising British tabloid reporter. Though he accepted a congratulatory bottle of champagne, the former lighting director was far from illuminating regarding his future plans. In the months before the wedding there was much speculation both inside and outside the family about whether Meghan's father, a shy man with underlying health issues, would even attend his daughter's nuptials. As his son Tom Junior told me: 'My father worships the ground Meghan walks on. I know how proud he will be to take her arm and walk her down the aisle. But I also know how terrified he will be. If he doesn't go he will regret it for the rest of his life. He has to know that he is not just representing his family, he is representing America.'

Tom Junior had found himself on the front pages for all the wrong reasons in January 2018 when his girlfriend Darlene was jailed for the night following a noisy and boozy New Year's Eve celebration at their Oregon home. The incident came a year after he was arrested for the 'unlawful use of a weapon and menacing'. Though these charges were dropped, Tom later told me that the constant media attention had been hard on the family.

The ghosts from Meghan's past kept arriving to haunt her. She was less than thrilled to learn that her ex-husband Trevor Engelson had sold a pilot comedy drama to Fox TV, which he was slated to produce, based on the idea of a recently divorced man whose wife has married into the Royal Family. He had the idea when he was discussing his chequered love life with fellow producer Dan Farah. Though at the time of writing the show remains in development purgatory, Meghan has had to get used to becoming a figure of fun. In the no-holds-barred Channel Four comedy *The Windsors*,

Kathryn Drysdale played her as a relentless name-dropper, while Harry is so dumb he cannot even read. And talking of dumb, the US cable network Lifetime announced that it would release *Harry and Meghan: The Royal Love Story* just before the wedding. Their previous offering, entitled *William and Kate: The Movie*, which they produced in 2011, was described by *The Guardian* newspaper as 'toe-curlingly, teeth-furringly, pillow-bitingly ghastly'.

What was no laughing matter was the decision by Meghan's lifelong friend Ninaki Priddy, who was her maid of honour at her first wedding, to sell her photograph albums and story to the highest bidder, receiving a six-figure sum for her memories. Though palace officials had warned Meghan that some of her friends may decide to sell their stories, it didn't ease the sense of betrayal she felt.

Perhaps more worrying in the long term was the racial and class prejudice that began to seep into public discourse about the newest arrival into the House of Windsor. Two faces of Britain were on display during their early engagements. In January 2018, when the couple made their second joint official visit together, they toured the social enterprise radio station Reprezent 107.3 FM in Brixton, South London, home to many of the capital's African and Caribbean communities. As the excited crowd chanted, 'We love you,' Meghan smiled, waved and blew kisses. When the noise reached a ragged crescendo, she coyly put her hand in front of her mouth.

During her tour of the station, which trains hundreds of young people in media and related skills every year, the gender-equality campaigner singled out twenty-four-year-old presenter YV Shells, asking him about his reputation as a young man who supported women DJs, empowering women and creating a space that is not so male-driven. 'I think that's incredible,' she remarked.

On a walkabout outside, she met with American students Jennifer Martinez and Millicent Sasu from Baltimore. Jennifer approved of the American import: 'She's black, she's white, she's an actress, she's American. She brings a bit of everything and has so many different qualities. She brings so much to the table.'

Not everyone thought so. During her time on the TV reality show *Celebrity Big Brother*, former Member of Parliament Ann

Widdecombe described Meghan as 'trouble', saying that she was worried about the 'background' and 'attitude' of Harry's fiancée. Matters got uglier as racist remarks made by the girlfriend of Henry Bolton, the then leader of the pro-Brexit UK Independence Party, were made public.

In a series of text messages, glamour model Jo Marney told a friend that Meghan would 'taint' the Royal Family with 'her seed' and pave the way for a 'black king'. She went on to say that she would never have sex with 'a negro' because they are 'ugly'. Many of the party's front-bench spokesmen walked out in protest when Bolton refused to quit.

He was eventually ousted after a vote by the party's shrinking membership. The vote took place before the alarming revelation in February 2018 that a letter containing a white powder and a racist letter was sent to Meghan and Prince Harry at Kensington Palace. While the white powder was deemed harmless, it brought back memories of the anthrax scares in America a week after the 9/11 attack in 2001, when various senators and others were sent the deadly powder through the mail. This act of domestic terrorism left five dead and seventeen others affected by the anthrax spores. The incident involving the royal couple, which was officially treated as a race hate crime, was a further example, if any more were needed, that racial prejudice is still a potent issue in multiracial Britain.

⁂

Meghan and Harry had to tune out what she calls 'the noise' and focus on the job in hand – organizing their wedding. Unlike her first marriage, which she left largely in the hands of a wedding coordinator in Jamaica, Meghan wanted to control every detail, the big day reflecting what their spokesman described as the 'fun and joy' of their 'fairy tale'.

Communications secretary Jason Knauf announced: 'The couple of course want the day to be a special, celebratory moment for their friends and family. They also want the day to be shaped so as to allow members of the public to feel part of the celebrations too and are currently working through ideas for how this might be achieved.'

First item on the agenda was the wedding dress. This was the choice for Meghan and Meghan alone. Her spouse, her supporters and the eager public would have to wait until the wedding day for the first glimpse of this unique creation. Only the Queen would be privy to a private viewing at Windsor Castle before the big day. Initially, the bookies' favourite was the Queen's designer, Stewart Parvin, who made a wedding dress for Zara Phillips, the daughter of Princess Anne. Other runners and riders included Erdem Moralıoğlu, Stella McCartney, Roland Mouret and Victoria Beckham.

As this was the bride's traditional surprise, the identity of the designer and the dress were smothered in secrecy. She had already given a few clues about the type of dress she would choose during the run-up to her TV wedding in the final season of *Suits*. She said that she was communing the simple but classic wedding dress worn by Carolyn Bessette Kennedy, wife of John F. Kennedy Junior, on her big day in 1996. Numerous designers sent their preliminary sketches and ideas in the hope of being chosen, but Meghan had her target almost from the get-go. She picked out Birmingham-born Clare Waight Keller who, as a child, had dreamed of being a designer.

Meghan felt an instinctive connection to this working mother who had raised three children while employed by Pringle of Scotland as well as Chloé, and had recently become the first female artistic director at the French house of Givenchy. She ticked all the boxes: British-born but with an international pedigree and sensibility, and a woman who was able to succeed in juggling the demands of home and work. Keller was feminine and a feminist, a juxtaposition that Meghan had come to appreciate close up while meeting successful female politicians, charity workers and community leaders. By her choice of designer, Meghan was able to highlight the achievements of a leading British talent while, according to Kensington Palace, admiring her for her 'timeless and elegant aesthetic, impeccable tailoring and relaxed demeanour'.

In order to keep their discussions confidential, they met just once before Christmas 2017 in a thirty-minute conversation at

Kensington Palace. Apart from a few brief meetings and a cloak-and-dagger visit to Keller's South London studio in mid-February, most interactions were by telephone. In the later stages, Keller even altered the dress by herself. Such was the secrecy that Keller's own family didn't realize what she had been making until the morning of the wedding. 'It was a very discreet communication between us – literally just us,' she later told *Vogue*. 'There was no one else involved. For those five months, that was so special.'

Besides the classic simplicity of the dress, it was the veil that really made a regal but contemporary statement. Meghan came up with the idea of embroidering the national flowers of fifty-three nations of the Commonwealth into her veil. She also added two personal favourites: wintersweet which grows in the grounds of Kensington Palace, in front of Nottingham Cottage where she first stayed, and Californian poppies to reflect her birthplace. Her choice was not only a compliment to the Queen, who has devoted her life to the Commonwealth, but also reflected their marital future, as Harry was about to be made youth ambassador for this multiracial, multicultural institution. For a well-travelled woman with a global vision, Harry's appointment suited her perfectly, Meghan experiencing what this family of nations truly means when she attended a Commonwealth Day service at Westminster Abbey in mid-March with the Queen and other senior royals.

She said later that her husband was over the moon at her thoughtful wedding veil design, as were other members of the Royal Family who showed their 'appreciation for the fact that we understand how important this is for us and the role that we play, and the work that we're going to continue to do within the Commonwealth countries'.

The veil was certainly a labour of love for the fifty or so workers from Givenchy's embroidery house who were tasked with producing the 5-metre-long garment. The gauzy creation took around 500 hours to hand-embroider, with workers washing their hands every thirty minutes to prevent dirtying the tulle and threads.

If the making of her gown and veil was like something out of a fairy tale, then her admission into that most holy of holies, the royal jewellery collection in the bowels of Buckingham Palace, was like a dream. 'Surreal,' she said to herself over and over as she was escorted to the small elevator which took her 40 feet or so into the basement where an Aladdin's cave of silver, gold and precious gems are kept. It is the last royal kingdom, a hidden realm of riches almost beyond comprehension. There are jewelled scabbards from the East, Great Seals of Office, diamond-encrusted snuff boxes, silver tureens that take two men to lift, great silver shields and platters, ornamental cutlasses, and memorabilia from the days of Emperor Napoleon and the heroic seafarer Admiral Nelson. Adding to the sense of wonder is the almost unnatural silence that pervades the white-walled strongroom, which is roughly the size of an ice rink.

Pride of place are the secure safes containing the Royal Family's diamond, sapphire and emerald tiaras, those headpieces redolent of regal history and pageantry. On this chilly February day, just to add to the sense of wonder, the Queen and her dresser Angela Kelly, who cares for the jewellery and insignias, joined Meghan. Prince Harry had also tagged along for this historic occasion. As she had with previous royal brides Kate Middleton, Camilla Parker Bowles and Sophie Rhys Jones, the Queen was inviting Meghan to choose one of the royal tiaras to borrow for her wedding. It was a function she delighted in undertaking, the Queen feeling that she was adding her unique touch to the bride's big day.

There were five tiaras on show. Though by rights the groom should not have been there, as soon as Meghan tried on the 1932 art deco diamond bandeau tiara which Queen Mary bequeathed the Queen in her will, he and the others all knew it was 'the one'. As Meghan later recalled for an exhibition of her wedding: 'That was the one that stood out. I think it was just perfect because it was so clean and simple ... an extension of what Clare [Waight Keller] and I had been trying to do with the dress, which was to have something that could be so incredibly timeless but still feel modern.'

The occasion was a satisfying and rather special bonding moment for the bride-to-be and Harry's grandmother, both women recognizing that in this generous act the Queen was personally welcoming her into the Royal Family.

She repaid the Queen's munificence with her own gesture of thanks. Though it was not necessary before the wedding, Meghan insisted on converting to the national faith, the Church of England, as a sign of respect to her. In early March she was baptized by the Archbishop of Canterbury, using holy water from the River Jordan, at a secret forty-five-minute ceremony at the Chapel Royal in the grounds of St James's Palace. Prince Harry was by her side, with the Prince of Wales and Duchess of Cornwall also present together with a select group of friends and supporters. Though the Queen, Prince Philip and the Cambridges were not present, the Sovereign appreciated Meghan's enthusiasm in accommodating herself within the strictures of the Royal Family. 'There was no pressure on her, she wanted to be baptized out of respect for the Queen,' noted an observer. After the ceremony, Archbishop Justin Welby commented: 'It was beautiful, sincere and very moving. It was a great privilege.'

As anticipated by her former Immaculate Heart theology teacher Maria Pollia, Meghan had struck up a firm friendship with the archbishop, who was impressed by her knowledge of the faith and willingness to adapt to her new family and country. With uncanny accuracy, Ms Pollia had previously observed that Meghan would 'utterly astound and delight' clerics when she took her studies for her induction into her faith.

In a sign of the radically changing times, Harry became the first member of the Royal Family to be granted a Church of England wedding in spite of marrying a divorced woman. Prince Charles and Camilla Parker Bowles married in a civil service while Princess Anne's second marriage to Commander Timothy Laurence took place in Scotland because of Church of England strictures regarding divorcees. At the first available Privy Council meeting in March, the Queen took the opportunity to confirm Harry's nuptials, giving her formal consent to their marriage in accordance with the 2013 Succession to the Crown Act.

Meghan, as shown with her conversion to the Church of England, was proving herself a team player. She closed down her social media accounts even though she had amassed an audience of more than 2 million. Enthusiastically, she had continued her quick-fire education of her new country by following up the trip to Cardiff with visits to the Scottish capital of Edinburgh and Belfast in Northern Ireland. Her first evening engagement at Goldsmiths' Hall in the City of London ignited memories of Harry's mother. In a moment of karmic symmetry, by an extraordinary coincidence this was the same place that Lady Diana Spencer made her debut evening appearance with Prince Charles. This time around Harry and Meghan were guests of honour at the Endeavour Fund Awards, set up by Harry's Royal Foundation, to celebrate and honour the achievements of wounded, injured and sick servicemen and women.

Unlike Diana, who arrived blushing and flustered, wearing a low-cut black gown that she almost spilled out of as she exited the car, Meghan plumped for a sleekly sophisticated Alexander McQueen trouser suit. The nineteen-year-old Diana would have surely been in awe of such effortless self-assurance as she was with the other former American actor she met on that first tricky public appearance, Princess Grace of Monaco.

Meghan's royal induction seemed complete when, in February 2018, she joined Harry, William and a pregnant Kate in a televised discussion about the future of the Royal Foundation, a charity where the 'Fab Four', as they were now called, were the founding patrons. It was a light-hearted family affair, Meghan telling the TV presenter that she couldn't wait to get the ball rolling on projects such as Heads Together, a mental-health charity set up by Harry and William. 'Wedding first!' interjected Prince Harry, to laughter from the audience, with Meghan replying, 'We can multitask.' Harry added, 'We're pretty tied up with planning a wedding at the moment, but we're really looking forward to working as a pair and as a four going forward, hoping to make as much of a difference where we can.'

Harry and William agreed that they had 'healthy' disagreements, some unresolved, though Harry insisted that they all had a passion to make a difference but with different opinions. While the headlines were uniformly positive – *Hello* magazine suggesting that 'the future of the monarchy was in safe hands' – there were concerning straws in the wind. 'Working as a family does have its challenges,' admitted Harry, 'but we're stuck together for the rest of our lives.'

※

Meghan had been welcomed with open arms by the Royal Family. As she sat on a flight to Los Angeles, heading to see her mother and show her some of the key sketches of her wedding dress, she never for a moment suspected that she was about to be betrayed by the man who had loved and nurtured her during her childhood and beyond. Literally as her flight was descending to land at Los Angeles International Airport, her father, Tom Markle Senior, was meeting with paparazzi photographer Jeff Rayner. Rayner, who ran an agency specializing in candid celebrity shots, had snagged a deal with Meghan's father. The idea was to take a series of photographs of Tom as the father of the bride preparing for the big day.

Though Tom had remained silent in the face of endless questions from journalists, his image was that of a dishevelled, careworn recluse leading a down-at-heel life in a rundown Mexican coastal resort. He had been variously photographed carrying a new toilet – or his throne, as it was dubbed – in a hardware store, holding a six-pack of ale or a plastic shopping bag, or sorting his washing at the local laundromat. Most days he was trailed by paparazzi, their long lens so insistently intrusive that he nailed plywood in front of the window of his apartment to give himself some privacy.

Rayner, who was a familiar fixture in the Mexican seaside town of Rosarito, convinced Tom to take part in the dubious enterprise. It would not only improve his image, argued Rayner, but also earn him a percentage of the proceeds. When Tom talked it over with his daughter Samantha she was fully in favour. So, as Meghan was proudly showing her mother the plans for her wedding dress, her father was collaborating with the notorious paparazzo in an initiative that would cast a shadow over the wedding.

During the day-long session, Tom was photographed at an internet café looking at pictures of his daughter on a computer, sitting in a coffee shop reading a book called *Images of Britain*, being fitted for a morning suit and working out, somewhat implausibly, on the site of the town's trash dump. The set of pictures were marketed as candid shots taken without Tom Markle's knowledge. Even to a casual eye that was a far-fetched claim – the clarity and proximity of the pictures indicated that the subject must have known what was going on.

Blindsided by her father, Meghan was also upset by her half-brother Tom who, for no obvious reason, penned a handwritten letter at the behest of a tabloid American magazine urging Prince Harry to cancel the wedding.

'As more time passes to your royal wedding, it became very clear that this is the biggest mistake in royal wedding history,' Tom Junior warned. 'Meghan Markle is obviously not the right woman for you.' For good measure, he described his half-sister as a 'jaded, shallow, conceited woman that will make a joke of you and the Royal Family heritage'. The fact that neither he nor any other members of the Markle family had been invited to the wedding seemed to be the reason behind such a sour missive.

Meanwhile, the wheels were coming off Tom Senior's photographic play. Internal surveillance footage captured inside the various stores that he visited proved without doubt that the shots were set up. The 'tailor' photographed measuring Tom for a morning suit was a worker in a party-goods shop, who was handed $15 in cash for brandishing the tape measure around Tom's circumference. Far from improving his image, this ludicrous escapade painted him as a buffoon, his behaviour the antithesis of Meghan's mantra to 'stay classy'. Eventually, even he admitted that the shots looked 'stupid and hammy'.

What was baffling about this episode was that, according to Tom Junior, his father owned a lock-up in Los Angeles filled with photographs of Meghan from birth to adulthood. He had once been a prolific photographer, proudly taking snaps of his daughter during her various theatrical performances at school and elsewhere. It would have been perfectly legitimate for him to compile a portfolio of his work and, with palace approval, see it published for a profit. When Sarah Ferguson married Prince Andrew, the Ferguson family did precisely that, releasing shots of their daughter, the resulting proceeds going both to the family and a charity of their choice.

As it was, after being exposed by the *Mail on Sunday* just days before the wedding, Tom Senior had to face the music. When Harry called him to ask if the news reports were true, he lied to him and told the concerned prince that in one of the shots he was simply being measured for a hoodie. The exposé was all the more embarrassing as the couple's press secretary had written to newspaper editors asking them to leave Thomas Markle Senior alone. Almost until the day of the wedding, Mr Markle's increasingly bizarre behaviour captured the headlines as the world – and Meghan – wondered if he would turn up for the wedding and walk his daughter down the aisle. Later, Meghan would use the word 'betrayal' when she discussed her father's conduct during an interview with Oprah Winfrey. Ironically, Oprah had bonded with Doria Ragland as they had both attended the same LA church and the TV presenter understood, having lived with endless scrutiny, the pressures that Meghan was under.

In the meantime, her father was taken to hospital after apparently suffering a heart attack. Harry called him again and, according to Tom Senior, said: 'If you had listened to me, this would never have happened.' What hurt Tom the most was that after the exposé Meghan informed him that he would not be allowed to make a speech at the wedding. Before hanging up the phone he told them petulantly: 'Maybe it would be better for you guys if I was dead ... then you could pretend to be sad.'

For the next few days, Harry and Meghan made frantic phone calls or sent texts to find out what was going on in his life – and in his head. A security team they had employed to mind him was dismissed while Tom's behaviour became more and more erratic. To all intents and purposes he went rogue, giving off-the-cuff interviews to the tabloid TV channel TMZ and ignoring endless calls from Kensington Palace. A text Meghan sent to her father shortly before the wedding gives a flavour of the confusion and bewilderment felt by the royal couple:

I've been reaching out to you all weekend but you're not taking any of our calls or replying to any texts ... Very concerned about your health and safety and have taken every measure to protect you but not sure what more we can do if you don't respond ... Do you need help? Can we send the security team down again? I'm very sorry to hear you're in the hospital but need you to please get in touch with us ... What hospital are you at?

In the space of a day, Tom Senior changed his mind three times about whether or not he would go to the wedding. Firstly, he told TMZ he wasn't going as he didn't want to embarrass the Royal Family. Six hours later he said he would walk Meghan down the aisle. This decision lasted a matter of hours before he announced that he would have to go to hospital to have a stent inserted into his artery as the stress of the last few days had given him a heart attack. Right up to the eve of the wedding, Meghan was calling and texting her father but in vain. As a close friend later told *People* magazine: 'It was like: "Please pick up. I love you and I am scared."'

For their last weekend before the big day, the couple stayed at a 4,000-square-foot barn on the Great Tew Estate in Oxfordshire in the forlorn hope of enjoying some peace and quiet. The unfolding saga of Tom Markle Senior put a spike in that ambition. They felt out of control, that the endless dramas surrounding their wedding were dominating their lives and draining a special occasion of any deeper meaning for them. It was their big day above all. They wanted to be celebrating their spiritual and physical union in a manner that spoke to their hearts.

As they pondered the issue they had the idea of 'marrying' privately before the day itself. It would give them a chance to say their own vows to one another in front of a religious leader. The Archbishop of Canterbury, Justin Welby, was willing to conduct a small private ceremony where the couple could exchange their own promises, handwritten vows that now adorn the walls of their home in California. 'You know, three days before our wedding we got married,' Meghan later confessed to Oprah during an historic TV interview. 'No one knows that.' They told Welby: 'Look, this thing, this spectacle is for the world, but we want our union between us.'

Inevitably there was much criticism of this apparent deception. Wedding guest and TV presenter James Corden was one of the kinder voices, joshing: 'I've got to tell you, I want my toaster back. That was a wedding present, not a three-days-after-the-wedding present. I was shocked the ceremony I went to wasn't real. It was a sham!' Archbishop Welby and a spokesman for the royal couple hastily emphasized that this was an exchange of vows, not an official ceremony. As the archbishop told the Italian newspaper *la Repubblica*: 'The legal wedding was on the Saturday [19 May 2018]. I signed the wedding certificate, which is a legal document, and I would have committed a serious criminal offence if I signed it knowing it was false.' The fact that Meghan had misspoken about something as personal as the date and day that she married did cast a shadow over some of her other statements.

The couple had no sooner exchanged their vows than they attended the final wedding rehearsal. It was every bit as fraught as these things can be, especially where small children struggling to fit into page-boy and flower-girl outfits are involved. It was, however, the adults who ended up in tears. A stressed Meghan, humiliated over her father's behaviour, was accused of leaving Kate, herself emotional following the birth of Louis, in tears. The spat apparently concerned Princess Charlotte's dress and the weighty question as to whether or not the flower girls should wear tights or go bare-legged. Kate felt that Charlotte, then three, and the other five girls should follow tradition and protocol and wear tights. Meghan demurred. Words were said, tears were shed, the two women, who enjoyed a brittle relationship at the best of times, parting in high dudgeon. Meghan's story, however, was diametrically opposite to the whispers inside the palace. She told Oprah Winfrey that it was Kate who had made her cry over the thorny issue of the flower girls' dresses. To further emphasize the point, Meghan described how the duchess personally brought a bouquet of flowers and conciliatory note to Meghan at Nottingham Cottage by way of apology. As Meghan told Oprah: 'It wasn't a confrontation, and I actually don't think it's fair to her to get into the details of that, because she apologized. And I've forgiven her.' Whoever was at a fault, it was clear that there was little love lost between these two high-profile royals.

At least the teary disagreement with Kate was private – albeit for the time being. The 'will he, won't he' saga of Meghan's father came to a head on the same day, Meghan finally issuing a statement confirming her father would not be coming. 'Sadly, my father will not be attending our wedding. I have always cared for my father and hope he can be given the space he needs to focus on his health.'

Amidst all the turmoil, she at least had the calm and steadying presence of her mother Doria, who had flown in from Los Angeles to support her. As generations of Brits have discovered, everything feels so much much better with a consoling cup of tea. It came courtesy of Prince Charles and the Duchess of Cornwell, who entertained Harry, Meghan and Doria over afternoon tea at Clarence House. Meghan had already bonded with Prince Charles over their interest in sustainable organic food, classical music and architecture – she and Camilla shared a love of fine wine and yoga – so Charles was immediately receptive when Harry asked if he would walk Meghan down the quire of the altar. Harry, who had a fractious relationship with his father, was eternally grateful when his father immediately said he would be delighted. 'Yes, of course, I'll do whatever Meghan needs and I'm here to support you,' he told him.

If the meeting with Charles and Camilla was a thrill, as far as Doria was concerned afternoon tea on the eve of the wedding with the Queen and Prince Philip was, apart from the wedding itself, the highlight of her flying visit. What could have been an awkward and tentative occasion was eased by Harry's presence and the stories he told about his much-loved grandparents.

Afterwards, Harry and his best man or supporter, Prince William, went on a ten-minute walkabout among the throngs of well-wishers gathering outside the walls of Windsor Castle. They were casual and relaxed as Harry prepared for his last night as a bachelor.

After the stresses and strains of the last few days, Meghan too was anxious to unwind and spend some downtime with her mother. The day before the wedding, they stayed in the £1,500-a-night Inchiquin Suite at the storied Cliveden House Hotel, the former stately home which over the years has played host to the likes of Winston Churchill and Mahatma Gandhi, as well as literary giants such as George Bernard Shaw. After a refreshing glass of vintage champagne, Meghan enjoyed a soothing facial from her long-time holistic therapist Sarah Chapman. During a relaxing bath, she exchanged texts with her close friends, the actor Janina Gavankar describing Meghan's mood as 'excited'. 'She gets to marry the love of her life,' she said.

She slept soundly, determined to enjoy her momentous day. Then, at 4.57 in the morning, she received a call from Mexico.

It was her father.

15

Wedding Belle

It was a moment of glorious, rapturous history. As Meghan Markle stood in her glowing wedding dress at the entrance to St George's Chapel on a sunny day in May 2019, Handel's transcendent 'Eternal Source of Light Divine', sung by the Welsh soprano Elin Manahan Thomas and accompanied by David Blackadder on trumpet, paused millions of conversations and provoked a waterfall of tears. While Meghan, alone, slowly made her way down the aisle, for a brief time all 'the noise' was stilled. No more discussion about Tom Markle Senior nor where the couple were going on honeymoon nor the identity of the dress designer – as Meghan had decided against a maid of honour, her designer Clare Waight Keller was waiting outside the chapel to make any last-minute adjustments. This was Meghan's moment. I was in a makeshift TV studio in Windsor Great Park, commentating for the American network ABC along with David Muir and Robin Roberts. Our response to her arrival was repeated in households around the world – a silent appreciation of the occasion.

It was also history in the making. In the last important royal wedding for a generation, Prince Harry's glamorous bride was the first dual-heritage divorcee ever to marry a member of the British Royal Family. At a stroke their union, blessed by Her Majesty the Queen, made the monarchy seem more inclusive and relevant in an ever-changing world. If nothing else, the wedding of the second son of Prince Charles and the late Diana, Princess of Wales, showed how much and how far the Royal Family – and the British nation – have evolved during the reign of Queen Elizabeth II. It was an occasion redolent with symbolism.

Since the romantic traumas surrounding King Edward VIII and Wallis Simpson, and Princess Margaret and Group Captain Peter Townsend, the Royal Family, like the rest of the world, has accepted, albeit reluctantly, the fact that divorce no longer carries the social stigma it once did. Yet even in the early 1980s, when Prince Charles was scouting the shires for a bride, the notion of a divorced American, let alone a dual-heritage American, marrying into the Royal Family was unthinkable. Then the priority was to find a white, Anglo-Saxon, Protestant aristocratic virgin. He found one in the winsome shape of Lady Diana Spencer, and the constitutional catastrophe of their marriage – and rancorous divorce – has caused the older generation of royals to pause before commenting on the chosen companion of the younger members of the family.

That Meghan divorced after a brief two-year union with a film producer hardly raised an eyebrow, let alone created a constitutional crisis. After all, the future king, Prince Charles, is a divorcee who married his former mistress, Camilla Parker Bowles, also divorced, in April 2005 in a civil ceremony just over the road from St George's Chapel. All very modern. Divorce, race and a racy past – the House of Windsor now welcomes all comers.

As he watched the American actor process slowly down the aisle, Prince Andrew, the Duke of York, may well have reflected on his own love life. Years before he was embroiled in the Jeffrey Epstein sex scandal, the prince was known as the world's most eligible bachelor and a war hero to boot. He was secretly dating another American actor, Kathleen 'Koo' Stark, who had starred in a tepidly erotic movie directed by arty aristocrat, the Earl of Pembroke. Once their romance became public, pictures were circulated of Koo in various stages of undress, provoking hysteria in both the mass media and among some Members of Parliament. Though she met the Queen and was considered the perfect match for Andrew, the stigma of that film, one of her first, poisoned any future prospects with Andrew. Their love affair was doomed. But for a fifth-rate movie, Koo Stark, not Meghan Markle, might have been the first American to marry a member of the Royal Family since Wallis Simpson.

Ironically, the girl who was about to make royal history had taken acting roles far raunchier than anything shot by Koo Stark. During her screen career Meghan was filmed snorting cocaine, teaching housewives the art of striptease and having sex in a file room. She appeared semi-naked in so many scenes of *Suits* that she complained that scriptwriters were deliberately crafting scenarios to show off her body.

❋

Despite the nerves and anticipation that had been building ahead of her momentous day, the girl at the centre of this historic royal occasion slept soundly through the night which, as she later remarked, was a minor 'miracle'. She had managed to miss her father's early-morning phone call. In any case, whatever he wanted to say to her, in Meghan's heart he was now consigned to history. Though she had a reputation for dropping people who were no longer useful to her, her father's self-indulgent behaviour at the most stressful time of her life put him beyond the pale. She would never forgive nor forget his betrayal.

It was as well that she had missed his call as she wanted to savour every precious positive moment of the day ahead. Her extraordinary journey began with a change of name. Early in the morning, it was officially announced that the one-time Valley Girl would, on marriage, become a fully minted royal, the Queen bestowing upon her the title of Her Royal Highness The Duchess of Sussex. Prince Harry would be made Duke of Sussex as well as Earl of Dumbarton and Baron Kilkeel. All that plus a coat of arms where the colour blue represented the Pacific Ocean and two golden rays symbolized the Californian sunshine. Three quills on her shield signified communication and the power of words.

As she prepared for the day ahead, she was joined by her mother and make-up artist Daniel Martin, who was under strict instructions from Harry to make sure his bride looked natural and to show off her pretty freckles. Martin duly obliged. As they chatted while he worked, the strains of 'Going to the Chapel', along with songs by Ella Fitzgerald, Billie Holiday and other favourites played in the background. Next up was hairdresser Serge Normant, Julia Roberts' long-time hairstylist, who swept Meghan's hair into a tousled chignon for the day.

Meanwhile, the Archbishop of Canterbury Justin Welby, proving that the Church of England was on brand, tweeted that he was praying for the couple and that he hoped it would be a day of 'joy and celebration'. He had his own concerns, the senior cleric later admitting that he was worried about dropping the wedding rings and getting the vows in the wrong order.

One of the wedding guests had also had to overcome a rather worrying problem. Oprah Winfrey, who arrived at St George's Chapel at the same time as actor Idris Elba, whom Harry had asked to DJ at the evening party, had had a dress disaster. While trying on her beige outfit the previous morning, she realized it might look too white on the photographs, which would never do. That colour is preserved for the bride. She sent out an urgent sartorial SOS to Stella McCartney and pleaded with her to run up another frock. Within twenty-four hours Oprah was able to go to the ball, in a blush-pink dress complemented by a vintage Philip Treacy hat.

As for a dual-heritage actor joining the Royal Family, Idris Elba, who has been widely touted to become the first black James Bond, was thrilled: 'As a strong woman marrying into our Royal Family, she's going to be a role model for any woman – black, white. The point is that of course our society is one of mixed heritage and it's nice to see Meghan within the Royal Family. It's great. She's going to be a beacon and of course she's going to be someone that people look towards.'

While Meghan's mother was the only member of the Markle family to attend the wedding, there were plenty of celebrities in the congregation, which led some cynics to suggest that they were there for that star wattage rather than friendship. The story originated from columnist Rachel Johnson, sister of the British Prime Minister Boris, who later reported that George and Amal Clooney had replied, 'We don't' when asked how they knew the royal couple. In fact, George and Harry had bonded years before over their love of motorbikes, the two couples becoming closer as they had properties near to one another in Oxfordshire. Weeks after the wedding, Harry and Meghan would join the Clooneys for a three-day holiday at their palazzo on Lake Como in Italy. They sat on Meghan's side near to her close friends Serena Williams, Priyanka Chopra, Abigail Spencer and Janina Gavankar. Other notable guests included singers Sir Elton John and James Blunt with their partners David Furnish and Sofia Wellesley, David and Victoria Beckham, actor Tom Hardy, funny man James Corden and of course the cast of *Suits*.

As the congregation were taking their seats, Meghan and her mother, who was dressed in a mint-green suit jacket and dress by the American designer Oscar de la Renta, carefully climbed into the Queen's claret-and-black Rolls-Royce Phantom IV. A tent had been erected from the hotel entrance up to the car door so that no prying eyes could see the wedding dress before the big reveal on the steps of St George's Chapel. On that steady thirty-minute drive, the enormity of the occasion began to sink in as Meghan and Doria passed thousands of well-wishers, some of whom had camped out overnight. Everything was building towards a very special day.

Meanwhile the other star of the show, Prince Harry, dressed in the uniform of the Blues and Royals, and accompanied by his supporter Prince William, made his way into the chapel to applause from the crowd. As the princes waited for the arrival of the bride, it was William who tried to keep a serious-looking Harry relaxed and calm – a turnaround from his own wedding in 2011.

Diana was very much in their thoughts, William asking Harry about something their mother used to say. Harry smiled and was seen to respond with: 'Yeah, I know.'

The other mother, Doria Ragland, made a significant statement in this ancient Christian venue. She chose a natural look for her hairstyle. As black broadcaster Dr Ateh Jewel wrote in the *Daily Telegraph*: 'Doria looked stunning in pistachio as she entered the church, but what has brought an unexpected tear to my eye is the fact this powerful, poised black woman is wearing her hair in locks – her natural state – with pride at one of the biggest historical televised events ever.' Her comment indicated that this would be no ordinary royal wedding. It was a celebration of all colours, cultures and creeds.

While Meghan is not the first mixed-heritage woman to marry into modern European royalty – that honour goes to Panamanian-born Angela Brown, now Princess Angela of the tiny but wealthy country of Liechtenstein – she is the first bi-racial American to take her place in the House of Windsor. Though race has aroused much debate in her own country – inevitably, because of America's past as a nation practising slavery and segregation – race relations have been largely ignored in conjunction with the Royal Family.

Ironically, when the engagement was announced in November 2017, moviegoers were enjoying *Victoria & Abdul*, the story of Queen Victoria's friendship with an Indian attendant, Abdul Karim. His presence in the Royal Household excited so much animosity that when Victoria died in 1901, her eldest son and successor, King Edward VII, personally supervised Karim's eviction and deportation back to India. As historian Carolly Erickson observes in her biography of Queen Victoria, *Her Little Majesty*: 'For a dark-skinned Indian to be put very nearly on a level with the queen's white servants was all but intolerable, for him to eat at the same table with them, to share in their daily lives was viewed as an outrage.'

Though Queen Elizabeth II does not, as author Penny Junor argues, recognize colour, only 8.5 per cent of those employed by the palace are from ethnic minorities whereas in London, where the majority of royal workers are based, just under 40 per cent of the population is from an ethnic minority. There are no figures for those from minorities who occupy senior positions within the institution. It has been argued that the Royal Family has missed an opportunity to take the lead on race and the palace has said 'it must do more' to recruit from minorities.

Race is not a subject that Meghan has shied away from discussing. Nor did it take her long to see that people of colour did not feature noticeably inside the palace. For all that, her very presence inside the Royal Family made the monarchy seem more inclusive and relevant to multicultural Britain, even as the nation struggled to come to terms with diversity in a post-Brexit world.

As Trevor Phillips, former chair of the Equality and Human Rights Commission, noted, the way in which Meghan handles herself will send out an important message. 'It is a very big deal that she has talked of her pride in her ethnicity. For people of colour that will be seen as a very positive, modern approach and immensely welcome.'

Doria Ragland's hairstyle was certainly a positive sign of pride in her black heritage and so too was the diverse arrangement of the wedding service. The hand of Meghan was very evident. Shortly after the arrival of the Queen and Prince Philip, who was still recovering from a fall, it was the turn of the star of the show. Accompanied by her two pageboys Brian and John Mulroney, who held her veil, she walked slowly and carefully, smiling at those she knew. It was a relaxed, easy performance of a woman in charge of herself and her big day. Body language expert Judi James was impressed, telling the Pod Save The Queen podcast: 'Meghan was brimming with confidence and I was nearly applauding, because that's rare. And it was so suitable for the occasion and I think suitable for feminists everywhere to see somebody that didn't go walking up the aisle looking like a nervous blushing bride who was about to pass out at any minute.'

Halfway down the aisle, she was met by Prince Charles, who took her arm and whispered, 'You look lovely – are you OK?' The duo then walked the remaining steps to where the groom and Prince William were waiting. Harry seemed nervous but utterly enraptured as he caught the first sight of the bride in her wedding dress. After greeting Meghan he said, 'Thank you, Pa,' in appreciation of his father's role in accompanying her over the last few steps. But his focus was on his bride, a broad grin creasing his face as he drank her in. 'You look amazing. Absolutely gorgeous.'

So far so traditional, with a welcome and an address by the Dean of Windsor, followed by the popular hymn 'Lord of All Hopefulness', the marriage declarations led by the Archbishop of Canterbury and a reading by one of Diana's sisters, Lady Jane Fellowes. Then Bishop Michael Curry, who had flown in from Chicago to give his address, entered the pulpit. He was due to talk for six minutes. He stopped at fourteen. But he could have continued for longer. Speaking on the theme of the redemptive power of love, he wove in quotations from the late Dr Martin Luther King Junior together with passages from the New Testament. His most memorable line was: 'Two young people fell in love and we all showed up.' It was a compelling sermon, one that drew smirks from some members of the Royal Family as they doubtless compared the passion and verve of the address by the first African American to serve as a presiding bishop in the American Episcopal Church with the rather more restrained style of the usual roster of preachers.

Then it was the turn of the Kingdom Choir led by Karen Gibson, who belted out a gospel version of Ben E. King's 'Stand By Me', which was originally written as a civil rights anthem. The song and the choir, like the hymns and other musical pieces, was recommended by Prince Charles – just as he had done for Prince William's wedding. Once the couple accepted his suggestion, it took twelve different arrangements by Karen Gibson before they hit on the 'right' one. Even the Queen was impressed, inviting the choir to attend a Buckingham Palace garden party.

Karen, who was mobbed when she left St George's Chapel, told the BBC that the initial call to perform came from Clarence House, the London home of the Prince of Wales. 'I understand that Prince Charles really likes gospel music. The couple were very intentional about what they wanted sung and how they wanted it sung, but the actual idea came from Prince Charles.'

While Prince Charles as musical impresario was unexpected, what came as no surprise was that the American feminist, like Lady Diana Spencer and Kate Middleton before her, omitted the word 'obey' from her wedding vows. Though the crowd erupted into cheers and laughter as Harry said, 'I will,' what the public couldn't see was that Meghan never took her eyes from her husband as she spoke her vows. It was, according to friends, a 'heart-warming' moment as it created a visible intimacy between them. As the couple went to sign the register, once again Prince Charles ensured that the other member of the Markle family, Doria, who was on her own, was looked after. He took her by the hand to witness the signing. 'It was a lovely gesture,' his wife, the Duchess of Cornwall, observed afterwards. 'It's something that moved everybody. It's the things he does behind the scenes that people don't know about. I don't think people realize quite how kind he is.'

He watched together with Doria and the rest of the Royal Family as the newly-weds made their smiling way down the aisle to the strains of their favourite song, 'This Little Light of Mine', sung by the Kingdom Choir. Meghan later told *Us Weekly* magazine: 'It was the music that we wanted playing when we started our lives together. Because, as we all know, darkness cannot drive out darkness, only light can do that.' At the top of the chapel steps, Meghan asked her husband, 'Do we kiss?' He replied, 'Yeah,' their moment of public intimacy provoking universal cheering and applause. The couple then embarked on a twenty-five-minute horse-drawn carriage drive, which gave everyone – the crowd was estimated at 120,000 – the opportunity to see them as they went by. It was such a happy, exultant event. Everyone was buoyed by the scene. Even my fellow TV presenters, David Muir and Robin Roberts, veterans of big-name interviews and occasions, were excited, leaping out of their seats to get a proper view of the royal couple as they went past the ABC television booth during their joyful perambulation.

It was an intimate family day but also a momentous event, a little bit of history in the making. As Rose Hudson-Wilkin, Britain's first black female Church of England bishop, told *Vogue*: 'The royal wedding of the Duke and Duchess of Sussex brought people together in many ways. It was such a positive moment for the Church of England, the Episcopal Church, the Royal Family and for Great Britain.'

The newly minted Duke of Sussex, exhausted after an age of smiling and waving, had one thing on his mind during the carriage ride. 'I'm ready for a drink now,' he told his bride, who was overwhelmed by the enthusiasm and size of the reception. 'Wow,' she kept repeating. Their day, however, had only just begun.

After the official family photographs, where cameraman Alexi Lubomirski – who took the engagement pictures – bribed the children with chocolate Smarties to get them to sit still, the couple, now running on nervous energy, attended a two-and-a-half-hour afternoon reception, hosted by Prince William, inside St George's Hall at Windsor Castle. Once again Charles showed his tender side in public as he referred to his son as 'my darling old Harry' and told him, 'I'm so happy for you.' He spoke of how touching it was, at this point in his life, to watch his little boy move on. A little boy whom he had winded so often as a baby and whom, he joked, might still have a bit of wind left.

Then it was Harry's turn. Not that he got very far with his speech. Every time the prince, who looked like the cat who had got the cream, said 'My wife and I', there was raucous cheering, applause and laughter. He managed to tell his guests: 'We make such a great team.' Harry also praised his bride for having 'navigated everything with such grace', telling her, 'I can't wait to spend the rest of my life with you.' After requesting that the American contingent not steal the swords, he asked the crowd if there was anyone present who could sing. Step forward Sir Elton John, who rattled through a medley of some of his biggest hits, including 'Tiny Dancer' which he dedicated to Meghan.

After a break it was time to party, the couple inviting just 200 guests to join them at Frogmore House, a place of happy memories for the newly-weds. It was here where they had enjoyed picnics in the gardens when they were first dating.

Though the guest list was cut dramatically – a significant omission was Harry's friend, Tom Inskip, who had blotted his copybook when he warned the prince about moving too quickly with his long-distance romance – there were plenty of celebrities in attendance including George Clooney who even helped to serve behind the bar. Comedy actor and talk-show host James Corden, who dressed as Henry VIII, compered the shindig and refereed a dance-off between Princes Harry, William and Charles, the trio quickly joined by Meghan and her mother.

As amusing as that was, the undoubted highlight of the evening was Meghan's decision to break with royal tradition and give her own speech. It was short and sweet, the duchess thanking the Queen, Prince Charles and her mother for their kindness and support. Finally, she turned to Harry and, to universal cooing, stated that finally she had found her prince. It was a tender moment which provoked George Clooney to tell his neighbour: 'I'm really enjoying this wedding because they actually seem to be in love, whereas I go to all these celebrity weddings and nobody seems to be in love at all.'

The other woman in Harry's life was uppermost in the minds and hearts of many. In their speeches, while Prince William and Harry's friend Charlie van Straubenzee joked about Harry's life as a ginger and his growing bald spot, they also both talked about how proud Diana would have been to see her youngest son so happy and how excited she would have been to watch him and Meghan start their lives together as a married couple.

There were other reminders of her presence, from the chunky emerald-cut aquamarine ring once owned by Diana, which Harry had given to Meghan, to the fireworks at the end of the evening, which had Harry reminiscing about the time Diana took her boys to Disneyland in Florida on holiday, where it had been a huge treat to see the evening firework display.

If she had been present, the Princess of Wales would have admired Meghan's chutzpah and self-confidence at taking the microphone. For years Diana was always the one who stood at the back in school plays and pantos, terrified of being given a speaking part. Though Meghan was self-assured and had enjoyed the spotlight from an early age, much still connected these two women, although they lived a generation and a world apart. Both women shared a humanitarian mission, both were charismatic and glamorous, and both recognized that they were invested with a power to do good in the world. In short, they both had and have a sense of destiny.

Diana was able to hurdle the barriers of class and ethnicity on both sides of the Atlantic, her appeal, which was to all races, lay as much in her vulnerability as in her star status. She was all the more attractive because of that sensitivity, especially to women trapped in unhappy relationships. Her social work, visiting those in hospices on their last lonely journey, was therapeutic, as healing for her as it was for those whom she comforted.

The word 'vulnerable' does not immediately spring to mind when assessing Ms Markle's many qualities. Empathetic certainly, but also self-possessed, sophisticated and poised, equally at home on a podium making a speech or on a photo shoot. She is a flag bearer for a new generation of confident, assertive women, determined to kick through the glass ceiling.

Her mantra, which she borrowed from her first husband, was that she wasn't going to invest five minutes in a project unless she was prepared to give it five years of her life.

She had married into the most famous and storied family in the world. It wasn't just five years' commitment that was demanded of her, but a lifetime.

16

In the Family Way

It was a silent act that spoke volumes. On 22 May 2018, when the Duchess of Cornwall, the future queen consort, held the hand of the new Duchess of Sussex during a garden party to celebrate Prince Charles's seventieth birthday at Buckingham Palace, this rare royal gesture was a sign of how quickly the American actor had been accepted and treated with genuine affection by the Royal Family. On that day, Camilla, Duchess of Cornwall, who had previously advised Kate Middleton on the finer points of protocol during her royal apprenticeship, was, without saying a word, signalling to the watching world that Meghan was now 'one of us'. Meghan had repaid the compliment in advance. Prior to the garden party, it seemed that she had carefully perused the royal rule book on style and had chosen to wear tights rather than opt for bare legs, which had been her favoured approach to royal engagements before the royal wedding. Her legwear, along with the fact that her outfit, hat and accessories were all British-made, underlined her commitment to 'the Firm'.

Not that Prince Charles would have minded. He dubbed his new daughter-in-law 'Tungsten' because he felt she was 'tough and unbending'. It was meant as a compliment as Charles, who likes strong, independent women, was thrilled by the newest member of the family, not only because she shared his interests in art and literature but also because she had made his second son, at times wayward and lost, complete. Indeed, her arrival seemed to have changed the dynamic between father and royal sons – for the better. Meghan, who was charmed by the future king, had perhaps encouraged her husband to appreciate the Prince of Wales a little more, reminding him of Charles's gallant behaviour during the wedding the previous week.

Certainly Harry's speech to the 6,000 guests, including representatives of the Prince of Wales's organizations and other charity workers, was affectionate and touching as the prince sang his father's praises: 'His enthusiasm and energy are truly infectious; it has certainly inspired William and I to get involved in issues we care passionately about and to do whatever we can to make a difference. In fact, many of the issues William and I now work on are subjects we were introduced to by our father growing up.' Later that summer, as a further sign of their closeness, Charles, Harry and their wives travelled to the far north of Scotland where they spent a weekend at the Castle of Mey, at one time the Queen Mother's remote retreat.

As affable as everyone was, Meghan's induction into the Royal Family still proved to be a steep learning curve. At the famous Trooping of the Colour ceremony in June, a somewhat nervy Duchess of Sussex was seen quietly asking Harry exactly when she should curtsy to the Queen. As he performed a neck bow, he whispered, 'Now.' During the traditional balcony appearance at Buckingham Palace, at which Meghan made a hesitant debut, Harry explained to her that there would be a fly-past and everyone would be watching the skies overhead.

Days later, her honeymoon with the Royal Family continued after the Queen sent an invitation for Meghan to join her on the overnight royal train for a day of engagements in Cheshire, in north-west England. Over breakfast on board the nine-carriage train, the Queen presented her with beautiful pearl earrings and a matching necklace. It was the perfect start to a momentous day. 'I really love being in her company,' Meghan recalled, comparing the Queen's warmth and welcoming persona with that of her own grandmother, Jeanette. As they watched a children's dance exhibition to celebrate the opening of the Mersey Gateway Bridge, Meghan felt comfortable enough with the Queen to essay an observation that had Her Majesty laughing.

Though she had read the chapter in the royal style guidelines about tights, it seems she had skipped the section on hats. She had been advised to wear one for that day's functions but had decided instead to go bare-headed. Unfortunately, the stiff breeze on the open platform had her long tresses whipping around her face. The Queen pretended not to notice. There was another moment of protocol uncertainty, too, when Meghan nervously hesitated about whether she should enter the royal Bentley before or after the Queen.

'What is your preference?' she asked Her Majesty.

'You go first,' replied the Sovereign.

'Oh, OK,' said the duchess.

It was reminiscent of so many early public outings for new arrivals – learning the minutiae of regal protocol on the hoof. That said, the Queen clearly had confidence in the royal ingenue. It was ten months before the previous commoner, Kate Middleton, was asked to join the Queen on a joint royal engagement which was also attended by the Duke of Edinburgh. 'The Queen made sure that Meghan knew what was going on and made her feel at home as it was her first trip,' said one observer.

To ensure that she was kept fully briefed, the duchess was provided with a formidable backroom staff. Even before the wedding, the Queen had shrewdly assigned her own experienced assistant private secretary Samantha Cohen to explain the workings of the monarchy and the Commonwealth to Meghan. As the Sussexes' temporary private secretary, 'Samantha the Panther', as she was dubbed, continued to advise and guide the duchess through the tricky early months of royal life. A keen student, Meghan acknowledged that she would be listening first, acting later. Writer Eleanor Steafel quoted a royal source as saying: 'It is going to be a very busy office. She has worked every day of her life. She is used to a demanding schedule.' Before long Meghan would become a familiar sight around the office, clutching folders of briefing and background notes.

Just as she seemed to have been enthusiastically accepted by the Royal Family, so the public also appeared to have taken her into their hearts. At Royal Ascot in June, she and Harry received a 'rapturous reception' from the cheering crowd during the traditional open-carriage parade. Wearing a white Givenchy dress and monochrome Philip Treacy hat, Meghan echoed Audrey Hepburn's style from *My Fair Lady*. Waiting for her in the royal box was her very own Professor Higgins, Prince Charles, who was ready and willing to discuss the finer points of the British constitution, the history of Ascot and his favourite works in the Royal Collection. A palace source later revealed to the *Daily Telegraph*: 'The duchess has shown a genuine interest in learning more about the history of the family she has married into and her father-in-law has been delighted to impart some of his knowledge.'

Keen, intelligent and inquisitive, Meghan was a willing pupil. She was a hit, a palpable hit, both inside and outside the Royal Family. Her life, though, was not just about fashions and parades, but about what she called 'the work', a life of service. It was no longer confined to the soup kitchens of Los Angeles and Toronto, but to the world stage. A reception for up-and-coming Commonwealth influencers at Buckingham Palace in June, which was attended by the Queen, former Prime Minister John Major and youth ambassadors David Beckham and comedian Lenny Henry, underlined the future direction of travel for the Royal Family's golden couple.

Harry, who had been appointed the Commonwealth's official youth ambassador by the Queen shortly before the wedding, told his audience of adolescent leaders: 'I guess you can say you're stuck with me. I, together with my wife Meghan, look forward to convening young people from around the Commonwealth to hear your ideas, work with you to build platforms for you to collaborate and form partnerships, and continue to meet with many of you as we travel around in our work on behalf of the Royal Family.'

This was the Queen's golden ticket for the duke and duchess to journey across the world to meet interesting, dynamic young people and encourage and enable them in their plans, schemes and dreams. For Meghan, who as a singleton caught planes to exotic locales like some people hail taxis, it was a dream come true, a perfect platform to project her core beliefs in gender equality.

Without articulating it, this global role would hopefully set the couple free from the now endless fashion, lifestyle and personality comparisons with William and Kate. The future king would focus on the British Isles, and Meghan and Harry would concentrate on the Commonwealth.

In reality the comparisons, particularly with Kate, continued unabated. Unfortunately it comes with the territory, the price to be paid for being a woman and royal. Over the years there have been parallels drawn between Sarah, the Duchess of York and Diana, Princess of Wales, the Queen Mother and Wallis Simpson, and of course the Queen and her younger sister, Princess Margaret, who appreciated more than anyone the penalty of living in her older sibling's shadow. As she is believed to have once said to the writer Gore Vidal: 'When there are two sisters, and one is the queen who must be the source of honour and all that is good, the other must be the focus of the most creative malice, the evil sister.'

Kate and Meghan, though, were neither sisters nor, unlike Fergie and Diana, friends before they joined the Royal Family. What is more, during the build-up to Meghan's wedding, Kate was experiencing her third difficult pregnancy and was focused on her own welfare. She did not have much energy to bond with her new neighbour. When they sat together in the royal box to watch the Ladies' Singles Final at Wimbledon in July 2018, the two women were still getting to know one another. During the match, in which Meghan's friend Serena Williams lost to Angelique Kerber, they chatted and clapped and cheered. Unlike Wimbledon 2016, when the cameras focused on Pippa Middleton and Anna Wintour and ignored the unknown American actor, this time they were fixated on the duo of duchesses. The spat concerning the bridesmaids' outfits now behind them, Meghan had since given Kate and her six closest friends gold bracelets designed by Californian jeweller Lisette Polny as a thank-you for their help and support. It was an elegant peace offering, both women professional enough to know that there was no gain in showing dissent or disdain. As royal author Katie Nicholl noted: 'Meghan and Kate have come to an agreement to get along, to make an effort, to be amiable and warm toward each other in public. They both realize it's in neither of their interests to have these catfight headlines. It's not what either of them want.'

Not only did they not know each other well, but there was little opportunity to develop a firm friendship away from public events. It was a practical matter as much as anything. Kate spent weekends and holidays at Anmer Hall, the Cambridges' country home in Norfolk, while Meghan and Harry were approximately three hours' drive away, living in a large, remote, rented property on the Great Tew estate in Oxfordshire. Harry's dream of two united happy families seemed a long way off. Here they entertained their own circle of friends, which included Serena Williams and her husband Alexis Ohanian, George and Amal Clooney, and Priyanka Chopra and Nick Jonas. It was a perfect place to relax and decompress, Meghan making sure that where possible the weekends were reserved just for the two of them. The arrival of an affectionate female Labrador that Harry named Pula, the official currency of Botswana where the couple fell in love, completed their country idyll.

Of course it couldn't last. Storm clouds were gathering over this bucolic scene. For once it wasn't the pesky paparazzi or the hostile TV pundits who rained on her parade, but her own father. Like a wasp at a summer-time picnic he refused to buzz off, telling the world what he thought of his daughter, son-in-law and the rest of the Royal Family whom he considered to be on a par with the cult of Scientology. All the while, his other daughter Samantha was spitting out sour tweets about the sibling she barely knew.

Initially, Tom Markle Senior's comments were headline-making but not mawkish or disparaging. That would come soon enough. He told the morning news show *Good Morning Britain* that Meghan had cried when he told her he would not be attending the wedding. The former lighting director added that he was upset to be 'a footnote in one of the greatest moments in history' and acknowledged that the staged paparazzi shots were a 'serious mistake'. He had the grace to admit that his daughter and Prince Harry were both very forgiving of his behaviour.

This, though, was just the opening salvo in a wearing summer of public recrimination and narcissistic complaint by both Meghan's father and her half-sister. Though Meghan affected to ignore his pleas and platitudes, the jabs and barbs cut deep. After all, this was the man who had raised and supported her. On the wedding's printed order of service, he was still named as the man to walk her down the aisle.

In his now interminable interviews with American and British tabloids, he painted a picture of a wronged father punished by a cold-hearted daughter for one mistake: his sham paparazzi pictures. He claimed that she had cut all ties with him, changed her phone number so that he couldn't reach her and ignored a text where he reported that his heart surgery was successful. Those close to the duchess said she never changed her phone number nor received his text. As for his claims that he missed the wedding because he had to undergo heart surgery, the hospital where the operation allegedly took place told the *Daily Mail* that no one named Markle had checked in for a procedure in mid-May. A friend of Meghan's stated: 'The whole story about Meghan's father undergoing heart surgery was made up. He had to come up with a good enough reason not to attend her wedding and avoid any further embarrassment after those staged photos went public. Don't feel sorry for him … feel sorry for Meghan.'

Tom Senior, though, continued to feel sorry for himself, threatening to show up at Kensington Palace unannounced for a showdown with his daughter. 'I don't care if she is pissed off at me,' he raged. In the event, his other daughter Samantha actually tried the same ploy in October 2018, and was turned away by a palace guard manning one of the security gates. The embarrassing encounter was conveniently photographed by waiting paparazzi.

Tom Markle's media moods, which veered from mawkish sentimentality to narcissistic self-pity, were in many ways more damaging than the original faked paparazzi pictures.

After another scathing tweet by Samantha saying: 'If our father dies, it's on you Meg', there were pictures, possibly staged, of him celebrating his lonely seventy-fourth birthday by picking up a McDonald's Happy Meal during a solo visit to Los Angeles.

Meghan felt helpless as Tom Senior continued his antics, seemingly oblivious to the pain and sorrow he was causing her. As a friend confided to *Us Weekly* magazine: 'She doesn't even know how to communicate with her dad without knowing he won't exploit her. She lives in fear that he'll leak their communication.' Though she cared about her father, the plain facts were that she could no longer trust him.

As his rants became more vituperative and personal, it became clear that the source of his complaint related to the fact that the public had not only responded so warmly and affectionately to his daughter, but also to his ex-wife Doria. Her dignity, discretion and elegance on the wedding day had earned her widespread respect and regard.

In the dysfunctional family dynamic, Tom Senior also wanted to be treated with similar courtesy, but had been denied as a result of his conduct. In one interview with *The Mail on Sunday*, he complained that he never got any praise for raising his daughter. 'Oh, she's a mummy's girl now and Doria gets a lot of the credit.' He continued bitterly, 'What riles me is Meghan's sense of superiority. She'd be nothing without me. I made her the duchess she is today. Everything that Meghan is, I made her.'

In one of his many self-pitying moods, he pondered: 'Perhaps it would be easier for Meghan if I died. Everybody would be filled with sympathy for her. But I hope we reconcile. I'd hate to die without speaking to Meghan again.'

Behind the scenes Meghan had had enough. As she prepared to celebrate her thirty-seventh birthday in early August, she sat down to write a heartfelt letter to her errant father. Now it was her turn to articulate her sadness, sense of betrayal and bewilderment over his behaviour and that of her half-sister.

In her distinctive elegant script she penned five pages, asking 'Daddy' why he had turned a blind eye to the pain he was causing. She continued: 'Your actions have broken my heart into a million pieces – not simply because you have manufactured such unnecessary and unwarranted pain, but by making the choice to not tell the truth as you are puppeteered in this. Something I will never understand.'

She went on: 'I have only ever loved, protected and defended you, offering whatever financial support I could, worrying about your health … and always asking how I could help.' She spoke of her 'horror' when she heard about his heart attack, but also begged him to stop lying, exploiting her royal connections and causing pain to her and Harry whom, she said, had only ever been 'patient, kind and understanding' towards him.

Nor did she overlook Samantha's conduct and the way her father tolerated her unsubstantiated insults. 'You watched me silently suffer at the hands of her vicious lies, I crumbled inside.' The duchess told him that only her Christian faith and her belief that a lie cannot live forever had helped her to sleep at night.

She sent him the letter by FedEx and for months he carried it with him in his briefcase. For once he remained silent about its contents. In response he wrote a four-page letter which concluded with a suggestion that the best way forward was to stage a photocall with Harry, Meghan and himself to show that they were a happy family. It was precisely the kind of bogus display that Meghan loathed. A private meeting, maybe. A public display, forget it. She told a friend: 'I'm devastated. My father's clearly been fully corrupted.'

Her father's now routine betrayals had a profound knock-on effect. Already wary of outsiders, Harry and Meghan became increasingly concerned about their privacy. At public events, royal rota reporters were kept further away from the couple, while in private the Sussexes deliberately kept a low profile. Friends were asked to say nothing under any circumstances to the media as Harry deliberately erected an emotional fortress around himself and his wife. As royal writer Camilla Tominey noted: 'The princes are both very private people and have tried their best to keep the press at bay ever since their mother's death. They are extremely protective of their wives and families and will do anything to avoid a repeat of the eighties and nineties, when they felt that Princess Diana was hounded.' An incident at the Sentabale Polo Cup in Windsor that

July, when the prince fired a ball at the press area, albeit accidentally, seemed to epitomize his increased hostility towards to the media. Even though he apologized, disgruntled cameramen pointed out that they were there to publicize his charity.

Photographers were most welcome, though, when Meghan and Harry attended the launch of a very special cookbook. It was inspired by the community of women in West London who came together following the tragic Grenfell Tower fire of June 2017, which claimed the lives of seventy-two people and left hundreds more homeless. For two days a week, women from all ethnic backgrounds gathered in the communal kitchen at the Al-Manaar Muslim Cultural Heritage Centre in West London where they cooked and prepared food for those in need. As word spread and more women joined, it became known as the Hubb Community Kitchen. In Arabic, 'hubb' means love.

After hearing about their work, Meghan went along to the Hubb kitchen in January 2018 to find out more and to help out. When the community organizers told her that they could only afford to be open two days a week, Meghan suggested compiling a cookbook to raise funds. She pulled some strings and eight months later *Together: Our Community Cookbook* was published. Meghan's brainchild was a runaway success, proceeds easily doubling the initial target of £250,000. In a promotional video, she recalled: 'I immediately felt connected to this community kitchen. Like these women I am passionate about food and cooking as a way of strengthening communities.'

In her first public speech since joining the Royal Family, at the official book launch she spoke for three minutes without notes, telling her audience of cooks and supporters gathered in the grounds of Kensington Palace that food was more than a meal, and that when you understood the story behind a recipe you got to know the person behind it. It was, she said, a celebration of 'what connects us rather than what divides us'.

The very fact that her proud mother Doria had flown over from Los Angeles especially for the launch was an indication of how passionately Meghan felt about this project. It was her baby, a tangible way of using her title and new position to effect genuine change in communities. As input from palace courtiers was minimal, the inevitable takeaway was that she could be more independent than perhaps the current hierarchy allowed.

It was a recipe for change, an acknowledgement that her own ethnic background enabled her to mix more readily with others from racial minorities. Without spelling it out, it was clear that Meghan had that special quality treasured by the Queen and the rest of the family – the ability to make the monarchy relevant to the wider world.

※

During Doria's visit, Meghan shared another secret with her mother – she was about to become a grandmother. The royal couple selectively spread the word a few days later when they were guests at the wedding of their friends Princess Eugenie and Jack Brooksbank at St George's Chapel. Although they were, perhaps inevitably, criticized for upstaging the bride, a mutual friend explained: 'It was a happy family event and that's where happy family news gets shared.'

As for the rest of the world, the Sussexes had a ticklish decision. They were due to fly out on their first official tour Down Under. As Meghan was already showing, they didn't want the visit to be all about pregnancy speculation. So when they landed in Sydney on 15 October, members of the press pack were informed shortly before the announcement was issued by Kensington Palace that Meghan was pregnant. Now she had to navigate the little matter of attending seventy-six engagements in Australia, Fiji, Tonga and New Zealand in sixteen days without succumbing to morning sickness – the illness that cursed the pregnancies of both Diana, Princess of Wales and Catherine, Duchess of Cambridge.

Even though it took her a week to get over the jet lag after the twenty-seven-hour flight, Meghan was indefatigable, throwing herself into engagements with such enthusiasm that Harry and royal aides pleaded with her to pace herself.

They were greeted by huge, at times hysterical, crowds who came to see what all the fuss was about. Though visits by members of the Royal Family are always popular, it was noticeable that the crowds were composed of more young people and ethnic minorities. Teenage girls particularly saw in Meghan a symbol of female empowerment or a familiar representative face. Sherry-Rose Bih Watts, a black social-enterprise entrepreneur, was impressed: 'For me, Meghan represents someone in the palace I never thought I'd see ... a major societal change. Her role in the Royal Family is extremely important and relevant. It's cool to think there are young girls who look at the Duchess of Sussex and think, "Hey, she kind of looks like me."'

Nor was it left to Harry to do all the talking. Meghan wrote and gave three speeches during the visit. She focused on the armed forces, equal rights, and at the University of the South Pacific in Fiji she returned to a favourite theme – female empowerment and the need for universal education. 'Because when girls are given the right tools to succeed, they can create incredible futures, not only for themselves but for all of those around them,' she said. The duchess found a new fan in New Zealand's Prime Minister Jacinda Ardern, who had given birth to her own baby in June. She lauded Meghan for 'the role she is playing at such an often tiring time. I have real empathy and I think she's incredible.' The two women became firm friends, emailing one another and meeting up when the Prime Minister came to London.

The royal couple returned to London in triumph, proving to the palace that their relaxed, open style – Harry only took two ties with him for the visit – made them relevant and relatable to a rising generation within important Commonwealth nations. It had been, as the Queen, Princes Charles and William, and other members of the Royal Family appreciated, damned hard work – but they had come through it.

As the icing on the cake, in a YouGov poll published in November, Harry was voted the most popular member of the Royal Family ahead of the Queen. Though Meghan came sixth, a month earlier she had received the accolade of being named in the 2019 Powerlist, an annual directory of Britain's most influential people of African and African-Caribbean origin. She joined British

Vogue editor-in-chief Edward Enninful, boxer Anthony Joshua and rapper Stormzy on the elite list.

When they arrived at the Royal British Legion Festival of Remembrance at the Royal Albert Hall with the rest of the Royal Family in November, there was no doubting who was the new star of the show. As *The Times* of London reported: 'All eyes soon turned to Harry and Meghan, whose entrance to a barrage of camera flashes prompted excited squawks on social media.' Meghan was 'glowing, smiling, baby bump growing and that's all that matters', tweeted one royal fan. Then the wheels came off.

17

Race and Relations

It didn't take long but the honeymoon was soon over. The honeymoon, that is, between the Duchess of Sussex and the mass media. Within a matter of months she went from Duchess Dazzling to Duchess Difficult, a Hollywood diva who tried to bend the thousand-year-old monarchy to her will and whim, offending everyone from the Queen downwards. The stories conformed to the age-old narrative of the unruly American individualist thumbing his or her nose at British class, hierarchy and tradition. Think Steve McQueen in the classic war movie *The Great Escape*. This time, though, it was a strong-willed American feminist who ruffled feathers.

For once it was not the tabloids who led the charge. In November 2018, just days after the couple returned from their successful tour Down Under, the venerable *Times* of London reported an extraordinary story. It stated that Meghan had thrown a 'tiara tantrum' shortly before the wedding because the tiara she wanted to wear was not available. Her prima-donna behaviour apparently earned a rebuke from the Queen herself, who told Prince Harry: 'She gets what tiara she's given by me.'

In the subsequent varied and often conflicting media accounts it seemed that initially she had favoured a tiara with emeralds, as the green of the stone would complement the outfits due to be worn by both the Queen and Meghan's mother Doria. However, according to *The Times*, because there was some question about the original provenance of the Russian Vladimir tiara, which was said to be Meghan's preferred headpiece, the Queen decided against offering it to her.

Meghan's growing fame, thanks to the success of *Suits*, ensured that plenty of goodies came her way. Known as a foodie, she was hosted around the island of Malta in 2015, where she tasted local wines and food. She also reflected on the fact that her great-great-grandmother Mary Merrill, the daughter of Mary Bird – a former housemaid at Windsor Castle – and a British soldier, was born here.

LEFT: On their second trip to Botswana in 2017, Prince Harry and Meghan celebrated her thirty-sixth birthday when they briefly stayed at the Meno a Kwena camp before driving to Victoria Falls. As William had proposed to Kate Middleton during a holiday in Kenya, the media, somewhat predictably, suspected that Harry would follow his big brother's lead.

BELOW: When Harry and Meghan officially attended the Invictus Games together on 25 September 2017, they caused a media frenzy. After they arrived at the Toronto stadium, they put on an affectionate show, knowing that their every gesture, whisper and smile would be photographed.

LEFT: Prince Harry and Meghan pose for photographers in the Sunken Garden at Kensington Palace after their engagement was announced on 27 November 2017. The Sunken Garden was one of Diana's favourite spots, which is why Harry chose this special place to tell the world of their love.

BELOW: On Christmas Day in 2017, the next royal generation – the Duke and Duchess of Cambridge along with Harry and Meghan – line up after church in Sandringham. Initially, they were dubbed the 'Fab Four' after The Beatles pop group. The reality was very different.

ABOVE: The duchess-to-be and her mother Doria wave to the crowds as they head to St George's Chapel, Windsor. Meghan's diamond tiara, loaned to her by the Queen, became a source of controversy after the wedding, which took place on 19 May 2018.

BELOW: At the last moment, Meghan's father Tom claimed he was too ill to walk his daughter down the aisle. Instead, Prince Charles met her part way, asking her if she was 'OK' after taking her arm. Prince Harry was simply bowled over by his bride.

ABOVE: The happy couple wave to the cheering crowds during a carriage procession down the Long Walk at Windsor Castle. It was a day of blue skies, broad grins and endless possibilities, their marriage seeming to make the monarchy inclusive and relevant once again.

BELOW: Meghan enjoyed her first flypast when she joined the rest of the Royal Family on the balcony at Buckingham Palace in June 2018. She was understandably nervous and Harry had to prompt her to look at the sky so she didn't miss the spectacular aerial display.

RIGHT: In June 2018, just days after the royal wedding, the Queen invited the Duchess to join her in a ceremony to open the Mersey Gateway Bridge in Cheshire. Meghan felt relaxed enough to essay an observation that had the Queen chortling.

BELOW: In September 2018 at Kensington Palace, Meghan launched a cookbook featuring recipes contributed by many of those touched by the Grenfell Tower fire in London.

LEFT: Delighted parents Harry and Meghan pose with their newborn son, Archie Harrison Mountbatten-Windsor, during a photocall in St George's Hall at Windsor Castle on 8 May 2019. Meghan gave birth at 5.26 a.m. on 6 May.

BELOW: In a jaw-dropping interview with Oprah Winfrey, Meghan laid bare the difficulties she had experienced in joining the Royal Family. She revealed that she felt isolated, lonely and almost imprisoned by the system. She even considered suicide.

The long goodbye. During her short royal career, Meghan bridled at the stiffness and formality of life inside the Royal Family. Once back in California, she enjoyed a relaxed lifestyle, doing open-air yoga and collecting eggs every day from her son's 'Chick Inn'. In June 2021, after the birth of her daughter Lilibet – whose name derives from the Queen's childhood nickname – she and Prince Harry took a five-month parenting break, but not before Meghan had launched a children's book, *The Bench*, which rapidly became a *New York Times* bestseller.

As it is one of the Queen's more familiar tiaras, worn variously for an audience with the Pope and at a banquet at Windsor Castle held in honour of the Irish President in 2014, this argument didn't hold water. Nor did the style of the Vladimir tiara especially complement Meghan's wedding dress, which went perfectly with the sleek 1932 diamond bandeau tiara. In any case, as previously discussed, Meghan and her designer Claire Waight Keller always saw the ornament as very much the Queen's ultimate choice. It was her gift.

However, where reports in several media outlets did overlap was with regard to Harry's behaviour. The prince, who needed acupuncture to stay calm in the run-up to the wedding, was overwrought when the chosen tiara could not be made instantly available for Meghan's hairdresser Serge Normant, who had flown from New York to work on the hair fitting. The Queen's formidable dresser Angela Kelly, who is the guardian of the Queen's jewellery, is said to have informed the irate prince that certain security protocols had to be adhered to in order to access the priceless piece. A source revealed that he was told: 'They're kept under very tight lock and key. You can't turn up and demand to have the tiara just because your hairdresser happens to be in town.'

Harry would have none of it, telling anyone who would listen: 'What Meghan wants, Meghan gets.' His ringing phrase did her no favours. Harry suspected, rightly or wrongly, that the old guard at the palace did not like Meghan and were deliberately trying to make life difficult for them. In the end he went directly to the Queen and organized a hair fitting. As reported by royal insider Emily Andrews, a royal source revealed: 'Harry and Meghan may have wrongly interpreted being told she couldn't have immediate access to the tiara as a snub, but Angela was following Palace protocol. It wasn't a snub, it's just the way the institution works.'

Though Harry was the prime mover in this episode, it was Meghan who took the hit. Almost overnight the narrative about her turned full circle, from Duchess Different to Duchess Dictatorial. Once that narrative was fixed in the popular imagination it was almost impossible to change. It was so noticeable that Sky News broadcast a report under the heading: 'Have we fallen out of love with the Duchess of Sussex?' In short order, she was accused of making Kate cry over Princess Charlotte's bridesmaid dress – a story that really, really rankled with her – and was blamed for the premature departure of royal staff, including her personal assistant Melissa Touabti, whom she also reduced to tears, along with temporary private secretary Samantha Cohen and her Scotland Yard bodyguard.

She was also deemed to be at the centre of the growing rift between the two hitherto inseparable brothers. Oh, and she wanted to use air fresheners in St George's Chapel to diffuse the musty smell – just like Kate did in Westminster Abbey before her wedding. It was quite a charge sheet.

What is truly remarkable is that Meghan's media narrative mirrored Princess Diana's early experiences inside the Royal Family. She too was blamed for a series of departures, from Prince Charles's valet, bodyguard and private secretary to friends and members of his social circle. In a matter of months she went from being a fairy-tale princess to, according to gossip columnist Nigel Dempster, a 'fiend' and a 'little monster'. Other commentators talked about 'Malice in the Palace'. At one royal engagement, the exasperated princess told veteran royal watcher James Whitaker: 'I am not responsible for any sackings. I don't just sack people.'

At a time when she was struggling with the eating disorder bulimia nervosa and post-natal depression following the birth of Prince William, dark thoughts of taking her own life scudded across Diana's psyche. Given her fragile mental state, the hostile step change in media coverage – and remember, this was before the Wild West of social media – could not have come at a worse time. As she told me for her biography: 'The thing is I never wanted to get rid of anyone. I never wanted to move anyone out. I just wanted to keep my head above water.'

Meghan may have sensed that history was repeating itself. What cut deepest was that there was never any formal rebuttal of the accusations made about the Duchess of Sussex by the palace press office. They were allowed to stand, further contributing to the construction of her negative image. The usual palace argument that if you deny one false story you would have to deny every piece of nonsense written about the Royal Family did not, in Meghan's eyes, cut it, especially as erroneous tales about other members of the Royal Family were officially refuted. As she later told Oprah Winfrey: 'But the narrative about, you know, making Kate cry, I think was the beginning of a real character assassination. And they [palace officials] knew it wasn't true. And I thought, well, if they're not going to kill things like that, then what are we going to do?'

In fact, the palace did not sit on its hands. From time to time, it did formally dispute stories, such as a tale that appeared in *The Sun* newspaper in early December suggesting that Kate had 'slapped down' Meghan for being rude to one of her staff. 'This never happened,' said the palace. Moreover, Kensington Palace spent hundreds of hours monitoring social media posts, particularly those relating to Kate and Meghan. It later unveiled a code of conduct for internet interactions on the Royal Family's platforms. Violent threats were reported to the police, and sexist and racist comments deleted.

During this time a BBC investigation exposed a shadowy neo-Nazi group which suggested that Harry was a 'race traitor' and should be shot. The organization also advocated the rape and killing of police officers. In June 2021, one of the group's leaders, politics student Andrew Dymock, was found guilty at the Old Bailey of fifteen offences relating to terrorism and hate crimes.

In an era of anonymous social media, vitriolic remarks about both duchesses, but especially Meghan, were a new and nasty fact of life. Exaggerated or distorted stories in the mainstream media gave the Twitter- and blog-spheres licence to feed their obsessive online hatred. Royal blogger Charlotte, who runs the sites Duchess Kate and Mad About Meghan, observed: 'Ardent fans known as "stans" online have driven the once affable online community into an incredibly divisive place filled with vile insults, abuse and inexcusable behaviour.'

It was, however, Meghan's continuing frustration with the palace's response to false stories about her that seemed to lead directly to a major article in *People* magazine in February 2019, where five of her friends, interviewed on the condition of anonymity, spoke out in her favour. This course of action would have unintended consequences.

Meghan and Harry now sensed a change towards them, not just in the ranks of the mass media but also inside the Royal Family. Harry later told Oprah Winfrey that the tour Down Under was 'the first time that the family got to see how incredible she is at the job. And that brought back memories.' He was referring to the famous 1983 tour of Australia and New Zealand by his parents, during which Prince Charles became jealous of Diana's popularity. In public, the Prince of Wales made light of the fact that during walkabouts the crowds would groan when he went to their side of the road; in private, he criticized his wife.

When we were working on her biography, the princess told me: 'The public side was very different from the private side. The public side, they wanted a fairy princess to come and touch them and everything will turn into gold and all their worries would be forgotten. Little did they realize that the individual was crucifying herself inside because she didn't think she was good enough. "Why me, why all this publicity?" My husband started to get very jealous and anxious by then, too.'

That jealousy, in Meghan and Harry's view, was now directed at them. They were too current, too fresh, too challenging for what they saw as the old guard. Harry had always been prickly at any suggestion of criticism of his wife, and from now on he seemed more sensitive and quick to take offence.

That said, there was a significant difference between Diana and Charles's visit Down Under and their own. His parents' experience highlighted the gulf between them as a married couple. As far as Meghan and Harry were concerned, they were united against the world – and that was beginning to include the Royal Family. 'I mean, here you have one of the greatest assets to the Commonwealth that the family could have ever wished for,' Harry told Oprah. When she reminded him that the marital drama between his parents during their Australian tour formed an episode of *The Crown*, he replied, 'Look, I just wish that we would all learn from the past.'

They were coming to appreciate that in the royal hierarchy, no matter how popular, inspiring or relevant they were to the outside world, they were low down on the royal totem pole. Both William and Harry were funded by their father and it was often the case that Harry's ambitions did not match Prince Charles's budget. His brother, as the future king, would always take priority. It may have been frustrating, it may have led to rows and jealousy, but that was the way it was and that was the way it was always going to be.

They were not the first nor will they be the last members of the family to experience the first rule of royalty: funding does not relate to popularity but position. In her heyday, Princess Margaret and her photographer husband Lord Snowdon were seen as the faces of the Swinging Sixties, the most glamorous, popular and photographed royals of the age. Yet they were still far down the pecking order, way below the Queen and her family.

The immutable hierarchy, palace politics and routine deference took Meghan, a girl in a hurry, quite some time to get to grips with. She slowly came to realize, as did Diana, that everything was not as it seemed in this looking-glass world. Indeed a generation later, Meghan's own observations of life in the goldfish bowl meshed remarkably with the princess's own feelings. Diana's first impressions of the palace world were: 'I couldn't believe how cold everyone was; how I thought one thing but actually another thing was going on. The lies and the deceit.' Meghan found herself being judged by the media-generated impressions of her rather than her actual life. As she told Oprah: 'It's easy to have an image that is so far from reality, and that's what was so tricky over those past few years, when the perception and the reality are two different things and you're being judged on the perception but you're living the reality of it. There's a complete misalignment and there's no way to explain that to people.'

※

During this pivotal month of November, when the day-to-day reality of royal life had started to sink in, Meghan and Harry first began to discuss their options and their way forward for the future. First item on the agenda was setting up their own Royal Household, which was essentially their own 'company' inside the family Firm. For all his adult life Harry had shared a household with his older brother, who as future king always came first. After William's marriage to Kate Middleton, Harry became the third wheel, happily trundling behind his sibling.

His years of Army life – he had a twenty-week deployment in Helmand Province in Afghanistan from 2012 to 2013 – ensured that his royal duties were minimal. It was only after he resigned his commission in 2015 that he became increasingly involved in the work of the Firm. Following his own marriage, there was now a sense that the time had come for Harry to go off on his own, even though it would mean additional expenditure for Prince Charles.

The first sign that times were a-changing came in late November 2018, when the couple announced that they were leaving their modest two-bedroom cottage at Kensington Palace for the storied Frogmore Cottage, a Grade II listed building on the Windsor estate. Not only did Frogmore hold a special place in their hearts, as it was in the grounds of the main house where they had enjoyed romantic picnics during their courtship, but it got them away from the goldfish bowl that is Kensington Palace. Though secure, the palace was also a place of gossip, prying eyes and endless salacious leaks about the prince and his wife. In any case Harry felt he needed a break from his brother and a chance to establish his own home life without any interference. Ever since William had questioned the fast pace of Harry's courtship, relations between them had been cool. It was time to start afresh.

However, the £2.4 ($3.4) million conversion of the historic building, paid for by British taxpayers, was another handy stick with which to beat the couple. What was lost in the shuffle was that the grace-and-favour building – one that is owned by the Sovereign or government and parcelled out at the Queen's discretion – had long been earmarked for renovation as it hadn't been worked on for some years and was deemed an official heritage site. It was, though, the Sussexes who found themselves in the firing line over the costs. It was suggested, wrongly, that Meghan had installed a yoga studio, insisted on an expensive sprung floor in the kitchen and splashed out £1 million on modern art.

Once more the stories of extravagance and indulgence were remarkably similar to those a generation earlier, when Princess Margaret and her husband Lord Snowdon were eventually allocated 1a Clock Court, currently the home of the Duke and Duchess of Cambridge, at Kensington Palace. Lawmakers and pundits attacked the couple for the cost even though the residence needed substantial refurbishment no matter who moved in, as it had been unoccupied for over twenty years and had fallen into disrepair. Lord Snowdon was so incensed by the inaccurate accusations of profligacy that he offered to show the media around the bomb-damaged palace.

When Harry and Meghan moved into their new home in April 2019, they *did* pay for the interior furnishings and the fixtures and fittings that were installed. Their friend, the writer Bryony Gordon, who visited them after they had settled in, poked fun at the couple's perceived lifestyle – 'sitting in sumptuous robes, throwing taxpayers' money into an expensive wood-burning stove, setting fire to the world they claimed to care so much about'. She wrote: 'Frogmore Cottage is not quite the lavish pit of taxpayers' money that the tabloids would have you believe. It's nice, of course, a great deal more than most British people could ever imagine living in, but it is by no means extravagant or palatial.'

Built in 1801 for Queen Charlotte, wife of King George III, the historic cottage had also been the home of Queen Victoria's Indian 'Munshi', Abdul Karim, until her death in 1901. As the Queen's favourite, Karim was loathed by her family and members of the Royal Household, and on Victoria's death, King Edward VII had him kicked out of the cottage and returned to India. On the King's orders all his correspondence with the late Sovereign was burnt. It was as though Karim had never existed inside the royal circle.

More than a century later, the ghosts of Karim and Edward VII – who is buried in St George's Chapel – hovered over the new tenants of Frogmore Cottage. Harry informed Meghan about an extraordinary conversation he had had with a member of his family. His royal relation, whom he refused to publicly name, had asked about how dark the new baby's skin might be. It was that issue, Meghan later implied, which was connected to decisions about her child's title and future security. In short, the darker the skin the more minor the title and protection. The mystery royal was not, Harry later pointed out, either the Queen or Prince Philip.

Meghan told Oprah: 'They were saying they didn't want him to be a prince or princess – not knowing what the gender would be – which would be different from protocol, and that he wasn't going to receive security. This went on for the last few months of our pregnancy where I was going, "Hold on for a second."'

She argued that the palace had allowed a 'monster machine', in terms of turning them into tabloid fodder, to grow up and it was therefore its responsibility to protect the new royal baby. While Meghan's child could take the courtesy title of the Earl of Dumbarton if he were a boy, according to royal protocol it was only the children and grandchildren of the Sovereign who could be made a prince or princess and be eligible for round-the-clock protection. As Meghan's baby was a great grandchild of the Queen, he or she would not have a full-time bodyguard.

The optics of precedence did not wash with the duchess. As she said to Oprah: 'But the idea of our son not being safe, and also the idea of the first member of colour in this family not being titled in the same way that other grandchildren would be ...'

Royal expert Robert Jobson explained: 'According to a 1917 letters patent issued by King George V, the title of HRH Prince or Princess passed to the children of any Sovereign of the United Kingdom and the children of the sons of any such Sovereign. Both Harry and Meghan know this.'

What was rather lost in this internal discussion was the fact that both Harry and Meghan had full-time bodyguards who, according to custom and practice, would also keep an eye on the child who would be, at least for the early years, confined to a pram or a cot. For the moment this debate took place only among the family. Not for much longer.

The distressing and insulting conversation pertaining to her unborn child could not have come at a worse time for the duchess. Unbeknownst to anyone – even her husband – Meghan was suffering badly during her pregnancy. Her anguish was such that in early January 2019, she harboured clear thoughts of suicide, thoughts sparked in part by the hate campaign against her.

In a touching and highly emotional confession, Meghan told Oprah that although she tried to avoid what was being said about her, her mother or her friends would call her up and say, 'Meg, they're not protecting you.' As she learned of the endless negative comments, she thought to herself: 'I realized it was all happening just because I was breathing.'

She nursed her secret shame, coolly and methodically assessing how and when to end it all. That impulse became so overwhelming that Meghan, who prides herself in bringing solutions not problems to her prince, finally confessed her distress to Harry. It was a decision she took reluctantly as she knew what a psychological burden he too carried with regard to the death of his mother. She confessed to Oprah: 'But I knew that if I didn't say it, that I would do it. And I … I just didn't … I just didn't want to be alive any more. And that was a very clear and real and frightening constant thought.'

She finally made her confession one morning in mid-January, the prince cradling her in his arms, reassuring her that they would pull through. That night they were scheduled to appear at a performance of *Cirque du Soleil* at the Royal Albert Hall to raise funds for Harry's Sentebale AIDS charity. He suggested that Meghan should cancel and stay at home. But she insisted on going and told him that if she was left on her own she might harm herself.

That night they held hands tightly, so tightly that the whites of their knuckles were evident. The couple were all smiles as they took their seats, but as soon as the lights went down, Meghan began to weep in the royal box.

What was as equally if not more distressing was that shortly afterwards, according to Meghan's narrative, she spoke to senior officials at the palace. She felt she needed to be hospitalized so that she could get professional help in order to cope with her suicidal feelings. She was met with sympathy but inaction. According to her account, the official said: 'My heart goes out to you because I see how bad it is, but there's nothing we can do to protect you because you're not a paid employee of the institution.' Eventually, it is believed, she contacted Harry's mother's good friend, Julia Samuel, founder patron of Child Bereavement UK, for support and a listening ear.

Clinical psychologist Dr Emma Svanberg, who specializes in mental health issues relating to peripartum – the time before, during and after childbirth – was unsurprised at the duchess's sorrowful story. As she explained to *The New York Times*: 'Meghan was a pregnant woman living in an unfamiliar country and isolated from her family and social support, with enormous and new pressures placed on her in her role as well as the pressures felt by all women in the perinatal period. I cannot begin to imagine going through this with criticism, hostility and judgement. How could there not have been an emotional fallout to that?'

For once the tabloids understated Meghan's sense of despair. When *Us Weekly* reported exclusively in January that 'Meghan has so much on her plate, between being pregnant and dealing with the public backlash, and she's finding the whole situation incredibly stressful', they were unintentionally on the money. Even though she was happily married to Harry, she felt a profound sense of isolation and loneliness, a feeling that she was somehow trapped in this unfriendly, unfamiliar and unforgiving new world in which she found herself marooned. When her passport, driving licence and keys were taken from her, she felt it was a symbolic moment of imprisonment.

Once again, comparisons with Diana are illuminating. Shortly after her engagement, she went to live at Buckingham Palace where she felt like she was a captive in a Grimm fairy tale. As the walls of the prison house closed inexorably around Diana, the public knew nothing about her ordeal, instead celebrating Prince Charles's good fortune. Her friend and Harry's godmother, Carolyn Bartholomew, recalled: 'She wasn't happy, she was suddenly plunged into all this pressure and it was a nightmare for her. She was dizzy with it, bombarded from all sides. It was a whirlwind and she was ashen, she was grey.'

Yet both Diana and Meghan had the ability to put on a brave face in public – Diana said she got that quality from her mother – and carry on regardless. This was just as well, as there was little respite from the royal treadmill – much of the work generated by Meghan herself.

In January, at the height of her mental anguish, Meghan, who had clocked up more than a hundred engagements during the first months of her royal life, took on the first four of her patronages. She agreed to champion the work of the Association of Commonwealth Universities, a clear fit with Harry's role of Commonwealth youth ambassador; the Royal National Theatre – she had already visited Brinsworth House, the Royal Variety Charity's nursing and care home for retired actors; Mayhew, an animal welfare charity, which was perfect for this animal lover; and Smart Works, a charity to help disadvantaged women find work through the provision of a new wardrobe and interview training. She had quietly dropped in on the centre several times during the previous year, on one occasion coaching a client before she faced a job interview. This was a scheme close to her heart as she had a long track record in the field of community and female empowerment. When she was at Northwestern University she participated in The Glass Slipper Project, which provided prom dresses and accessories to young women living in underprivileged districts.

That month she sent an unsolicited email to a man who knew all about the power of fashion, Edward Enninful, the first black editor-in-chief of British *Vogue* magazine. He was spending a few days in the Austrian mountains when the note, signed simply 'M', arrived in his in-box suggesting a meeting. Over tea in central London a week later, they discussed her association with Smart Works and how *Vogue* magazine could help. She followed up their first meeting with a text message in which she politely asked if he would consider co-editing a special issue of *Vogue* with her, to highlight the female change-makers who are set to reshape the planet in a positive way. He recalled: 'From activists to artists, prime ministers to climate change campaigners, we would gather faces from the front lines of fashion, film, technology, wellness and beyond to celebrate a special moment in time – and to ask the question: "What's next?"' He instantly agreed and the theme 'Forces for Change' was the beginning of the adventure that became the September 2019 issue of *Vogue* magazine. It was an endeavour that would occupy her during the long waiting days before she gave birth.

Like the Grenfell cookbook, it was very much her baby, conceived and created with minimal input from the palace, an organization that she increasingly felt did not have her best interests at heart. She had her own shadow court of American advisers who came up with suggestions and projects for her to consider. The quartet comprised her lawyer Rick Genow, business manager Andrew Meyer, talent agent Nick Collins and Keleigh Thomas Morgan of PR firm Sunshine Sachs, who organized her 2017 interview with *Vanity Fair* magazine. They were the guiding lights behind initial conference calls and then a meeting at Kensington Palace between Meghan, Harry and Jeffrey Katzenberg, the billionaire founder of Quibi, a US streaming start-up focused on short ten-minute content. Katzenberg, former chairman of Walt Disney Studios, and CEO Meg Whitman, a defeated Republican candidate for the governor of California, were keen to court the couple ahead of the launch of the platform in April 2020. While Harry was eager to discuss a sustainable travel show as well as his charity interests in Africa, the duchess was somewhat nonplussed by Katzenberg's big idea, a show on 'princesses and puppies'. It was classic Hollywood logic. People love puppies and adore princesses. Put them together and hey presto, a sure-fire ratings winner.

After the intellectual exhilaration of her discussions with *Vogue* magazine, this wasn't exactly what she had in mind. 'Meghan seemed to find that idea offensive and though she was gracious in the moment, people in the room were a bit appalled that this was the pitch to her,' a source told writer Caroline Graham. Nonetheless, these freelance discussions continued often without senior members of their staff knowing what was going on.

There was a sense, as the couple saw it, that as Meghan was not being protected by the palace they would have to do something about it themselves. The first immediate result was a February 2019 issue of the American magazine *People*, where five unnamed friends paid tribute to her empathetic and giving nature, and castigated the media for so savagely attacking a pregnant woman. Though Meghan's supporters claimed she was not aware of the article or its contents, the fact that *People* magazine felt confident enough to use copyright pictures of Meghan taken by her close friend and wedding planner Jessica Mulroney during their 2016 holiday in Italy rather undercut that argument. They stated that their aim was to 'stand up against the global bullying we are seeing and speak the truth about our friend'.

A former co-star expanded: 'Meg has silently sat back and endured the lies and untruths. We worry about what this is doing to her and the baby. It's wrong to put anyone under this level of emotional trauma, let alone when they're pregnant.'

Though they valiantly painted a portrait of a 'selfless' woman 'who was devoted to God', it was a reference to the exchange of letters between Meghan and her father which really made the headlines – and angered Tom Markle Senior. A friend described to *People* how Meghan's heart had been broken by his behaviour and how she had pleaded with him to stop victimizing her through the media. As royal writer Richard Kay noted: '[Her letter] was much more than the private thoughts of a wounded young woman. It was a cry for help from someone adjusting to a bewildering new life many thousands of miles from home.'

Her pal went on to briefly describe his letter of reply, where he suggested that they organize a photocall. That revelation was enough for Tom Senior to decide to go public and allow Meghan's letter to be published in the British tabloid, *The Mail on Sunday*. Not only did it drive a permanent wedge between father and daughter, but some months later it prompted a wide-ranging legal suit against the Sunday tabloid by the duchess. If the aim of her friends was to lower the temperature between Meghan, the media and Tom, it achieved precisely the opposite effect.

The most prominent voice of those condemning the publication of an intimate letter between father and daughter was George Clooney. 'She's a woman who is seven months pregnant and she is being pursued and vilified and chased in the same way that Diana was, and it's history repeating itself. And we've seen how that ends. I can't tell you how frustrating it is to see that. You're taking a letter from a daughter to a father and broadcasting it everywhere. She's getting a raw deal there, it's irresponsible. I'm sort of surprised by that.'

If any further proof were needed to demonstrate the similarities between Diana's treatment and that of the duchess, in January a helicopter hovering over the remote house that Harry and Meghan rented in Oxfordshire was another example of routine media harassment. Inside was a photographer working for Splash News and Picture Agency. The resulting shots – some of which were clear enough to show the furnishings inside their bedroom and living room – prompted the couple to abandon their weekend retreat and return to Nottingham Cottage where they could be assured of police protection. Once again the imperatives of security for themselves and their unborn child dominated their thinking. Given the level of online abuse and hate directed at Harry and Meghan, this was no longer a game. Harry subsequently sued the agency and won substantial damages which he donated to charity.

The clashes with the media were now routine, as was the criticism of Meghan for every gesture. In early February, a few days before the *People* magazine furore, she and Harry visited One25, a charity in Bristol that helps the city's sex workers to break free from the cycle of poverty and violence. During the visit she had the idea of using a Sharpie pen to write messages of support on the bananas that were included in food parcels given to the women. She drew hearts and notes, including the words: 'You are loved', 'You are strong' and 'You are brave'. Her idea, inspired by affirmations for American schoolchildren, was, according to the media, a banana skin and she had slipped up badly. The tabloid *Sun* newspaper reported that one of the charity's clients called the gesture 'offensive', while columnist Piers Morgan, her one-time drinking partner and now leading media detractor, described the episode as a 'humiliating farce that made a laughing stock of the very sex workers she claimed to be helping'.

When, a few days later, she flew to New York for a glamorous and expensive baby shower organized by Serena Williams and her old university friend Genevieve Hillis, it was open season on the duchess. During her five-night stay she was able to walk around the West Village incognito before the event, which took place in the penthouse of the ritzy Mark Hotel on the Upper East Side. The baby shower itself was very Hollywood, with banks of cameramen either side of the entrance waiting for the arrival of up to twenty guests, who included Misha Nonoo, Amal Clooney, broadcaster Gayle King and *Suits* actor Abigail Spencer. During the shower, the attendees were given a lesson in flower arranging, their efforts later passed on to a charity that distributes flowers to care homes and hospitals. Inside the shower guests were able to nibble on designer biscuits, including iced storks on lollipop sticks, trays of sweet bunnies with chocolate piping and biscuits in the shape of traditional English prams in blue icing.

The party was chic, sophisticated and, to use Meghan's favourite word, 'classy'. On-brand, too. All the vendors and gifts were name-checked, including the goodies in the baby shower thank-you bags. The laundry list of party details was very un-Buckingham Palace, leading royal writer Ingrid Seward to describe the event as 'trashy' and for Diana's former private secretary, Patrick Jephson, to accuse Meghan of confusing celebrity with royalty. The fact that she returned to London with Amal Clooney and her twins Ella and Alexander on board a private jet paid for by the Clooneys raised even more eyebrows – especially as the duchess was linked to environmentally conscious charities. Inside the palace the optics of the flashy baby shower had some aides shaking their heads, though they accepted it was entirely paid for by the duchess and her friends.

As she was flying back to London (remember, this was a woman who claimed that her passport was confiscated when she joined the Royal Family), she was told about a tribute paid to her and her work by one of the world's most influential black couples, Beyoncé and Jay-Z. When they accepted the prize for Best International Group at the BRIT Awards via video-link, they did so with a portrait of Meghan by artist Tim O'Brien hanging behind them. Adorned with jewels and a diamond crown, Meghan looked every inch the regal princess.

Beyoncé later explained on her own website why they had decided to pose in front of the portrait of the American duchess. 'At the wedding her culture was front and centre, and she and Prince Harry have continued to push the race-relations dialogue forward.'

It was clear that in spite of the constant sniping in the mainstream media, Meghan had a cohort of influential followers and admirers around the world. She even impressed the sternly unimpressible Anna Wintour, editor-in-chief of American *Vogue*. At a Women in the World summit in 2019, the fashion maven told host Tina Brown that Meghan was 'really bringing modernity to the Royal Family in a way that is inspiring. I think the image that I have in my mind [was] the Duchess of Sussex walking down the aisle by herself that to me was representative of a modern woman.'

Certainly the Queen had confidence in her, in March 2019 appointing the duchess Vice-President of The Queen's Commonwealth Trust, of which the Sovereign was patron. The Trust exists to champion, fund and connect young leaders around the world who are driving positive social change and serving their communities. In her new role, Meghan would focus on the Trust's work in supporting women and girls. In celebration of International Women's Day and to mark this appointment, she joined former Australian Prime Minister Julia Gillard, musician and activist Annie Lennox, and other women's rights campaigners for a televised panel discussion on women's issues. Journalist Anne McElvoy, who chaired the discussion, was impressed by Meghan's ability to hold her own intellectually in a gathering of political and cultural heavy hitters. Introduced as a 'royal not afraid to embrace full-on feminism', McElvoy found her shrewd common sense and authentic approach instantly endearing. At the same time it did not take her long to identify the Markle paradox: 'The right think that she is irritating and preachy, while the new, punitive, left is not keen to identify with rich royals with extensive shoe collections.' As Meghan and Harry were promoting a progressive agenda, they would be judged more rigorously by the media. In short, if you preach about climate change, be careful with your use of helicopters and private jets. So when Harry attacked the media for 'distorting the truth' in front of a cheering audience of teenagers at Wembley Arena on WE Day UK, this acted as catnip for the media, which gleefully pointed out his own use of helicopters to fly from London to Birmingham for an engagement instead of using the train.

The Queen had seen it all before with other members of the family and simply shrugged it off. It was the price paid for being royal. She clearly approved of the way in which Meghan and Harry were conducting themselves publicly for, after much back and forth, she agreed to Harry and William splitting their households to allow the Sussexes to go their own way. William and Kate would stay and work at Kensington Palace, while the Sussexes would have their household office at Buckingham Palace and home at Frogmore Cottage in Windsor. Ninety-five per cent of funding would be provided through Prince Charles's fiefdom, the Duchy of Cornwall, with the Sovereign Grant covering the remainder. It was hoped that the space would be good for the brothers' relationship. At the time Harry appreciated the fact that William had fought his corner so that the split was effected with sensible levels of funding to enable them to properly staff their administrative and communications offices.

The new recruits – an early appointee was heavy hitter Sara Latham who had worked for the Clintons – would have their work cut out. For all the criticism they attracted, there was no doubting the Sussexes popularity. When they launched their official Instagram site, @sussexroyal, they attracted a million followers in under six hours. By January 2020, 11.3 million fans had joined their site. Their popularity concerned some courtiers who saw shades of Diana, the charismatic royal duo potentially overshadowing the rest of the Royal Family, particularly the two immediate heirs, Charles and William. 'The danger to them is that Meghan is going to be bigger than Diana,' a source revealed to Tim Shipman, *Sunday Times* political editor.

Harry's camp was more down to earth. They realized that the media caravan moves on. In just over a decade the spotlight would be on William and Kate's children, and Meghan and Harry would no longer be flavour of the month. They felt that they had to use the influence they enjoyed to make a change and support the causes they believed in.

Added into the mix was further work on the plan for the Sussexes to be the Royal Family's 'soft power' abroad, particularly in the Commonwealth, and the Cambridges to be based in Britain. The Queen's former private secretary, now Permanent Lord in Waiting, Christopher Geidt, and former British ambassador to the United States, Sir David Manning, were appointed to put more flesh on the bare bones of this plan. It would give Meghan and Harry the chance to carve out their own family life – as the Queen had done during two halcyon years in Malta with her naval officer husband – and give them all a breather from the divisions that had plagued the various households over the previous few years. While suggestions that Harry become Governor-General of Australia or New Zealand or the couple be made trade envoys were dismissed as impractical, work continued on developing a bespoke role for the royal rock stars. The focus was on a base in Africa, Harry's home away from home.

But it was their new home in England where they wanted the baby to be born, the couple shunning the traditional royal birth at the private Lindo Wing of St Mary's Hospital in Paddington, central London. It was intended that the infant would be the first royal baby born at home since Prince Edward at Buckingham Palace in 1964. However, as April flipped over into May and Meghan's due date passed, doctors advised a hospital-assisted delivery for the child who would be seventh in line to the throne. The couple's concern about discretion and security led them to choose the private five-star Portland Hospital where the Duchess of York had given birth to Princesses Beatrice and Eugenie.

On 6 May at 5.26 in the morning, Archie Harrison Mountbatten-Windsor, who weighed in at a healthy 7 lb 3 oz, entered the world to the utter delight of mother and father. Of course, even the birth of their first baby could not take place without controversy as confusion arose after Buckingham Palace put out a misleading statement that Meghan was in labour at 2 p.m. that day when she had in fact given birth hours earlier. No matter, Meghan was relieved to have her 'beautiful, sweet little boy' in her arms.

As they informed aides, they had decided against accepting a royal title for Archie, who they would be registering for dual citizenship, until he was old enough to choose for himself what he wanted to do. Moreover, they both feared the day when Prince Charles became king as it would mean that Archie, as the new monarch's grandson, would be eligible to be made a prince. They were so worried by this possibility that they asked the Prince of Wales if he would issue new letters patent to change this when he acceded to the throne. As a senior aide told writer Omid Scobie: 'To not have a senior role in the Royal Family but have a title is just a burden.'

Their thinking directly contradicted the claims that Meghan made when she told Oprah Winfrey that the style and seniority of his title would essentially be awarded according to his skin colour and that the couple wanted him to be a prince in order to secure more official protection. As with so many of their assertions over the next few years, their truth was not necessarily *the* truth.

For instance, when Oprah observed that things started to change when the royal couple decided against the traditional baby photocall, Meghan was quick to call out the false story. 'We weren't asked to take a picture. That's also part of the spin that was really damaging. I thought, "Can you just tell them the truth? Can you say to the world you're not giving him a title, and we want to keep him safe, and that if he's not a prince, then it's not part of the tradition? Just tell people, and then they'll understand."' A curious assertion, especially as the couple didn't want a title for him and had even lobbied Prince Charles to ensure this was achieved.

Instead of the traditional photocall, Harry wanted to tell the world the good news himself. He expressed his delight to select media who were gathered in St George's Hall at Windsor Castle. Harry was the one carrying the baby, a clear sign that this modern man was going to share the chores of day-to-day parenting. And so it proved.

Later, their photographer Chris Allerton recorded the intimate moment the Queen, Prince Philip and Doria Ragland met with baby Archie and his proud parents, this time Meghan carrying the infant.

It was a charming tableau: inquisitive great-grandparents, a proud grandmother and two ecstatic parents all focused on the tiny bundle of joy. Ingrid Seward, the editor-in-chief of *Majesty* magazine and frequent critic of the Sussexes, was won over. 'It was a very lovely mixture of formality and informality. The hair was a bit messy. If she was trying to give a message – if she had the energy to give a message – it was a feminist message that you don't have to look slim and slick the moment you've had a baby, which has been her mantra all the way.'

On their first wedding anniversary on 19 May, the couple enjoyed a traditional Sunday roast for lunch at Frogmore Cottage in the company of Doria, with Archie napping nearby in a cot. They had always dreamed of having a baby before they celebrated their first anniversary.

As they looked at the sleeping infant, they were thankful that suddenly they were a family and their dream had come true.

18

Walking in Diana's Footsteps

The ghost of Diana, Princess of Wales loomed large over the lives of Harry and Meghan. She was essentially the third wheel in their marriage. Not a day went by without a reference, a memory or, perhaps more importantly, a decision relating to Harry's beloved mother.

Her cause-driven life and the tragic manner of her death, after being hounded by a pack of paparazzi, shaped Harry's world view and coloured his relationship with his family, the media and the wider public. Privacy and the protection of his wife and baby son were his commanding priorities, balanced also with a desire to serve the Crown. The notion that a monarch and her immediate family were public figures whose private lives were fair game did not wash for a moment with the Sussexes. Precedent and protocol were concepts to be challenged rather than accepted. Over the next few months, Harry and Meghan did more to unmask the inner workings of the Royal Family than even his mother, who spoke frankly to me for her 1992 biography, *Diana: Her True Story*, and appeared in an infamous TV interview on the BBC's *Panorama* programme in 1995.

The birth of Archie merely reinforced their desire for privacy, the couple introducing him to the public on *their* terms rather than adhering to the recent royal convention of a mass photocall on the steps of a central London hospital. This policy of privacy and protection continued with his christening in July 2019 at the Queen's private chapel at Windsor Castle. Once again they thumbed their noses at protocol by refusing to publicly name their son's godparents.

It was a move that stirred a hornet's nest of criticism, especially as it came just weeks after the announcement that the Royal Foundation, the charitable umbrella of the Cambridges and Sussexes, was to split, with Meghan and Harry planning to form their own royal charity later in the year. The parting was agreed by both couples just sixteen months on from the Royal Foundation forum in February 2018, where the 'Fab Four', as they were once called, made their debut. It was further proof, if any more were needed, that Harry and William were travelling on very separate paths.

The decision to keep the names of the godparents secret was another issue, one of many, that perplexed William. He, like others inside the family, felt that those chosen to guide and counsel a future royal prince, seventh in line to the throne, should be identified. Harry and Meghan thought otherwise. They explained that the godparents were genuine friends, not celebrities or public figures, and had joined with the royal couple in preferring privacy.

Though Meghan and Harry had broken with media tradition, it was a traditional ceremony. Archie was baptized with holy water from the River Jordan by the Archbishop of Canterbury, Justin Welby, and the infant wore a replica of the Honiton lace gown originally commissioned by Queen Victoria for her first child. Diana, too, was present in spirit; the Duchess of Cambridge sported the same pearl drop earrings worn by the late princess for Harry's christening in 1984, while Diana's sisters Lady Jane Fellowes and Lady Sarah McCorquodale featured prominently in the christening photographs.

Although Harry and Meghan wanted to organize the christening their way, disgruntled critics argued that, as the taxpayer had funded the revamp of Frogmore Cottage, the public should be able to witness the build-up to the baptism of the latest member of the Royal Family. As royal author Penny Junor complained: 'They can't have it both ways. Either they are totally private, pay for their own house and disappear out of view, or play the game the way it is played.'

She was closer to Harry's thinking than she could have imagined, as the prince and his wife pondered how best to shield and raise their child as a commoner but without the intrusion that some felt was justified because their lifestyles were, in part, paid for by the taxpayer. The solution lay in Junor's complaint – simply break the stick used to beat them with, namely money. If they were self-funding, set apart from the Sovereign Grant and Prince Charles's largesse, they would simply sidestep the tsunami of harsh comment that came their way. It was an idea that was ripe for fruition. In preparation for that day, in June 2019 they trademarked the name 'Sussex Royal' for their possible future use, but also to prevent others from buying the domain name.

The censure over the private christening in July dovetailed with sour comment that Meghan had thrown her weight around at Wimbledon when she and her friends Lindsay Jill Roth and Genevieve Williams (née Hillis) went to watch Serena Williams in a second-round match on Court One on American Independence Day. Not only was Meghan wearing jeans in the members' enclosure, which was a big no-no, but her security detail stopped members of the public from taking pictures, even though the trio were the focus of the BBC cameras and the massed ranks of accredited photographers. Spectator Hasan Hasanov, who was trying to take a selfie featuring tennis star Roger Federer on court, was asked to 'please give them privacy' by the duchess's minder and warned not to photograph her. The amateur cameraman was nonplussed as he had no idea that Meghan was even there.

TV presenter and three-time world real tennis winner Sally Jones was also told not to take pictures of the duchess, even though she was trying to snap Serena Williams and was also unaware of Meghan's presence. Afterwards she said angrily: 'Harry and Meghan see themselves more as A-list celebrities rather than royals carrying out their duties. It's control-freakery.' There was more: an All England Club source informed *The Times* newspaper that Meghan was a 'nightmare' to accommodate thanks to her casual attire and 'self-regarding paranoia'. All so ironic, bearing in mind that three years earlier she had attended Wimbledon in the vain hope of getting her picture in the papers.

Ironic too that, given her plea for privacy, nine days later Wimbledon became the venue for Meghan and Kate to publicly express their friendship and simultaneously confound the endless rumours about a feud between the sisters-in-law. The duo of duchesses, as well as Kate's sister Pippa, watched Serena Williams lose to Simona Halep in the Ladies' Singles Final, the trio chatting warmly in the July sunshine. Earlier in the week the two royal wives had put on another united front when they watched their husbands compete in a charity polo match. Kate's children and Archie were also on parade in their first public playdate together. The two events were, in the view of the well-informed royal author Katie Nicholl, 'deliberate and calculated efforts' to stem the unceasing rumours about a dispute between the Sussexes and the Cambridges. For a time they succeeded, *People* magazine reporting that the two women had bonded over motherhood. The truce didn't last long – at least in the tabloid imagination.

Royal rivalry erupted once more with the birth of Meghan's other baby, the September issue of *Vogue* magazine, which she had secretly been working on since January. Her guest issue, which was called Forces for Change, inevitably drew comparisons with a 2016 cover that had featured just the Duchess of Cambridge. For her front cover, Meghan chose fifteen different change-makers – and a mirror to suggest that the reader could make a difference – but no image of herself. Meghan's comment that it would be too 'boastful' to do so was seen as a put-down of Kate and a renewal of the catfight between the duelling duchesses.

Once again Meghan was in the media cross hairs. Although Kate had guest-edited the Huffington Post UK website in 2016 to raise awareness of children's mental health, Prince Charles had focused on environmental issues when he had twice edited *Country Life* magazine, and even Harry had edited the *Today* programme on BBC Radio Four without undue controversy, it was Meghan who aroused the ire of conservative commentators.

With her hand on the editorial tiller, she and *Vogue* magazine were described as too 'woke', opportunist, hypocritical, narcissistic and self-absorbed. Choose your pejorative. In any case, they raged, why didn't she put the Queen on the cover? Her Majesty was a change-maker. Hmm. Debatable.

The furore over Meghan's special edition of *Vogue* was part of an enduring issue. Overwhelmingly, the commentators who attacked Meghan were nationalist conservatives. Meghan was a foreigner, a woman and a progressive whose philosophy, as she made clear in the magazine, was about 'the power of the collective', that people, especially women, were 'stronger together'. It was a recipe for conflict.

This wasn't just personal, it was political. 'Our royals should keep their political opinions private,' opined the right-wing *Sun* tabloid.

This complaint was nothing new for members of the Royal Family; the Duke of Edinburgh was regularly attacked during the 1950s and 1960s for his trenchant views on conservation, while Prince Charles was ridiculed when he championed the cause of organic farming and admitted that he talked to his plants. Meghan was the latest in a long line of royal Aunt Sallies.

In spite of the cacophony of criticism, though, Meghan had the last laugh. Her September 2019 *Vogue* issue, which included her interview with Michelle Obama, Prince Harry talking to primatologist Dr Jane Goodall and also featured climate change activist Greta Thunberg and New Zealand Prime Minister Jacinda Ardern, as well as promotions for grassroots organizations and charities like Smart Works, was the fastest selling in the magazine's 103-year history, having sold out in just ten days.

Her critics simply changed tack. That summer, the Sussexes offered them a gift. Not only did Harry hitch a ride on a private jet to make a speech about climate change to the Google Camp conference of tech giants, philanthropists and activists in Sicily, but he and his family also enjoyed several excursions on private jets to locations such as Ibiza, where they rented a villa for £108,000 a week to celebrate Meghan's birthday, and the south of France to stay at Sir Elton John's villa. 'Prince Harry's heir miles,' proclaimed *The Sun*, helpfully printing a map showing the couple's various trips. Elton John mounted a staunch defence of the duke and duchess, condemning the media's 'distorted and malicious' reporting and arguing that the flight was fully carbon offset.

He also invoked the spirit of Harry's mother when he stated: 'Diana, Princess of Wales was one of my dearest friends. I feel a profound sense of obligation to protect Harry and his family from the unnecessary press intrusion that contributed to Diana's untimely death.' Celebrity friends like Ellen DeGeneres and Pink also came to their rescue, describing the royal couple as 'down to earth' and 'compassionate'. Pink observed: 'The way people treat her is the most public form of bullying I have seen in a while.'

However, the argument that flying private was for their security and protection was made to seem self-indulgent when Prince William and his family boarded a budget Flybe flight from Norwich to Aberdeen, with the future king holding tickets that cost just £73 each. If he could do it, why not the sixth in line to the throne?

Money-making was now suspected in their every move. It had long been rumoured that Meghan was keen to return to Los Angeles with her prince in tow. Fuel was thrown on to the flames of speculation when Harry, at the premiere of *The Lion King* movie in London in July, mentioned to the then Disney CEO, Bob Iger, 'You know she does voiceovers,' a reference to Meghan's narration of the *Elephant* documentary. The film clip, which went viral, implied that Harry was lobbying for work on behalf of his wife in preparation for their departure from Britain and the Royal Family.

At that time they were indeed looking towards America, but primarily to promote their Sussex Royal charitable foundation. To that end they used the contacts and influence of the New York-based Sunshine Sachs PR agency. If the agency applied its dark arts to try to burnish Meghan and Harry's tarnished image, all well and good. Indeed, their upcoming ten-day visit to South Africa, Angola, Botswana and Malawi in September was seen as the perfect opportunity to recalibrate the relationship between Meghan,

Harry and the mass media. The focus would be on their charities, Commonwealth patronages and, of course, baby Archie.

With the hiring of several new all-female members of staff, notably high-flying British diplomat Fiona Mcilwham as their private secretary and Karen Blackett, once described as the most influential black person in Britain, as the director of their Sussex Royal Foundation, the couple showed that they meant business inside the family Firm. As Diana used to say to me about serious overseas visits, it was all 'very grown up'.

Shortly before they flew to Cape Town with baby Archie in tow, Meghan essentially outlined her humanitarian mission at the launch of the first capsule collection of Smart Works, the charity set up to help women back into the workplace. During her speech she urged the public to donate items that helped to get them where they were now, rather than unwanted cast-offs. She saw these donations not as an act of charity but of community, women helping and empowering one another through the act of giving. It was a theme she returned to frequently during the African tour.

First stop after they arrived was Nyanga township in Cape Town, dubbed South Africa's murder capital, where they visited an initiative led by the Justice Desk, a human rights organization that educates children about their rights and helps to empower girls through self-defence classes. Later, they both made speeches and, in a last-minute addition to hers, Meghan made reference to herself as a 'woman of colour'. As she stood on a tree stump, microphone in hand, she told her audience: 'On one personal note, may I just say that while I am here with my husband as a member of the Royal Family, I want you to know that for me I am here with you as a mother, as a wife, as a woman, as a woman of colour and as your sister.' While it wasn't quite on the scale of President Kennedy's 'Ich bin ein Berliner' ('I am a Berliner') speech at the height of the Cold War, it was a very public statement by Meghan. She was identifying as one of us, not one of them. All very unroyal and it set the tone for the tour.

On the second day she posed for a selfie, which she sent to her friend Michelle Obama, and on the third she showed off Archie to the world during a thrilling meeting with Nobel Peace Prize-winner Archbishop Desmond Tutu.

It was turning into a classic modern royal tour, the couple's celebrity projecting grassroots, communal charities, fashions – Meghan deliberately dressed in eco-friendly, locally sourced garments – and local Commonwealth organizations onto the world stage. This was royal magic in action.

When Harry flew first to Botswana and then to Angola on his own, he made global headlines when he retraced his mother's steps in Huambo. Back in 1997, Diana walked through a cleared Angolan minefield, but now it was a bustling shopping and community centre. During the visit, he donned the same body armour as his mother when he walked through a similarly marked-out minefield nearby, the prince remotely exploding a mine during the event. The pictures reminded the world of Diana's legacy and gave Harry a global platform to talk about the progress that had been made – and the giant task that still remained, the prince pointing out that 60 million people still live in areas containing uncleared minefields. He said: 'It has been quite emotional retracing my mother's steps.' He subsequently added: 'I lost her twenty-two years ago, but the memory of her is with me daily and her legacy lives on.'

It was all going so very well. Then, shortly before the end of the tour, the couple publicly launched three lawsuits against a powerful trio of newspaper groups. Their decision to announce the legal proceedings during an official tour left local British diplomats blindsided and bewildered. It completely overshadowed the very good work that they had done on the visit. There was also a great deal of head-scratching inside Buckingham Palace, after once again being caught flat-footed by a serious announcement made without consultation.

If anything, the lawsuits gave an insight into the growing disconnect between the royal couple and senior courtiers who privately thought that the Sussexes had a financial 'death wish' thanks to their decision to face off against the massed ranks of the tabloid media. In the lottery of the High Court, there are few winners – except the lawyers.

Harry, though nervous about the uncertain outcome, felt that he had a duty to take on what he described as a toxic institution that was damaging the country. He sued News Group Newspapers, owners of the *Sun* and the now-defunct *News of the World*, and Mirror Group Newspapers, publishers of the *Mirror* titles, for illegally intercepting his phone calls between 2001 and 2005. This was part of the notorious phone-hacking scandal which had led to the jailing of several journalists as well as huge cash payouts to the numerous victims. The case had been rumbling on for years, which was why the timing came as such a surprise. Apparently, the lawsuits were brought at this moment because of a change in procedures within the High Court which could in future be more favourable to publishers.

In turn, the duchess took *The Mail on Sunday* to task for an invasion of privacy relating to the publication of a private letter that she had written to her father concerning his behaviour before and after the wedding. She also pointed out numerous stories in the Sunday tabloid – most notably that she had bought a £5,000 copper bath and splashed out £500,000 on soundproofing Frogmore Cottage – which Meghan deemed 'false and absurd'. Her lawyers also highlighted a feature about Meghan eating avocados, the story juxtaposing her dietary choice with human rights abuses, murder and environmental devastation. It was beyond parody, though the Sussexes didn't see the funny side. As the Mail group decided to vigorously contest the lawsuit, Meghan was faced with the unhappy prospect of possibly appearing in court against her own father, as well as being burdened with costs, not all reclaimable, that would quickly run into seven figures.

In a statement, Harry explained that the couple had decided to go ahead with the lawsuits because Meghan was the latest victim of a 'ruthless' tabloid campaign of bullying and it was now time to call a halt to it. Notwithstanding the legal merits of his argument, it is worth noting that Meghan was not around during the phone-tapping farrago and, as it was her father who volunteered her letter to *The Mail on Sunday*, the lawsuit was provoked initially by the actions of her own family.

Nonetheless, Harry went on to argue: 'I have been a silent witness to her private suffering for too long. To stand back and do nothing would be contrary to everything we believe in.'

Threaded through the statement was his fear that Meghan would suffer the same fate as his mother. 'Though this action may not be the safe one, it is the right one,' he explained. 'Because my deepest fear is history repeating itself. I've seen what happens when someone I love is commoditized to the point that they are no longer treated or seen as a real person. I lost my mother and now I watch my wife falling victim to the same powerful forces.'

His statement and Meghan's undoubted distress had a strong impact. A month after they arrived back in London, seventy-two female MPs signed an open letter backing the duchess's stand against 'distasteful and misleading' media coverage and blasting 'outdated colonial undertones' of numerous stories. Meghan subsequently called lawmaker Holly Lynch to thank her and her colleagues for their support.

Though the lawsuits gave the impression that the couple were in control of their world, it was clear to their friends and supporters that they were struggling to cope. Their friend and TV presenter Tom Bradby, who was making a documentary about their trip, *Harry & Meghan: An African Journey*, had known Harry and William for a number of years and was the one who originally exposed the phone-hacking scandal. He first met Meghan before the wedding and noticed that she was already finding the attention difficult to deal with, especially with journalists offering friends and family money for information. Shortly before their visit to South Africa he visited them at Frogmore Cottage. This time he discovered a couple who were 'defensive' and who, as he saw it, were under 'extreme pressure' and in danger of 'buckling beneath it'. Harry looked burnt out. Bradby said later: 'Both of them in this trip came across as more vulnerable and bruised than the spoilt, petulant, arrogant and entitled caricatures that are sometimes tied to the public whipping post.' Yet the Africa visit had only been short, just ten days, and the media coverage had been friendly and positive. Compared to the ten-week tour of South Africa by the

Royal Family in 1947 or even Diana's six-week trip to Australia and New Zealand in 1983, this was closer to a walk in the park. Bradby found himself asking the question: 'If they can't cope with this, then what?'

His ITV documentary captured the angst, bewilderment and frustration of a couple who wanted to make the world a better place, but found their path obstructed at every turn, either by the palace or the media. During the programme Meghan admitted that she 'didn't get it' when her British friends warned her that the tabloids would 'destroy your life'. At a 'vulnerable' time in her life, being pregnant and then with a newborn, she admitted that the attention had been 'challenging'. Forget the stiff upper lip, the duchess found herself holding back the tears when Bradby asked her if she was OK. 'Not many people have asked if I'm okay, but it's a very real thing to be going through behind the scenes,' she replied, her complaint a familiar one among new entrants to the Royal Family, including Diana who was hurt that no one ever said, 'Well done.' As royal author Penny Junor explained: 'It is a strange family and not one that has supported one another very well. They don't praise one another and never call each other up just to say, "That was a great speech."'

Meghan admitted that her life since joining the Royal Family had been a struggle. Her mantra was that 'it's not enough to just survive ... you've got to thrive'. All too often both she and Harry were simply surviving.

During the documentary Harry also admitted that he had his own issues, particularly with his brother. He told the TV presenter: 'We're certainly on different paths at the moment, but I will always be there for him and as I know he will always be there for me. We don't see each other as much as we used to because we are so busy, but I love him dearly.'

At the beating heart of his profound discomfort with being in the public eye was the death of his mother. No matter how friendly the media could be, as far as Harry was concerned every camera whirr and click reminded him of her terrible fate. He could not let that feeling go: 'Every single time I see a flash, it takes me straight back. So in that respect, it's the worst reminder of her life as opposed to the best.'

Psychologically, all roads led back to Diana. It was evident that until he resolved this childhood trauma he would not be able to play a complete or effective role as a senior member of the Royal Family. All the plans in the world meant nothing until he could cope with Diana's death and go on to live a full and positive life. As his brother had shown, it was not impossible.

As for Meghan, she had to come to terms with a relentlessly hostile media. It would not be easy. She was both a divisive but also a popular figure. While she could be consoled to know that around 55 per cent of the British public, according to a *Tatler* magazine poll, thought she was good for the monarchy, there was still a substantial minority who held the contrary view. Worldwide, a statistic reported in *The New York Times*, based on Google searches about the Sussexes and the Cambridges between November 2017 and January 2020, revealed that Harry and Meghan accounted for 83 per cent of international interest about the two royal couples. For the Duke and Duchess of Sussex, the frustration was that while they were hugely popular, inside the palace their lesser position in the line of succession meant that they were always also-rans in the race for funding and publicity.

As she reviewed this social media landscape, Meghan told her writer friend Bryony Gordon, who visited her shortly after the South Africa trip, that she didn't want people to love her – she just wanted them to be able to hear her. As the writer observed: 'I have found that this is what the Duchess of Sussex stands for: using her voice to help give one to people less privileged than her.'

Brave words but it remained a struggle, Meghan's eyes glistening with tears when Gordon initially asked how she was. An undoubted strain too for Harry, a palace aide telling the BBC that his mental health was a cause for worry and concern for William and various members of the Royal Family.

Like many others, Prince William breathed a sigh of relief when Harry and Meghan announced that they were stepping back from royal duties for six weeks or so and spending Thanksgiving and Christmas in North America. The couple ended up in a remote luxury mansion on Vancouver Island loaned to them by a patriotic Canadian businessman.

Palace aides, who had been urging the couple to slow down, were pleased to see them take a breath. They had seen at close quarters Meghan working on the *Vogue* edit, the Smart Works collection, holding meetings with lawyers while remaining engaged in quotidian office details. She was a hard worker with a reputation for driving herself and her staff to the brink – 5 a.m. emails were not uncommon. As one member of the household told journalist Victoria Ward: 'We were saying to her, "Wow, this is not what a maternity break looks like, you need to slow down."'

Another team member was even more blunt: 'I told her last week to "Please just turn your brain off. Enjoy Thanksgiving. Focus on cooking some pies."'

While they watched Archie grow and change in their Canadian retreat, it was clear that Meghan and Harry were cooking something up – but it wasn't pies.

19

The Long Goodbye

It had been apparent for some months that Harry and Meghan were unhappy with the unrelenting media criticism and what they saw as a lack of support from inside the institution. Before Christmas, Harry had spoken to the Queen and Prince Charles about stepping back as senior royals and raising funds privately to enable them to relinquish the Sovereign Grant which, according to their accounting, only paid for 5 per cent of their outgoings. As semi-private citizens, they would no longer be at the beck and call of the media and yet continue to serve the monarchy in a more limited capacity.

They used as their example Prince Michael of Kent, who undertakes some royal duties but also has a private business career. In the meantime, Meghan explored ways of monetizing their foundation, Sussex Royal, focusing on Hollywood celebrities and big American business as a path to exploit their international reach.

One source who has known Meghan for years told *The Daily Telegraph* that this was a long-held dream. 'This is a mission that Meghan has been on for a long time. Even in her younger years in Hollywood, she wanted to work towards creating an international charity changing lives. Now that she has the platform and profile of being a British royal, she can truly build this plan.'

However, it was clear that there were many unanswered questions and difficult decisions that remained to be resolved, not least the simple fact that, as the Queen herself pointed out, it was virtually impossible to be half in and half out of the Royal Family.

It was like being slightly pregnant. When Harry first formally broached the subject, Prince Charles asked his son to put down all his thoughts and arguments in writing. Harry, fearing a leak, was reluctant. Sure enough, details from his position paper were made available to *The Sun* newspaper, which ensured that these confidential discussions now became front-page news. As far as Harry and Meghan were concerned, this was the final straw.

The royal couple suspected that the entire institution was conspiring against them. As they saw it, the evidence was all around them. To mark the new decade the Queen released a formal photograph of herself and her direct heirs, Prince Charles, the Duke of Cambridge and Prince George, which was taken in the Throne Room at Buckingham Palace, the picture of the quartet illustrating change within continuity. The unspoken code was straightforward: the future of the monarchy was assured, with or without Meghan and Harry.

This sense that, despite their international popularity, they were low down the royal totem pole was confirmed when Harry arranged to meet the Queen for a grandson-to-grandmother chat in early January. At the last minute the meeting was postponed. Harry suspected classic internal politics, his family concerned that anything the Queen agreed during informal conversations would be used by Harry as a negotiating tactic.

In the fetid atmosphere of distrust and suspicion, on 7 January *The Sun* announced its front-page scoop under the headline 'We're Orf Again', detailing the Sussexes' plans to step back and spend more time in Canada. Meghan and Harry were incandescent, deaf to the entreaties of their officials who pleaded with them not to 'go nuclear' and issue a pre-emptive public statement themselves. They argued that the couple should remain silent and continue to conduct the negotiations behind closed doors. Harry and Meghan would have none of it.

Before making their bombshell announcement, Harry, once again, spoke to the Queen. As was to become a familiar refrain, versions of the conversation differed. According to one narrative, she made it clear that he should not go public with his plans, whereas a source close to Harry told *The Times* that she told him it was fine.

What was undeniable was that the Queen, his brother, his father and the rest of the family were given ten minutes' notice before their statement was released on 8 January. That afternoon Meghan visited the National Theatre, of which she was patron. The real theatrics, though, were taking place offstage.

Curtain up was at 6.30 p.m. when the news was posted on Instagram: 'After many months of reflection and internal discussions, we have chosen to make a transition this year in starting to carve out a progressive new role within this institution. We intend to step back as "senior" members of the Royal Family and work to become financially independent, while continuing to fully support Her Majesty The Queen.'

They planned to divide their time between Britain and North America, an endeavour that would enable them to raise Archie 'with an appreciation for the royal tradition into which he was born' and focus on the launch of their new charity, Sussex Royal.

The couple were insistent that they were not walking away from the Royal Family, just stepping back. Harry later explained his thinking to his friend James Corden, on *The Late Late Show*: 'It was a really difficult environment, as I think a lot of people saw. We all know what the British press can be like, and it was destroying my mental health. I was like, this is toxic. So I did what any husband and what any father would do. I was like, I need to get my family out of here. But we never walked away.'

For her part, Meghan emphasized that they were only asking to function like several junior members of the Royal Family, that is to support the Queen when required and earn a living professionally. She later told Oprah: 'So we weren't reinventing the wheel here. We were saying, "OK, if this isn't working for everyone, we're in a lot of pain, you can't provide us with the help we need, we can just take a step back. We can do it in a Commonwealth country."'

Harry denied blindsiding the Queen, explaining in the Oprah interview that he called her three times to discuss matters and his father on two occasions – until Prince Charles had refused to take his calls. The duke and duchess were adamant that they would have stayed inside the institution if they had received more support from the family.

Within ninety minutes of the Sussexes releasing their statement, the Queen authorized a brief response from the palace, which was conciliatory in tone but signalled the difficulties that lay ahead.

It read: 'Discussions with The Duke and Duchess of Sussex are at an early stage. We understand their desire to take a different approach, but these are complicated issues that will take time to work through.'

The bland wording masked a buzz of indignation emanating from the various palace households. The general feeling was that the Queen had been treated shoddily, while everyone inside the Royal Household felt stabbed in the back. One senior courtier told veteran royal watcher Robert Jobson: 'This hasn't been properly thought through. It is incredibly self-indulgent and the way they made this announcement showed little or no respect to the Queen or the Prince of Wales who have given a lifetime of service to the Crown. It is shocking, just shocking behaviour.'

For once royal officials were not holding back. There was real fury within the family; William and Charles were said to be 'incandescent with rage'. One official who briefed *Daily Mail* royal correspondent Rebecca English, stated: 'People had bent over backwards for them. They were given the wedding they wanted, the house they wanted, the office they wanted, the money they wanted, the staff they wanted, the tours they wanted and had the backing of their family. What more did they want?'

The problem was that the entity that Prince Philip called the 'Firm' was not some faceless corporation, but a family of flesh-and-blood individuals who felt pain and nursed resentment. Harry might have been hurting, but so too was his brother. A friend of William briefed *The Sunday Times* about the prince's feelings. 'I've put my arm around my brother all our lives and I can't do that anymore; we're separate entities. I'm sad about that. All we can do, and all I can do, is try and support them and hope that the time comes when we're all singing from the same page. I want everyone to play on the team.'

The couple's friend Tom Bradby articulated the view from Vancouver Island. 'Harry and Meghan feel like they've been driven out,' he said. 'The rest of the family just felt they were impossibly difficult. Their attitude is: "We want our freedom – if you want to take everything away, that's OK, we'll live with it and we'll support ourselves."'

No matter what everyone thought, the Queen made it clear that she was not prepared to let this crisis drag on. For years it had been her policy to kick the can down the road – as with the separation of Charles and Diana – and hope something would turn up. Not this time. After a series of phone calls between the royal quartet, aides were ordered to work 'at pace' to find a way forward within a matter of days.

This suited Harry. He was concerned that Meghan was 'on the brink' of just walking out and he realized he had to take swift action to ensure her happiness. For Harry it was either Meghan or the monarchy. When the American actor realized in her heart that the royal world was not for her, she was impatient to move on. She found life inside the royal institution slow, repetitive and, quite frankly, unimaginative. Her own endeavours, particularly the Grenfell cookbook and the capsule collection she had overseen for Smart Works, were the type of projects she wanted to work on – and they could take place outside the royal world.

There were other, more personal grievances about life in the 'Firm'. She and the Duchess of Cambridge had never had any real rapport and Meghan resented playing second fiddle to her. According to royal writer Camilla Tominey: 'The two women rarely spoke and severed all communication on a family WhatsApp group. Their fallout at the time of the wedding was never really healed and wounding words were uttered which were left to fester.'

If Kate was cool, then her husband was a bully; not physically, but verbally. The Sussexes felt that they had been driven out by the 'bullying' attitude of Prince William. As a source told *The Times*: 'If you are Meghan and Harry, and you have had two years of constantly being told your place, constantly bullied as they would see it, constantly being told what you can't do, Meghan has been thinking, "This is just nuts. Why would anyone put up with this?"' Both brothers united to make a rare public statement denying the claims.

It was clear that Meghan had ruffled feathers in the family and that they felt she and Harry were very difficult to deal with. For her part, Meghan found some of its members – not the Queen or Prince Philip – unfriendly and jealous. At a personal level, then, their departure from Britain was quietly welcomed by some in the Windsor family and their courtiers, but on an institutional level it was a heavy blow.

That blow was delivered at a brief and businesslike family conference in the Long Library at Sandringham in mid-January 2020. Princes Charles, William and Harry, together with the Queen and the royal quartet's private secretaries, met to resolve the key issues surrounding the unprecedented situation.

While the Sandringham summit was not on the seismic constitutional scale of the abdication of King Edward VIII in 1936, in the weeks since Harry and Meghan had made clear to the Queen and Prince Charles that they wanted to step back from the family and royal duties, there had been turmoil inside the venerable institution. Anonymous briefing and counter-briefing merely added to the discord. Such was the venomous atmosphere that diplomat Fiona Mcilwham, Harry's private secretary, joked that it might have been easier to have run the Iran desk at the Foreign Office, a post she was offered before taking on the royal position.

Before formal discussions commenced at 2 p.m., Prince Harry and his father joined the Queen for lunch. Significantly, William arrived just fifteen minutes before the opening of the momentous meeting. It was clear that he did not want to make small talk with his brother. Just over ninety minutes later, in what turned out to be a curiously quick, workmanlike and bloodless affair, enough was agreed for Buckingham Palace to release a 153-word statement confirming that Harry and Meghan were no longer part of the Royal Family and were giving up public funding and moving to

Canada. It was a very personal statement from the Queen, one tinged with regret and sadness that the Duke and Duchess of Sussex had chosen a life outside the Royal Family. The word 'Megxit' – a derivation of Brexit, Britain's exit from the European Union – was quickly coined in journalistic circles to define the departure of the royal couple.

They may have been considered difficult inside the institution but the simple fact remained that Meghan and Harry appealed to an audience that the Royal Family – indeed many such long-established organizations – found hard to reach: a young, progressive, multicultural and multiracial community. Though many voices inside the institution asked, 'What more could we have done for them?', the public, especially the American public, didn't see it that way. By allowing Meghan and Harry to leave, the Royal Family was missing a trick and confirming, in the public's mind, that the monarchy was backward-looking and out of touch. An article in *The New York Times* by black British journalist Afua Hirsch gave the Royal Family a taste of the wider response.

Under the headline 'Black Britons Know Why Meghan Markle Wants Out', she wrote: 'If the media paid more attention to Britain's communities of colour, perhaps it would find the announcement far less surprising. With a new prime minister whose track record includes overtly racist statements, some of which would make even Donald Trump blush, a Brexit project linked to native nationalism and a desire to rid Britain of large numbers of immigrants, and an ever-thickening loom of imperial nostalgia, many of us are also thinking about moving.'

For his part, President Donald Trump also got in on the act. He described the turmoil inside the Royal Family as 'sad' and extended his sympathy to the Queen. 'I don't think this should be happening to her,' he told Fox News.

After days of negotiations, where it was clear from the outset that Harry and Meghan's half-in and half-out model was unsustainable, the couple agreed to a severing of links with the Royal Family. They would step back from royal duties, no longer receive funds from the Sovereign Grant, and while they could keep their titles they would not use the appellation HRH. Shortly afterwards, the duke and duchess were also informed that they would not be able to use their trademarked Sussex Royal Foundation, a brand they hoped to utilize to promote their charities and themselves. It came as a shock, requiring a complete rethink and redraft of their business plan. While Harry and Meghan had found freedom, it had come at a high price.

In a statement issued on 18 January, the Queen put a positive and affectionate gloss on what was an unhappy situation, thanking the royal couple for their work and singling out Meghan for the way she had integrated herself into the Royal Family. 'Harry, Meghan and Archie will always be much-loved members of my family,' she declared. 'I recognize the challenges they have experienced as a result of intense scrutiny over the last two years and support their wish for a more independent life.'

For Meghan, she was simply moving back to Canada, a country she had lived in from 2011 to 2017. While she had embraced her life in Britain enthusiastically, she would be the first to admit it was not her home. That was California. For Harry, he was saying farewell to the Queen whom he adored, the military – the organization which had made him – and the country he loved and had defended. Unsurprisingly, he was said to be 'heartbroken' and found giving up his military patronages and titles, especially as Captain General of the Royal Marines, particularly hard.

As with the 1936 abdication, when Wallis Simpson was blamed by the British public for the departure of their darling king, so Meghan was deemed mainly responsible for the hard 'Megxit'. She told a friend: 'I gave up my entire life for this family. I was willing to do whatever it takes.' At some level too, Harry, who loathed the media and all the endless attention, had always been looking for a way out – but on very different terms. As a friend told Omid Scobie: 'Deep down, he was always struggling within that world. She's opened the door for him on that.'

The royal babes in the wood were now on their own in the big bad world. Exactly how bad Harry would discover shortly after he was reunited with Meghan on Vancouver Island. He learned that while his wife and son were out for a walk, they were 'ambushed' by a paparazzo hiding in the foliage. He immediately took legal action as he did on every occasion they were 'papped'. If they thought they had escaped the dark outriders of the mass media, they were sadly mistaken. Nor had they broken free from the outpourings of Meghan's father, Tom Markle Senior. Not only did he file a statement on behalf of *The Mail on Sunday*, with regard to the private letter she wrote to him, but he was also the centrepiece of a ninety-minute television documentary about his life. The *Daily Telegraph* television critic described it as 'ugly tittle-tattle'.

For the most part, though, Harry and Meghan were able to go hiking, enjoy local restaurants and shop without the attentions of freelance photographers. Inside their Vancouver bubble they had the time and opportunity to take a breath and reflect. They were both millionaires in their own right – Harry, thanks to his mother's legacy – so there was no immediate imperative to earn a living. Though Harry later told Oprah Winfrey that his father cut him off financially in the first quarter of the year, in fact royal accounts show that he was bankrolled for a 'substantial sum' by Prince Charles during this period of transition. Clarence House accounts, first made public in June 2021, reveal that William and Harry shared a total of £4.4 million, ample funds for Harry and Meghan to start their new life without dipping into Diana's inheritance.

Their future was an endless panorama of possibilities, from lucrative speaking engagements to media and commercial deals that aligned with their social values, as well as a yet-to-be named and fully realized charitable foundation.

In the meantime, duty called. In late February, Harry returned to the UK where he gave a keynote speech at the eco-friendly travel company Travalyst in Edinburgh, and also joined Bon Jovi at the storied Abbey Road Studios to record 'Unbroken', a song to raise funds for the Invictus Games, of which Harry was still patron.

The highlight of the visit was a long Sunday lunch with the Queen at Windsor Castle, during which they discussed his future and that of his family. The Sovereign made it clear to him that he was a much-loved and missed member of the Royal Family and that he would be very welcome if he chose to return. She had always had sympathy with Harry, knowing that the 'spare' never has an easy time within the system. They have the profile but not the position. Even though it was a different era, she remembered all too well how difficult it was for her younger sister Princess Margaret to find a useful role inside the Royal Family. Outside the system, though, life might be even more challenging. Better the devil you know.

Indeed, the complexity of his decision to step away from the family was made abundantly clear when the Canadian government announced that it would no longer pay for their security at the end of March 2020, the date that 'Megxit' would come into effect. An anxious Meghan says that she wrote to senior royal officials asking for their security to be retained, if not for her and her child, but for Prince Harry who was born royal. 'I see the death threats, I see the racist propaganda,' she later told Oprah. Her request fell on deaf ears.

They still had security when, in early March, Meghan joined Harry in the UK to fulfil their final engagements. During their brief visit, the Royal Family and their supporters were given an insight as to what might have been. The couple were treated like returning rock stars. Meghan was mobbed when she spoke at a school in Dagenham, East London, for International Women's Day and together they received a prolonged standing ovation at the Royal Albert Hall when they attended the Mountbatten Festival of Music. It was the last time that Harry would wear his dress uniform as Captain General of the Royal Marines and he had difficulty in holding back the tears. Even in the rain they were showstoppers – a photograph of the couple looking lovingly at one another when they attended the Endeavour Fund Awards for injured servicemen and women would later snag a top award for photographer Samir Hussein who captured the iconic moment.

For all the smiles and tears and hugs with departing staff and well-wishers, the aching divide inside the House of Windsor was exposed for all to see at the Commonwealth Day service at Westminster Abbey. Meghan and Harry were not included in the royal procession as they had been the previous year. Instead, they were seated before the Queen and the rest of the royal party arrived. To ameliorate the snub, the Cambridges also opted out of the procession and sat, stony faced, in front of the Sussexes. Meghan and Harry only spoke to Prince Edward and his wife, Countess of Wessex. The body language between the Sussexes and Cambridges seemed cold, awkward and hostile, the two couples barely exchanging a civil word before or after the ceremony. William uttered a terse: 'Harry' to his brother, but ignored Meghan – as did his wife. What had been an opportunity to wish the Sussexes 'bon voyage' and no hard feelings became just another unhappy episode in the long-running saga of the War of the Windsors. Once the hour-long ceremony was over, Meghan could not wait to sink into her first-class seat for the ten-hour flight back to Vancouver where her darling Archie was waiting.

Her joy at leaving Britain for Canada was short-lived. The inexorable spread of the deadly Covid-19 virus changed everything. In late March, the UK went into lockdown. Businesses, schools, pubs, clubs, almost everything closed. Around the world the streets fell silent as the pandemic took hold. Everyone had to stay indoors to help keep the modern plague at bay. A handshake, a hug or a kiss could and did spell death for thousands. Prime Minister Boris Johnson was lucky to survive when he caught the virus and ended up in a central London hospital on a ventilator, fighting for every breath, for his life.

Everyone was both paralysed and consumed by the dreadful news as the numbers of those dead or seriously ill rose inexorably, the tide of sickness threatening to swamp the health service.

Amidst this mounting turmoil, Harry and Meghan had a decision to make. Their security was due to end around the same time that the border between America and Canada was scheduled to close. Though they would be safe inside their Canadian retreat, it wasn't where they wanted to be in the long term. Then Oprah Winfrey, who was making a TV series on mental health with Harry, came to the rescue.

Early in the morning of 14 March, a week before the closure of the American–Canadian border, the royal trio boarded a private jet owned by Oprah Winfrey's long-time friend and business partner, billionaire actor and studio owner, Tyler Perry. They were flown to his $18 million mansion near Beverly Hills where they were to stay for the next few weeks. Here they were guaranteed safety – and the company of Doria Ragland and Meghan's LA friends. The duchess later recalled: 'We needed a house and he offered his security as well, so it gave us breathing room to try to figure out what we were going to do.'

Before the world realized that they had moved countries, Meghan was able to drive the royal formerly known as HRH Prince Harry around her favourite neighbourhoods without fear of the lurking paparazzi. It was a few hours of bright escapism in a world where darkness was closing in.

On the Covid-19 front, it was not just the British Prime Minister who was sick but Harry's own father. The prince was shocked to learn that Prince Charles, who at seventy-one was in the vulnerable category, was self-isolating at Birkhall on the Balmoral estate. His wife Camilla was with him but stayed away from his quarters. While Prince Charles's condition was made public, with the Prime Minister very seriously ill, Prince William, who also contracted the dreaded disease, decided that at a time of national crisis he should keep his diagnosis a secret. Later reports suggested that the prince, although fit and healthy, was struggling to breathe.

Harry's phone calls to his father and brother helped in a small way to bridge the distance between them. He also contacted his grandmother to wish her luck before she made her historic and highly emotional 'We Will Meet Again' speech from Windsor Castle. Almost 24 million people, the second-highest audience of the year, watched as she invoked wartime memories and imagery, telling her huge and anxious audience: 'We should take comfort that while we may have more still to endure, better days will return: we will be with our friends again; we will be with our families again; we will meet again.' The address left many in tears. Indeed if anything was going to make Harry homesick then this was it, his beloved ninety-three-year-old grandmother leading her country at a time of crisis. Obviously, the pandemic made the transition even more challenging. As a friend observed: 'He had a much more established life in England and he doesn't really know anyone in LA. I imagine he might be feeling a bit of what Meghan felt over in the UK – lonely and directionless.'

The closure of their Sussex Royal Instagram site on 31 March, the agreed cut-off point, brought it home to the couple that they had to sink or swim by their own endeavours. This new life perhaps came a little easier to Meghan. She had always been a self-starter and self-promoter, the endless acting auditions she attended hardening her to the daily yin and yang of success and failure. By contrast, Harry had spent his life in rule-driven institutions of one kind or another, be they schools, the Army or the monarchy. For the first time ever, he was on his own with a family to care and provide for. It was an exciting if daunting new chapter in both their lives.

20

Happy Ever After?

With the whole world now gripped by a once-in-a-century viral pandemic, the royal couple tried to keep in touch and stay as busy as they could. They joined the Zoom generation, checking in on their UK patronages via video call. In April 2020, they publicly discussed their latest brainchild, a non-profit charity empire which went under the name Archewell, through which they wanted 'to do something of meaning and to do something that matters'. The word 'arche', which means 'source of action' in Greek, had already been the inspiration for their son's name. The couple's plans included running emotional-support groups, a well-being website and volunteering services, but the scheme was still at the drawing-board stage and would face numerous legal and trademark challenges in the coming months before it was ready to launch.

'They are settling into a new life, a new era,' said a source. 'This is about getting it right and making sure they are able to make the difference they want to make.' To this end they reached out to senior officials at both the Bill & Melinda Gates Foundation and the Obama Foundation for advice. Before the pandemic took hold, they had flown to Stanford University in Palo Alto, California, where they met with professors and other academics to brainstorm ideas.

More practically, Harry and Meghan spent Easter Sunday delivering food parcels in Los Angeles for a local charity called Project Angel Food. They also asked that £90,000 – a percentage of the cash generated from the BBC's coverage of their wedding broadcast – be directed to the charity Feeding Britain. There was, though, no charity for Britain's tabloids, the couple announcing in April that they were ending all cooperation with newspapers such as *The Sun*, *Daily Mirror*, *Daily Mail* and *Daily Express*. In future, their press team would not even answer calls from them. So of course there was undisguised glee within tabloid circles when the judge in Meghan's privacy case threw out parts of her legal argument which were deemed 'vague' and 'irrelevant'. In the legal lottery she had entered, Meghan now had to pay Associated Newspapers, publishers of the *Daily Mail*, almost £68,000 in costs. She may have lost round one, but she was in it for the long haul.

Just like their stay in California. They needed to put down roots that would endure, and where better than Montecito, an upscale community by the sea which was home, unsurprisingly, to their fairy godmother Oprah Winfrey and a pantheon of celebrities who included Ellen DeGeneres, Rob Lowe, Tom Cruise and Gwyneth Paltrow. After reviewing numerous properties online, they fell in love with a 14,500-square-foot home, known locally as 'The Chateau', which featured nine bedrooms, sixteen bathrooms, a games room, gym, spa, wine cellar and a five-car garage. The estate, which had the feel of an English country garden, boasted tiered rose gardens, cypress trees, olive trees, a now very famous chicken coop, as well as a tennis court. Even Prince Charles, whose garden at Highgrove in Gloucestershire is world-famous, would be envious of the variety and scale of planting in his son's estate. A few years earlier, the previous property owner, Russian tycoon Sergey Grishin, had tried to sell the property for $34 million. Harry and Meghan, who needed a $9.5 million mortgage, paid just shy of $15 million for their starter home in June 2020, moving in the following month. Their interim host, Tyler Perry, sent them a $100,000 redwood grand piano from his Beverly Hills home as a house-warming gift, although neither Meghan nor Harry have displayed any particular musical talent.

In June, to help pay off the mortgage, the couple signed up with the prestigious Harry Walker Agency, which represents the Obamas and the Clintons in regard to speaking engagements. Social issues such as racial justice, gender equity and mental health would be their primary focus, while charging $1 million a pop to take the stage – and only then if conditions about branding, choice of moderator and other limitations met with their approval.

No longer living out of a suitcase, Harry and Meghan worked out a more civilized work-life balance, one minute collecting the eggs laid by their hens, the next backing a campaign to combat hate speech via Zoom or acknowledging Ellen DeGeneres' dinner suggestions – she recommended San Ysidro Ranch, the exclusive Montecito hotel where the Kennedys enjoyed their honeymoon. When Harry went for a bike ride on the beach, or up in the hills with Archie on the back in his baby seat, he was barely acknowledged. Those paparazzi who did attempt to take pictures knew that they would be sued. He and his celebrity neighbours had their own early-warning system. Orlando Bloom, who lived down the street, would send him messages about paparazzi who had been spotted nearby, and sometimes he would pass on pictures of them. Unsurprisingly, security and safety was a high priority for Harry and Meghan. All their trade visitors had to wear masks, and before they could gain admission to the property they were tested for Covid-19 in the garage complex, which doubled as a security point.

The locals affected disinterest. As the small town of Montecito itself is awash with old money and celebrities, it is seriously uncool to point and stare at the latest headline arrivals. 'I've seen Brad Pitt in Whole Foods and it is no big deal,' recounted one property agent. From time to time, a group of 'ladies who walk' would pass by their home and drop a cheery curtsy in front of the security cameras. It was all very friendly and laid-back, the Sussexes quietly and quickly absorbed into the local community. His near-neighbour, actor Rob Lowe, joked with James Corden on *The Late Late Show* that Harry was so reclusive that spotting him was akin to seeing the Loch Ness Monster. There was an expectation that he would join the Santa Barbara Polo & Racquet Club, and there was even talk of a charity tournament involving the two princes – William has already been a guest of the club.

With the beach close by and hills surrounding them, their home was ideally placed for hiking, cycling and surfing. Inside the compound there were eggs from 'Archie's Chick Inn', and herbs and vegetables from the extensive gardens. This was indeed the good life.

Then, in July, shortly after moving into their forever home, Meghan felt a sharp cramp and knew instinctively that she was losing the baby she was carrying. She vividly described the pain of that loss in an op-ed piece for *The New York Times* to mark Thanksgiving.

'Hours later, I lay in a hospital bed, holding my husband's hand. I felt the clamminess of his palm and kissed his knuckles, wet from both our tears … Losing a child means carrying an almost unbearable grief, experienced by many but talked about by few … Yet despite the staggering commonality of this pain, the conversation remains taboo, riddled with (unwarranted) shame and perpetuating a cycle of solitary mourning.'

Her 1,075-word essay won praise, especially from other women who had suffered a miscarriage and were reluctant to talk about this solitary heartache. Along with applause came its inevitable handmaiden, the duchess criticized for wanting a private life but publicizing such a deeply intimate experience. Author Matt Haig, whose wife suffered a miscarriage, would have none of it. He argued: 'To people saying: "why is Meghan Markle sharing her story if she doesn't want negative media attention?" It is very simple. There is a difference between sharing your own pain, and having others cause it. You have a right to your own truth. And a right to tell it.'

Whatever she did, Meghan was a divisive figure, the duchess sadly acknowledging that in 2019, when she was pregnant or a nursing mother for much of the year, she was still the most trolled figure on social media. She found that level of vitriol and reflex hatred 'almost unsurvivable', especially during a year where she was so physically vulnerable.

As Princess Grace once said to Princess Diana when she complained about the constant publicity: 'Don't worry, it will get a lot worse.' Meghan too had pause to reflect on the wisdom of the last American actor to marry a prince.

Not only was 2020 dominated by the pandemic, but it was also defined by race protests and worldwide demonstrations after numerous police killings stateside, most notoriously of African American George Floyd. The justifiably angry emergence of the Black Lives Matter movement, the destruction of statues of Confederates and slave owners and the upcoming presidential election placed all debate into a political context. Though in their public comments Meghan and Harry had tried to navigate through the political undertow, whatever they said was interpreted as partisan. In the commencement address that she made to students at her former school, Immaculate Heart, she became the first member of the Royal Family to talk about the Black Lives Matter movement. In her online speech in June 2020, she told the graduating class: 'I know you know that black lives matter. So I'm already excited for what you are going to do in the world.'

When she and Harry spoke to young people involved with the Queen's Commonwealth Trust via a video call on 1 July, Harry argued that society could only move forward if we acknowledged the 'uncomfortable' past of the Commonwealth. It was a statement that drew ire from British historians. During Black History Month in October, the couple called for an end to structural racism in Britain, while in an interview with *GQ* magazine later that month, Harry admitted that he too was guilty of unconscious racial bias and was only made truly aware after 'walking in Meghan's shoes' for a few days.

In August, Meghan's sit-down conversation with feminist icon Gloria Steinem in her backyard for the MAKERS short-form video platform, a media project to empower women, was another attempt by her to dance on the head of a political pin. She discussed with Steinem her concerns regarding voter suppression – a subject she had previously talked about with the influential Democratic lawyer and activist Stacey Abrams – as well as the importance of the presence of Kamala Harris, who was potentially the first black female vice president, on the ballot.

With the impending presidential election in November, Meghan actively used her platform to encourage American citizens, especially the young and women, to exercise their right to vote. It was a recurrent theme, in August telling *Marie Claire* magazine why she was voting and urging others to make their voices heard.

In a knowing dig at her time inside the Royal Family, she said: 'I know what it's like to have a voice and also what it's like to feel voiceless.' It was a refrain she repeated to Emily Ramshaw, founder of The 19th, a Texas-based and independent non-profit news organization. She lamented the 'devastating' state of affairs in her home nation with the undercurrent of racism and unconscious bias. Though she was careful not to endorse the Democrats, critics felt that her comments in support of social-justice campaigns and voter-turnout drives were inappropriate. In a poll carried out by *Tatler* magazine in September 2020, more than two-thirds of respondents felt that the royal couple should be stripped of their titles. The precedent was simple: traditionally, the Royal Family stays scrupulously above party politics. For the Queen's grandson and his wife to be involved in the thrust and parry of a presidential election, however obliquely, was an absolute no-no.

Eventually, further comments that she made urging voter registration, this time during a broadcast of a Time100 TV special, earned her the ire of President Donald Trump. He spoke out about the duke and duchess at a White House briefing in September: 'I'm not a fan of hers and I would say this – and she probably has heard that – but I wish a lot of luck to Harry, cos he's going to need it,' a jibe suggesting that he was under her thumb. His remarks provoked a formal palace intervention, the monarchy distancing itself from the royal couple. 'The Duke is not a working member of the Royal Family and any comments he makes are made in a personal capacity,' said a spokesperson.

There were compensations for the beleaguered royals. At least 100 million of them. In September, around the same time as their constitutional tiff with Trump and others, Harry and Meghan signed a major multi-year deal with Netflix to make documentaries, feature films, children's programmes and scripted shows. The deal was estimated at between $100 and $112 million, and was similar to that brokered by agents for the Obamas in 2018 at the end of the presidency. That a media giant was prepared to invest such an emphatic sum in the couple showed that, irrespective of the naysayers, Meghan and Harry enjoyed a considerable and enthusiastic constituency. They had also, according to *Variety*, had meetings with other media companies, notably Apple, Disney and NBC Universal, before landing with Netflix.

In a statement, the Sussexes indicated where their attention and energy would be directed: 'Through our work with diverse communities and their environments, to shining a light on people and causes around the world, our focus will be on creating content that informs but also gives hope.' With Netflix having 193 million subscribers worldwide and counting, Harry and Meghan were assured of a global audience and viewing figures that would dwarf shows in Britain. They were in the big time now.

It was made clear that Meghan would be behind the camera, not in front of it, the duchess being eager, according to the *Daily Mirror*, to make her first movie about Black Lives Matter co-founder Patrisse Cullors. 'She thinks her story needs to be told – and she would love to be the one to make it,' a source revealed.

The royal couple were certainly keen to follow in the highly successful media careers of Barack and Michelle Obama. They were particularly impressed by the way the former President and First Lady had built a thriving and dignified life after leaving the White House. Their first Netflix production, *American Factory*, about globalization and American–Chinese relations, earned them an Academy Award for Best Documentary Feature.

The ink was hardly dry on the Netflix contract before Harry paid back the £2.4 million that had been spent on renovating their other home, Frogmore Cottage, on the Windsor estate. It was loose change now for the multi-millionaire media mogul. 'Our life is great now,' Harry told Oprah. 'We've got a beautiful house, I've got a beautiful family – and the dogs are really happy.'

It was not long before they took another page from the Obama playbook and began discussions with Spotify, the podcast and music giant that had signed up Michelle Obama. The Sussexes also agreed a multi-year partnership to produce podcasts through their newly formed audio-first production company Archewell Audio. Meghan was the driving force behind the deal, which was worth many millions of dollars, the actor demonstrating to executives that she had a clear vision of how their podcast should be presented. As with Netflix, the couple wanted to 'spotlight powerful and diverse voices and perspectives'.

Their first offering was a Christmas holiday special that they themselves hosted, during which they recalled the heartbreak and hope in the year of Covid. They reached into their commodious little black book to snag Sir Elton John, James Corden, tennis star Naomi Osaka, their West Coast host Tyler Perry and British activist Christina Adane. The episode ended with nineteen-month-old Archie wishing listeners a 'happy new year'.

The year 2020 was crowned with the couple successfully winning another legal case against the old enemy, a paparazzi picture agency, for taking snaps of Archie – possibly using a drone camera – when they were living in Vancouver. 'This settlement is a clear signal that unlawful, invasive and intrusive paparazzi behaviour will not be tolerated,' said their legal spokesperson.

The tabloid culture took another hit when, in February 2021, after a two-year battle, Meghan won her high-wire legal case against *The Mail on Sunday* over the publication of a private letter to her father. 'For these outlets, it's a game,' she said in a statement. 'For me and so many others, it's real life, real relationships and very real sadness. The damage they have done and continue to do runs deep.'

They wanted to shape their lives – using one of Meghan's favourite words – 'authentically', not defined by the tabloids or palace tradition. To celebrate Valentine's Day she and Harry were pictured shoeless, he sitting against a tree and she lying down with her head in his lap, in a black-and-white shot captured by their photographer friend Misan Harriman. In an Instagram post, the couple revealed that they were expecting their second child. It was all very Meghan, considered and thought through, the date coinciding with the news, released on 14 February 1984, that Diana was pregnant with Prince Harry.

✖

Ultimately, all roads lead to Diana. In years gone by she too had welcomed Oprah Winfrey into her Kensington Palace apartment. The American talk-show host was very much approved of by those who worked closely with the princess, her then private secretary Patrick Jephson thinking Oprah a sensible and sensitive media adviser. Of course, she flew over from the USA for lunch with the princess in the hope of securing an interview.

She was one of a squadron of famous TV personalities vying for that first fireside confessional. Then the unknown BBC reporter Martin Bashir swooped in, scared Diana half to death with his dark tales of deadly Establishment conspiracies, and snagged the interview that made history. Oprah had to wait a generation, with a chat with Sarah Ferguson in 1996 the equivalent of hors d'oeuvres, before her next chance of interviewing a high-profile royal. It was worth the wait, though, as her conversation with Meghan and Harry would become worldwide water-cooler television.

Oprah first called Meghan in February or March 2018, weeks before the wedding. Meghan later complained that her communications team was in the room during the telephone conversation, so she didn't have the chance or choice to say 'yes' to Oprah's offer of her own volition. Instead, she parried her request by saying it wasn't the right time. It was a wilfully naïve remark. As Meghan had discovered early on in her TV career, interview requests to on-screen stars, such as when Meghan appeared in *Suits*, are routinely filtered through the press office. The same is true of politicians, business people and, of course, members of the Royal Family.

In spite of the initial but friendly rebuff, contact continued, Meghan inviting Oprah to Kensington Palace in March 2018. The TV veteran offered friendship and guidance to the duchess, as she had nearly a quarter of a century before to the Princess of Wales. Three years later, though, Oprah was first in line: the only question mark concerned the timing.

In the end, it was far from ideal, the interview with Meghan and Harry announced on the same day that Prince Philip, then ninety-nine, was taken to hospital after complaining of feeling unwell. It coincided too with the formal announcement that, after a year of transition, the Sussexes were not returning as full-time working members of the Royal Family. As a result, they were permanently relinquishing their royal patronages and Harry's honorary military appointments. Though the Queen stated that Meghan and Harry were 'much loved members of the Royal Family', the suspicion remained that the couple had decided to speak to Oprah as an angry tit for tat for being stripped of their remaining functions. This was amplified when they released their own statement in which they emphasized their commitment to duty and service. 'We can all live a life of service. Service is universal,' they argued.

While probably unintentional, their words were seen as a direct rebuke to Her Majesty, the couple behaving in a manner that was described by a source reported in *The Sunday Times* as 'petulant and insulting to the Queen'.

Amidst this by now predictably sour and hostile atmosphere, Oprah herself explained why Harry and Meghan had chosen this particular moment to speak out. It was the age-old reason: to give their side of the story, to set the record straight. 'When you have been lied about for a series of years … if in your own office or in your family, somebody is saying things about you that are not true … how hurtful that is,' Oprah told *Town and Country* magazine.

Before the big interview, which took place in a lush Montecito garden, others decided that they wanted to have their say about Meghan – and it wasn't pretty. On 2 March, *The Times* revealed that Meghan faced formal complaints of bullying by two personal assistants, as well as of unacceptable behaviour that was undermining the confidence of a third staff member. She had reduced one member of staff to tears, while another 'could not stop shaking' before a confrontation with Meghan. The complaints were made in October 2018 – just five months after the royal wedding – by Jason Knauf, the couple's then communications secretary. Though Harry pleaded with him not to pursue the matter – the prince's lawyers have denied this allegation – Knauf felt duty-bound to send an email to the Human Resources department. The response at the time was: 'How can we make this go away?'

A palace source told *The Times*: 'Senior people in the Household, Buckingham Palace and Clarence House knew that they had a situation where members of staff, particularly young women, were being bullied to the point of tears. The institution just protected Meghan constantly. All the men in grey suits who she hates have a lot to answer for, because they did absolutely nothing to protect people.' In addition, aides working unsung behind the scenes did much more to help Meghan find a role than has been publicly acknowledged.

These accusations meshed with a now familiar but negative narrative about Meghan, which suggested that she was a cold-eyed social climber who had ditched her father, LA friends and first husband when she found fame on *Suits*. These stories, though, did not align with the positive portrait of the young girl who stood up to bullies at school and would go on to champion women's empowerment.

A spokesperson for Meghan described the allegations as a 'calculated smear campaign' based on 'misleading and harmful misinformation'. An official statement also revealed: 'The duchess is saddened by this latest attack on her character, particularly as someone who has been the target of bullying herself and is deeply committed to supporting those who have experienced pain and trauma.'

Harry witnessed at first hand her pain. He recalled: 'Before the Oprah interview had aired, because of the combined efforts of the Firm and the media to smear her, I was woken up in the middle of the night to her crying in her pillow – because she doesn't want to wake me up because I'm already carrying too much. That's heartbreaking. I held her. We talked. She cried and she cried and she cried.'

These new negative headlines, as well as a light-hearted TV appearance in which Harry joined James Corden on an open-topped LA sightseeing bus, served as the warm-up act for the main event. It did not disappoint. At times Meghan's allegations and Harry's accusations were simply jaw-dropping. Never in history had a royal prince and his consort turned their anger and contempt onto the venerable institution of the monarchy in this way. Even the criticism of the Royal Family by Diana's brother, Earl Spencer, at her funeral in Westminster Abbey was mild by comparison.

Predictably, in *Oprah with Meghan and Harry*, the host started by chatting about the wedding, moved on to Meghan's first meeting with the Queen and then dealt with the altercation with Kate over the bridesmaids' outfits. Meghan talked about her loneliness, her sense of isolation and her profound suicidal thoughts – all so very reminiscent of Diana's conversations with me for her 1992 biography, *Diana: Her True Story*.

When Meghan went for help, after finally telling Harry about her dangerous mental condition, she claimed she was turned away by officials. The question of why she went to Human Resources rather than a doctor or therapist was not asked by Oprah.

She also felt silenced and trapped by the system; her passport, driver's licence and keys were taken away from her as though she were entering an open prison. That didn't stop her, though, from making numerous speeches on female empowerment, equality and other issues while travelling around the world on private and commercial aircraft. It was a curious kind of muzzling.

She also claimed that over one four-month period, she had only twice left the house, again indicating that she was a lonely prisoner hidden away by the men in grey. Yet she was seen out on numerous occasions: dinner and lunch appointments in Notting Hill, beauty treatments in Kensington and various shopping trips. Though she was snapped by the paparazzi, British newspapers declined to buy photographs of these excursions. While she endured this lonely existence, she told Oprah that she had had no training on how to behave in a regal manner. However, her semi-official biographer Omid Scobie described how she had similar coaching to Kate, everything from how to exit a limousine gracefully, how and who to curtsy to and how to act in a potential kidnap or other crisis situation.

But it was the couple's allegation that an unnamed member of the Royal Family had wondered aloud about the colour of Archie's skin, leading Meghan and Harry to interpret this remark as relating to the boy's protection and title, that really captured the popular imagination. Oprah's theatrical 'What?' drew the watching millions into reflecting in that moment on the racism at the heart of the Royal Family. This was an entertainment masterclass, if not a slice of investigative journalism or piece of evidence that would never have survived rigorous cross-examination in a court of law. Their story remained *their* truth, if not *the* truth.

Their claim, for example, that they were officially married three days before the wedding ceremony at St George's Chapel was debunked by the Archbishop of Canterbury himself. Harry's churlish accusation that his father had 'cut off' all funding when he moved to Canada was later undermined by the Clarence House accounts, which showed that the Prince of Wales had settled £4.4 million on his sons, part of which was to keep Harry financially afloat during this period of transition. While there was some debate about when the funding started and stopped, Harry's phrase that he was 'cut off' by Prince Charles was utterly misleading. It was also later revealed that the couple's decision not to give their son the title 'Earl of Dumbarton' had nothing to do with race or keeping him a commoner, but because they didn't want Archie being made fun of because it contained the word 'dumb'.

Whatever the misstatements, exaggerations and untruths in their historic interview, there was no denying that the worldwide takeaway, a generation after the beloved Diana had walked away from the Royal Family, was damning. As a final withering attack on the institution that had nurtured him, Harry confessed he had felt 'trapped within the system' and believed that the same applied to his father and brother, who were condemned to this narrow, stultifying life: 'They don't get to leave. And I have huge compassion for that.' The prince admitted that he had been rescued by Meghan, his sentiments reminiscent of those who have escaped a malign cult. It was hardly a ringing endorsement for the institution that sits atop Britain's social hierarchy. As ever, the last word went to Diana, the woman who first set the ball rolling with her own TV confessional. Because all she had ever wanted was for her children to be happy, Harry thought she would feel 'very angry' and 'very sad' by the current state of affairs: 'I think she saw it coming. I certainly felt her presence throughout this whole process. I'm just really relieved and happy to be sitting here, talking to you, with my wife by my side. Because I can't begin to imagine what it must've been like for her, going through this process by herself all those years ago, because it has been unbelievably tough for the two of us. But at least we had each other.'

In the dramatic finale, the couple concluded that Meghan had saved Harry and Harry had saved Meghan. Theirs was a story, as they saw it, with a happy ending.

It was an interview watched by a worldwide audience of over 60 million. In Britain the popular reaction was hostile, Harry and Meghan branded 'selfish' and 'nauseating' by the tabloids. They deplored the harm and pain they had caused the Queen.

Long-time Meghan critic Piers Morgan stormed off his own breakfast TV show following a heated discussion with weatherman Alex Beresford over Morgan's scathing and disbelieving comments about Meghan's mental health, a rant that generated a record 57,121 complaints, including a formal complaint from Meghan herself. The conflict certainly divided the generations. Young Brits, Americans and ethnic minorities took the view that Meghan, the first dual-heritage American royal, had every right to air her grievances in public. Older Britons felt that she should have thought more carefully before signing up to the position, and that the couple had wilfully and selfishly damaged an institution to which the Queen and Prince Philip had devoted their lives.

Former First Lady Michelle Obama and singer Beyoncé applauded Meghan for speaking so openly about race and mental health, while the White House press secretary Jen Psaki made clear that President Joe Biden felt the same way about addressing mental-health struggles. Influential *LA Times* columnist Patt Morrison wrote: 'I think the monarchy is perceived generally as very fuddy-duddy and out of date. The expulsion and the wish to depart from the Royal Family by Harry and Meghan was another indicator of that. This is a family that can't keep up.' *New Yorker* writer Doreen St Félix believed that moments from the interview 'might drain the dying British monarchy of its last dredges of cultural esteem'.

While the debate raged, the Royal Family was considering its response. There was much resentment at Harry's accusation that his brother and father were trapped, anger at his complaint about being financially cut off and resentment at the couple's casual and inaccurate playing of the race card. Initially, there was a desire to make a point-by-point rebuttal. In the end, some sixty hours after the Oprah bombshell, Buckingham Palace issued a sixty-one-word statement. It was notable for its terseness and unwillingness to take the Sussexes' word as gospel: 'The whole family is saddened to learn the full extent of how challenging the last few years have been for Harry and Meghan. The issues raised, particularly that of race, are concerning. While some recollections may vary, they are taken very seriously and will be addressed by the family privately.'

Prince William put the family's position succinctly when quizzed by a reporter during a visit to a school in East London. 'We are very much not a racist family,' he said.

Early talks between Charles, William and Harry to discuss some of the issues at stake were unproductive, not least because William, according to *Vanity Fair*, was worried that anything he said to his brother would appear in the American media.

Other royals, like Prince Albert of Monaco, believed the dirty laundry should have been aired behind closed doors, while Prince Philip's pithy view was the same as when Prince Charles and his wife separately discussed their affairs on prime-time TV: 'Madness.'

The Duke of Edinburgh never had the chance to tell Harry his thoughts face-to-face. On the morning of 9 April 2021, a month after the Oprah interview, Prince Philip died. In his personal tribute Harry called his beloved grandfather 'master of the barbecue, legend of banter, and cheeky right till the end'.

Amidst the many recollections of the Queen's husband, the abiding concern was how the Royal Family, in particular Princes Charles and William, would respond to the arrival of Harry at the royal funeral. It was perhaps as well that a heavily pregnant Meghan had been advised not to make the 11,000-mile round trip. With numbers in St George's Chapel at Windsor Castle limited to thirty, it was a dignified if modest farewell.

Diana would have been so pleased with her boys. Their gaze was unwavering, their stance upright, proud of their place in the family procession behind their grandfather's coffin. What a difference from that day, almost twenty-four years previously, when William and Harry, their heads bowed, walked behind their mother's funeral cortege. William, as he later admitted, tried to hide his face behind his fringe. These days he has no fringe to cover his face – not that he would have wanted to.

This time around there was no fuss or wailing and gnashing of teeth. Prince Philip's motto in life, 'Just get on with it', was expressed in the brisk funeral arrangements which had a remote dignity, symbolized by the Queen sitting silently on her own in the pews, kept apart from her family by the demands of Covid-19.

After the service Kate had a few words with Harry, who was walking alongside William, and then stepped back a pace to allow him to speak to his brother. All three were acutely aware of the optics, knowing that everyone was waiting for some kind of public reconciliation. Not a bit of it. Once out of camera range and after a few words to the Queen and Prince Charles, William and Kate headed back to Kensington Palace to be with their children.

Harry had his own personal concerns about attending the funeral in the first place. This was not about the chilly reception he expected from his family, but to do with coping with his own anxiety when he was back in London. This was a place where he felt trapped and hunted, the prince using coping skills he had learned in therapy to help still his 'pounding' heart in the presence of cameras.

'I was worried about it, I was afraid,' Harry told the Associated Press while promoting *The Me You Can't See,* the show on mental health and well-being that he co-executive-produced with Oprah Winfrey.

In the emotional first episode, first broadcast in May 2020, Harry revealed that it was Meghan who, early on in their relationship, encouraged him to go for counselling to deal with his anger. Much of his resentment was focused on his father. He explained that Prince Charles refused to question the self-imposed hardships of royal life.

'My father used to say to me when I was younger, "Well, it was like that for me, so it's going to be like that for you."' Harry took issue with this parental philosophy, saying: 'That doesn't make sense. Just because you suffered, that doesn't mean that your kids have to suffer, in fact quite the opposite. If you suffered, do everything you can to make sure that whatever negative experiences that you had, that you can make it right for your kids.' He continued: 'Isn't this all about breaking the cycle? Isn't this all about making sure that history doesn't repeat itself?'

As with the Oprah interview, he accused his family of turning a blind eye to his and Meghan's mental-health struggles. Harry complained: 'I thought my family would help, but every single ask, request, warning, whatever it is, just got met with total silence or total neglect.'

Ironically, he and William have long championed the importance of mental health. In 2016, the royal brothers and the Duchess of Cambridge launched Heads Together, an initiative designed to encourage people to speak up and not be ashamed to ask for help when mental well-being is at stake.

In a podcast with popular broadcaster and actor Dax Shepard, he made it clear that he no longer wanted to be part of the monarchical set-up. He described his life before Meghan as 'a mix between *The Truman Show* and living in a zoo': 'It's the job, right? Grin and bear it. Get on with it. I was in my early twenties and I was thinking I don't want this job, I don't want to be here. I don't want to be doing this. Look what it did to my mum. How am I ever going to settle down and have a wife and family when I know it's going to happen again? I've seen behind the curtain, I've seen the business model and seen how this whole thing works and I don't want to be part of this.'

He was, though, going to profit handsomely from his experience behind the curtain, after it was revealed that for the best part of the year he had been discussing his life – the good times and the bad – with Pulitzer Prize-winning journalist and author J.R. Moehringer. It promised to be the definitive and, in his word, 'honest', account of his turbulent times inside the Royal Family.

As Moehringer had ghostwritten tennis star Andre Agassi's life story, which particularly emphasized the difficult father/son relationship, it seemed certain that Prince Charles would have more than an unwilling walk-on part in his son's memoir. There were even reports, denied by Team Sussex, that Meghan and Harry had negotiated a four-book deal with the publisher, one to be released only after the Queen's death.

Either way, the ghostwritten memoir of Harry's life and times was not due to be published until after the Queen's Platinum Jubilee. This news had nervous royal officials fretting that the revelatory tome would cast a long shadow over the celebrations of the Queen's life of service.

The irony was that this outpouring of resentment and contumely against the institution was balanced by Harry and Meghan's respect and adoration for the woman who had been the head of that same establishment for almost seventy years, namely the Queen. They demonstrated their loyalty to Her Majesty and her family in the naming of their second child, Lilibet 'Lili' Diana Mountbatten-Windsor, who was born at Santa Barbara Cottage Hospital on 4 June at 11.40 a.m., weighing in at 7 lb 11 oz. In a statement, they said: 'Lili is named after her great-grandmother, Her Majesty The Queen, whose family nickname is Lilibet. Her middle name, Diana, was chosen to honour her beloved late grandmother, The Princess of Wales.'

While there was no surprise in the name of 'Diana', there was, as is inevitable with this couple, a groundswell of irritation that they had chosen such an intimate family nickname which dated back to King George V, the Queen's grandfather. He called Princess Elizabeth 'Lilibet' in an imitation of her efforts to pronounce her own name when she was a toddler.

A brief but stiff leader in *The Times*, known as the paper of record, articulated the view of the Establishment over the use of such a cherished name. 'If the name was intended as an olive branch, a gesture of reconciliation after a year of bridge-burning, then it misjudges the mood. There is surely more work to do after their hatcheting of the Royal Family, and more authentic commitment to service to the country and to the integrity of the institution that is so ably represented by the woman they call Lilibet.'

Harry made it clear that he had spoken to the Queen before announcing their daughter's name and that she had signalled her approval. The BBC's royal correspondent Jonny Dymond broadcast a different version, quoting a senior palace official as being 'absolutely adamant' that no such permission was granted. The furious couple instructed their lawyers to inform other media outlets not to repeat what they called a 'false and defamatory' report.

Besides the 'did they, didn't they inform the Queen' mystery, the takeaway from the naming of their daughter Lilibet showed how deeply they were still invested in the Royal Family. In the Oprah interview and beyond, they had complained about an organization that was racist, abusive and indifferent to their mental suffering, and yet by calling their newborn Lilibet, they harked back firmly to royal tradition, allying themselves with continuity not change. They may have unmasked the monarchy but that gesture only went so far. While they had given the institution a necessary jolt, they did not start a revolution. Indeed, just three months after the couple made allegations of racism against the Royal Family, the palace admitted it 'must do more' to employ more staff from ethnic minorities. The Royal Household's annual accounts revealed that 8.5 per cent of staff were from minorities compared with around 13 per cent of the UK population (according to the 2011 census).

Meghan and Harry had scored a point but not overturned a dynasty, because when Prince Charles becomes king, Lilibet will be entitled to be a princess and her brother a prince. Meghan might be dubbed a Hollywood princess, but her daughter will be unique – the first ever real-life British princess born in America.

'Lili becomes the fourth generation of amazing, strong women in the family – behind Meghan, Diana and Her Majesty the Queen,' the couple's friend, Dean Stott, told *People* magazine.

With Lilibet's birth, the couple's family was complete, the duo announcing that they were going to spend the next five months on parental leave. But not before the indefatigable duchess had released *The Bench*, a children's picture book based on a poem she had written for her husband's first Father's Day to celebrate the joyous, loving union between Harry and Archie.

In the inscription she wrote: 'For the man and the boy who make my heart go pump-pump.' Within days of its publication the book became a *New York Times* bestseller, prompting Meghan to write: 'While this poem began as a love letter to my husband and son, I'm encouraged to see that its universal themes of love, representation and inclusivity are resonating with communities everywhere. In many ways, pursuing a more compassionate and equitable world begins with these core values. Equally, to depict another side of masculinity – one grounded in connection, emotion, and softness – is to model a world that so many would like to see for their sons and daughters alike.'

This wasn't her first attempt at authorship. When she was in eighth grade, aged thirteen or fourteen, she wrote a charming tome about her freckles. Its title came from words uttered by her own father, who used to say to his young daughter, 'A face without freckles is a night without stars.'

Now Tom Markle Senior was reduced to lamenting on television that he saw little if any chance of ever seeing his grandchildren. There were no stars in his life.

This is the heart of the paradox that is Meghan Markle. Much as she talks of inclusivity and compassion, her father and the rest of his family remain outside her emotional orbit, cast into the outer darkness. For all her lobbying and discourse about female empowerment, she faces a lengthy and potentially damaging inquiry into written allegations that she bullied a number of members of household staff, mainly female. She took a leaf out of the Trump playbook, doubling down on her protestations of innocence while demanding access to every memo, email and letter.

Of course she is not the first American to face unrelenting hostility from the British Establishment. That dubious honour goes to Wallis Simpson, who was blamed for causing King Edward VIII to abdicate and in the process wrecking the hitherto amicable relationship between the Sovereign and his brothers, particularly his unwilling successor, King George VI. There were high hopes in this modern Cain and Abel conflict that William and Harry would be publicly reconciled at the unveiling of the statue of their mother, on what would have been her sixtieth birthday on 1 July 2021. While the brothers were at ease and chatted amiably with the small group of attendees, mainly members of the Spencer family, there was no public overture of friendship. In a joint statement, the princes remembered their mother's 'love, strength and character – qualities that made her a force for good around the world, changing countless lives for the better'.

Though the new mother stayed in California during the ceremony, comparisons between Diana and Meghan were inevitable. Both were and are controversial women who were agents of change in their own contrasting ways. Diana's philosophy was captured in her phrase, 'Anywhere I see suffering that is where I want to be, doing what I can.' Her ambition, as she famously remarked, was to be the 'queen of people's hearts'. While Diana responded to individuals, Meghan's work is centred around the collective, empowering communities to make a change. Her battle cry, as she has made on numerous occasions, is that she doesn't want to be loved but rather wants to be heard.

Diana became an independent humanitarian, linking her name to existing institutions like the Red Cross. By contrast Meghan, with Harry by her side, is rapidly constructing their own working charitable foundation, which began effective operation during the pandemic. Diana also dreamed of starting her own foundation and talked of raising money to fund hospices around the world. Sadly, that ambition was never realized.

Of course, as Harry pointed out, Diana was on her own during this journey, a factor that has irrevocably coloured his view of his father. Not only does Meghan have the unconditional love and support of her husband, but she also has an effective, combative and well-connected court, mainly American, who have not been afraid to speak out on her behalf.

A media mogul, a charity maven, a bestselling author, a friend, a mother and a wife, Meghan has achieved a remarkable amount during her brief time inside the Royal Family. During her journey, or their journey, she has become a figure who inspires adoration or contempt. She and Harry have been prepared to discuss issues such as race and inclusion that the monarchy – and the country – have traditionally shied away from.

She was initially seen as a bridge between the monarchy's past and future, that sunny day in May 2018 a signpost of a glorious inclusive tomorrow. For many reasons, some racial, she was not absorbed into either the Royal Family or the country. She became a standing and articulate rebuke to those unwilling to accept difference and diversity. Her complaints had a familiar ring. Meghan's feeling of loneliness, isolation and lack of support echoed Princess Diana's experience many years before.

Unlike Charles and Diana, Meghan and Harry are in lockstep. When they went into self-imposed exile, they did so together, their isolation reminiscent of the Duke and Duchess of Windsor. Unlike the Windsors, who spent the rest of their lives in sybaritic but bored splendour in the south of France, New York and Palm Beach, Meghan and Harry are determined to make a difference.

Meghan has, in her eyes, reclaimed her life and is living it on her own terms, unable to combine the fulfilment of her individual needs and ambitions with serving an institution that did not command her respect or allegiance.

Her dalliance with the Royal Family is largely over. As for the future, the adventure is just beginning.

Picture Credits

PHOTO INSERT 1

Page 1: MEGA

Page 2: Mail on Sunday / Solo Syndication (both)

Page 3: Mail on Sunday / Solo Syndication (top); The Sun / News Licensing (bottom)

Page 4: MEGA (top); The Sun / News Licensing (bottom left); © Tameka Jacobs (bottom right)

Page 5: MEGA (both)

Page 6: Moviestore / Shutterstock (top); Frank Ockenfels / Dutch Oven / Kobal / Shutterstock (bottom)

Page 7: Mike McGregor / Getty Images for Cantor Fitzgerald (top); DOD Photo / Alamy (bottom)

Page 8: Nicholas Hunt / Getty Images

PHOTO INSERT 2

Page 1: Kurt Arrigo / MEGA

Page 2: The Sun / News Licensing (top); Christ Jackson / Getty Images for the Invictus Games Foundation (bottom)

Page 3: Facundo Arrizabalaga / EPA-EFE / Shutterstock (top); Paul John Bayfield, Camera Press London

Page 4: Oli Scarff / AFP via Getty Images (top); Jonathan Brady / AFP via Getty Images (bottom)

Page 5: Tolga Akmen / AFP via Getty Images (top); Samir Hussein / WireImage / Getty Images (bottom)

Page 6: Jeff J. Mitchell / Getty Images (top); PA Images / Alamy (bottom)

Page 7: Dominic Lipinski - WPA Pool / Getty Images (top); Chris Jackson / Getty Images (bottom)

Page 8: Kurt Arrigo / MEGA

Index